The Economic Thought of Michael Polanyi

T0359049

Michael Polanyi is most famous for his work in chemistry and the philosophy of science, but in the 1930s and 1940s he made an important contribution to economics.

Drawing on rich archival materials of Polanyi and his correspondents, Gábor Bíró explores their competing worldviews and their struggles to popularize their visions of the economy, economic expertise and democracy. Special focus is given to Polanyi's pioneering economics film and postmodern ideas.

This volume will be of interest to advanced students and researchers of the history of economics, philosophy of science, and science and technology studies.

Gábor Bíró is an Assistant Professor and Vice Chair of the Department of Philosophy and History of Science at the Budapest University of Technology and Economics, Hungary.

Routledge Studies in the History of Economics

For more information about this series, please visit
www.routledge.com/series/SE0341

The Economic Thought of Michael Polanyi

Gábor Bíró

Routledge
Taylor & Francis Group

LONDON AND NEW YORK

First published 2020
by Routledge
2 Park Square, Milton Park, Abingdon, Oxon OX14 4RN

and by Routledge
605 Third Avenue, New York, NY 10017

First issued in paperback 2021

Routledge is an imprint of the Taylor & Francis Group, an informa business

British Library Cataloguing-in-Publication Data
A catalogue record for this book is available from the British Library

Library of Congress Cataloging-in-Publication Data
A catalog record has been requested for this book

ISBN 13: 978-0-367-78506-2 (pbk)
ISBN 13: 978-0-367-24563-4 (hbk)

Typeset in Bembo
by Wearset Ltd, Boldon, Tyne and Wear

To my mother, Éva Pénzes

Contents

Acknowledgements

This book was written in the inspiring intellectual and scholarly milieu of the two Polanyi societies, The Polanyi Society and the Michael Polanyi Liberal Philosophical Association. It owes much to excellent scholars who dedicated their lives not only to study Polanyi but also to introduce novices to the tacit dimension of science: the fiduciary framework which makes the scientific community more than a sum of its parts, and more than what could be grasped by the finest-grained scientometrics. I was particularly lucky to be able to learn from the earliest days of my PhD from Phil Mullins, president of the Polanyi Society, former editor of *Tradition and Discovery: The Polanyi Society Periodical*, and a remarkable scholar of Polanyi from the 1970s. Mullins played a pivotal role in shifting my scholarly interest towards the economic thought of Michael Polanyi. I remember one of our first discussions in Budapest back in 2014 about Keynes, Hayek and the undiscovered economic thought of Polanyi. Without this discussion, my research could have taken a very different path and, probably, this book would have never been written.

Special thanks are due to Márta Fehér and Tihamér Margitay for making available a plethora of Polanyi materials they collected through the last two decades. I feel privileged to get regular advice from Fehér, who was the most influential in shaping my perception of Polanyi's liberalism and epistemology. Special thanks must also go to Gábor Áron Zemplén for grating me access to the Polanyi materials donated to the department by Mihály Beck (mostly Polanyi's early chemical writings), and for providing me early Hungarian literature on the Polanyi family written before the Hungarian Democratic Transition. I feel honoured to have had illuminating talks with Eduardo Beira, a remarkable Polanyi scholar and a great translator of Polanyi's works, who has recently rediscovered Polanyi's economics film and made it available to study for others. I am particularly grateful for his invitation to the *Trade, Employment and Public Policy: Polanyi Then and Now* workshop (November 2017) co-organized by the MIT and the Polanyi Society where I had the chance to present my research leading to this book.

This book has indissoluble ties to the Philosophy and History of Science Department at Budapest University of Technology and Economics and its Doctoral School of History of Philosophy of Science. One cannot wish for a more open atmosphere or a more inspiring scholarly milieu. I am particularly thankful to those who were working tirelessly to maintain and develop this great community, most importantly to Márta Fehér, Tihamér Margitay, Gábor Forrai, Benedek Láng, János Tanács, Gábor Zemplén, István Danka, Mihály Héder and Krisztina Szabó. They all influenced my thinking as a scholar for which I will always be grateful. I want to express my sincere thanks to Tibor Frank and Karl Hall, who influenced my research towards exciting new directions. I am thankful for the close reading and the useful advice of Phil Mullins. His exemplary scholarly guidance was a beacon for me through the years of writing this book. Several colleagues listed above have offered insightful feedback on earlier drafts, and three anonymous reviewers gave thoughtful suggestions for improving the manuscript.

I am grateful to Natalie Tomlinson, editor of the *Routledge Studies in the History of Economics*, for her support of the project from 2018. I could always rely on her precious guidance and comprehensive expertise when it was most needed. I owe many thanks to Lisa Lavelle, editorial assistant for economics at Routledge. Special thanks must go to Steve Turrington for his dedication and excellent editing, and to Pip Clubbs for her outstanding professional guidance. I am very grateful to John C. Polanyi and the Special Collections Research Center of the University of Chicago Library for giving me permission to publish direct quotations from the papers of Michael Polanyi. Part of the research of this book appeared elsewhere, helping to refine my ideas through peer review. Elements from Chapter 3 appeared in *Changing Knowledge in the Early Economic Thought of Michael Polanyi* (Springer, 2018); from Chapter 2 in my dissertation, *Projecting the Light of Democracy: Michael Polanyi's Efforts to Save Liberalism via an Economics Film, 1933–48*.

Throughout this journey, my family's support, love and patience have been unwavering. Much love always.

Introduction

Nowadays, Michael Polanyi is mostly known among scholars for his fundamental early work in physical chemistry and his later pioneering contributions to philosophy of science. What is less known about him is that between the two, from about 1933 to 1948, he was reimagining economics on a postmodern basis. This book explores the personal journey of Michael Polanyi and his *vanguard vision*[1] through various social worlds, with the aim of portraying his threefold mission to craft a heart for economics, to revitalize liberalism and to save the West from the growing shadow of totalitarian régimes. Following in the footsteps of Sheila Jasanoff, this book intends not to go beyond imagination but with imagination. Its pursuits take place both in fictional and non-fictional realms, utopian and dystopian landscapes, subjectively-drawn topographies of power inhabited by accounts of economies and experts who claim to know them. It does not provide an objective general overview of the economic ideas, social theories and political movements of the United Kingdom in the analysed period, nor claims to do so or that such feat would be even possible. Instead, by mining the rich archival materials of Polanyi and his fellows, it shows how they saw, through their socially constructed eyes, what is happening, and how they encountered each other in their struggles to draw others into believing specific visions of the economy, economic expertise and democracy. It is a yet untold story of giving birth to a *postmodern economics*,[2] but it is also a story of a handful of intellectuals who were carving their social niche to attain power, authority and the promise of a better tomorrow in the economic and political turmoil of the 1930s and 1940s.

Although the primary aim of this book is to present the personal road taken by Polanyi's postmodern economics and his related film, it might also be seen contributing, perhaps in a less direct way, to ongoing discourses of social constructivism and science and technology studies (hereafter STS). One cannot praise enough Mary Jo Nye's *Michael Polanyi and his Generation: The Origins of the Social Construction of Science* (2011), a pioneering book which put Polanyi on the radar of contemporary studies in the sociology of scientific knowledge (SSK) and social constructivism and, by doing so, paved the way for further related studies. Following this innovative opening, this book gives a glimpse into the social epistemology of interwar economics through the eyes of Polanyi and his correspondents. But it pushes the social analysis further with recent tools and perspectives of STS on at least three fronts. First, by analysing Polanyi's *Unemployment and Money: The Principles Involved* (1940), the first educational film ever made to portray a certain economic theory and not the economy itself, one is tempted to re-examine the role of materiality in social sciences. Second, by discovering how Polanyi and his correspondents summoned examples from the literary realms of Charles Dickens, Thomas Mann and others to argue for or against certain economic theories or economic policies and, conversely, by exploring how economics and economists were depicted in fictional realms, one might shed some new light on the social thickness of economic ideas. And, last but not least, by presenting how an individual vision of postmodern economics was imagined to make democracy flourish by recrafting the minds and eyes attached to the relevant epistemic and political practices, one might better understand the significance and the versatility of the idiom of *co-production*.[3] The latter part of the introduction should then not only map this current contribution onto the wide interdisciplinary canvas of Polanyi scholarship, but should also explain how the book relates to the major STS approaches and, particularly, to the most relevant studies which are analysing the economy or economics and defining themselves as belonging to the corpus of science and technology studies.

From the birth of the field in the mid-1970s, comparatively few scholars have chosen to study social sciences and the economy instead of natural sciences and nature. The maturing of science and technology studies in the last two decades has brought, among many other things, the emergence of specializations focusing on the so-called soft sciences and certain aspects of the economy. Perhaps one of the most significant of these specializations and the most relevant to our topic is the sociological study of finance and, particularly, the pioneering work of Karin Knorr Cetina and Alex Preda.

In *Framing Finance* (2009), Preda argued that inquiries into the "spirit of capitalism"[4] should not be primarily concerned with "collection of abstract beliefs, existing only in the minds of market players" or with an "ideology concealing hidden meanings". Instead they should focus on where, and through which "instruments, techniques and knowledge forms", the modes of "public access"[5] to financial markets are being generated. The perspective of this book is different. Following in Polanyi's footsteps, belief is not considered to be abstract but personal: an aspect of knowing always already tied to other aspects. Unlike Preda's account, the focus is therefore not on the commonly used "observational boundaries" between economy and society but on how a specific group of scientists, scholars and other intellectuals imagined the economy of the past, present and future and the fields studying it. This book portrays the micro-social depths of these imaginations having attachments to a plethora of fictional and non-fictional realms and being driven by moral charges and normative dimensions lying outside the focal area of Preda's accounts. It intends to focus less on what becomes mainstream or common concepts of economy and economics and more on mining the relevant imaginations of Polanyi and his fellows. Imaginations, embracing various concepts of economic disciplines and, in most cases, having implications towards possible futures of utopian or dystopian flavour. The scope of this book therefore is not limited to the sociological studies of economy and economics through the socially constructed eyes of a few dozen connected intellectuals in the 1930s and 1940s. It also aims to map how these imaginations related to fictional and non-fictional literature, technological advances, social orders, political movements, democratic and totalitarian régimes, and even to the struggle of civilizations in the eyes of these intellectuals. With the latter approach, the book intends to avoid the anachronistic and disciplinary skeletonization of the economic views analysed and aims to provide a gradually built social thickness by drifting with the examined line of thoughts to a certain degree. One might say that defining the degree of this drifting is where anachronism, yet in a more disguised form, necessarily appears. And it would be hard to argue with this statement. But it would be even harder to argue that drifting provides a less anachronistic way, and that less anachronism is the better for making historical accounts.

Jasanoff identified a weakness of actor-network theory (hereafter: ANT) which she succinctly summarized as the "flatness of networks".[6] Being in agreement with her critique, this book refuses to accept the symmetry postulate of ANT which attributes the same kind of agency and importance to human and non-human agents, and emphasizes that emotions, morals, interests and imagination lie in the heart of the realm of men but not of things. Attributing symmetrical agency to human and non-human agents might be useful for scaffolding the claims of passive and morally neutral networks, but making such horizontal complexity visible does not come without its cost: making multiple vertical complexities invisible. Without the "topographies of power"[7] and the planispheres of the morals, interests and dreams of the people involved one can only draw things together in a quite insensitive, inhuman and mechanistic way. Practices of "flattening" the world are not only the subject of ANT accounts, the creation of these accounts is also a kind of *flattening*. Human actors in ANT accounts, like the polygons (except A Square) and line segments in Edwin A. Abbott's *Flatland: A Romance of Many Dimensions* (1884) are deprived of the capacity to see, think and dream unlike the others. They have a symmetrical task to do and they are not permitted to do anything else. The outcasts of the poorly imagined and invented worlds of actor-network theoreticians are manifold: interests converging and diverging from different perspectives at the same time; dreams about various contingent pasts, presents and futures; "moral valences"[8] and personal beliefs crossing material and social assemblages, and in doing so, transform and being transformed by what they encounter.

It has been previously pointed out that Latour's framework suggesting that first "immutable mobiles"[9] are being created which are then being disseminated from "centers of calculation"[10] lacks a fine-grained socially constructed eye to power (Jasanoff and Kim 2015). Another point to be raised is that different people can see the same thing differently, even if it is material like a film on a screen or an economic theory on a sheet of paper. Nothing ever is really immutable. Better said, there is no objective way to judge the immutability of anything. Labelling something as immutable is always arbitrary whether we admit it or not. Immutability, therefore, is just a fancy word for disguising complexity-blindness. One is even tempted to suggest a surrogate term, *transmutable mobiles*, to refer to such a state of permanent transformation in which an idea, a concept or a cumulation of inscriptions is being carried over from one place to another. There is no such thing as a finished representation of anything. Things are being presented and represented endlessly. The related practices never cross an imaginary finish line fixed by some timeless consensus of all those who walk the earth. We like to think that there is such a finish line and that we know exactly where it is. But whether a representation becomes seen as "immutable" or not is not fixed by a timeless consensus but determined by various kinds of arbitrary power. Power decides which actors have their preferred shades of being and meaning accepted more easily in a wider circle, and which actors need to struggle for the acceptance of their views with considerably lower chances. Blinding ourselves to power when making accounts about how science works is like making tea and forgetting about the water. People and their practices are always already embedded in multiple dimensions of power. As the following chapters will show, accounts about what is 'out there' in the economy and what is the desirable economic expertise we should rely on are being framed in a complex political environment. Some expertises and claims are more likely to be seen as compatible with certain political ideologies, constitutional systems, social theories, economic interests, visions and religions than others. Some claimants realize this and attempt to use it to extend their authority versus their rivals. Others do not see it, and notwithstanding get entangled in narratives they do not always want to get involved with. After sharing certain ideas with Joan Robinson, the latter characterized Polanyi as a supporter of laissez-faire liberalism, which was far from what Polanyi really was or how he wanted to be seen. Another example might be the case of Max Born, who warned Polanyi that being anti-capitalist, anti-liberal and an ardent opposer of every economic theory does not necessarily make him a socialist despite what common sense suggests. Science, expertise and authority is not being made in a social and political void but in a ruthless and quite unpredictable environment where people, as well as their practices, ideas, tools and visions have to fight for survival in moving arenas. The complexity of this fight is genuinely grasped by the concept of *sociotechnical imaginaries*.[11]

The theory of sociotechnical imaginaries offers to make conventional dichotomies of descriptive and normative, material and mental, agency and structure lose their charm by giving a more fine-grained analytical tool cutting through previous theoretical frames and being capable of providing novel insights. Sociotechnical imaginaries are "collectively held, institutionally stabilized, and publicly performed visions of desirable futures"[12] which are "animated by shared understandings of forms of social life and social order attainable through, and supportive of advances in science and technology".[13] The focus has shifted from attempting to give depersonalized accounts of the interconnectedness of science, technology and society towards attempting to follow individuals and their personal visions while these are entering into versatile public arenas and imaginary realms of past, present and future. This book tries to go one step further by portraying several clashes and concords of these subjectively drawn realities through unpacking immensely rich and mostly unstudied archival materials. The perspective that the historical pursuit of science or economics should be concerned about how the individuals imagined the past, present and future of the world they were embedded in, offers an uncustomary burden of archival research on the one hand, and a plethora of exciting stories on the other. By excavating the minutiae of individual beliefs and understandings, one can go beyond common labels like liberal, socialist, conservative, anarchist and many more, revealing that political history and the history of economic disciplines is far more complex than most accounts suggest. Embracing this historiographical multiverse, and treating imaginations of science, economic disciplines and political systems as being "produced by people with bodies, situated in time, space, culture, and society",[14] having interests, feelings and dreams and "struggling for credibility and authority"[15] makes the way for more fine-grained insights.

Mirowski, in his *Machine Dreams* (2002), showed that inquiries into the history of technology and the history of economic ideas can be mutually impregnating. His magnum opus compounded Cold War history and the history of postwar economics to show how parallel tendencies of dehumanization and mathematization of economic science gave birth to American neoclassical economic theory. Although Mirowski's contribution was pioneering and excellent in many respects, it did not come without having certain asymmetries. Mirowski was more interested in writing a history than writing histories. His narrative was strenuously being driven towards portraying what and how was driving the increasing cyborgness of economics, and paid less attention to depict other influences. Mirowski tracked the role and impact of natural sciences on the structure and content of orthodox economics, commonly called neoclassical economics.[16] He argued that

> without the computer, it would still be obligatory to bend a knee to the mantra that economics really was about "the allocation of scarce resources to given ends" and not, as it now stands, obsessed with the conceptualization of the economic entity as an information processor.[17]

This book shows that it was not obligatory to bend a knee to such a Robbinsian concept, and that a couple of intellectuals were, in fact, busy developing alternatives for the field entitled to explain the economy in the 1930s and 1940s (although in some cases not under the label of economics).

Perhaps, without the rising of what Mirowski calls *cyborg economics*, we would not have stuck to the 'older view' of economics patterned on classical mechanics in a physical sense, and instead, would have embraced another kind of economics driven by neither mechanistic nor mathematical machine dreams but economic dreams of a different nature. This book does not primarily intend to deconstruct or disassemble Mirowski's cyborg economics. Nevertheless, it might be seen refining some of his arguments on a couple of points. Mirowski analysed "the history of economics and the history of natural sciences as jointly evolving historical entities"[18] in his pioneering work, and, by doing so, made a forceful step towards slaying the commonly worshipped demon of writing internal disciplinary histories.

Mirowski has pointed out that one does not simply write a history of her own science without being concerned about others. He was making an interdisciplinary bridge visible between economics and natural sciences. One might wonder, whether he was also making other bridges invisible or less visible by doing so. By tracking Polanyi's attempts to craft a heart for postmodern economics, this book delves into other social realms which were confidently and heedlessly banished from most accounts of the history of economics. A freshly crafted eye paying less attention to the beaten paths of historiography of economics and more attention to the archival materials might explore quite neglected but immensely strong ties of economics to realms of economic policy, social and political movements, fictional and non-fictional literature and technological devices. Exploring a little slice of the history of economics, not through the austere official record of those who later became seen as the field's celebrated heroes, but by following a few dozen interrelated intellectuals of all kinds through their micro-social personal journey in manifold social realms, can provide new insights even to such excellently well-written, anti-dogmatic and original accounts like Mirowski's *Machine Dreams* (2002).

But *Machine Dreams* (2002), like every scholarly account, has certain flaws. Describing von Neumann as "the single and most important figure in the history of twentieth-century economics"[19] seems a bit anachronistic and arbitrary because Neumann was nowhere on the radar of expert economic discourses in the 1930s and 1940s while, for example, Keynes, Hayek, Robbins and Hicks were on the rise. Mirowski's argument is convincing about the computer being a "Promethean device"[20] and a "protean machine".[21] But why and on what basis did he choose to put this device into the focus of reimagining the history of economics instead of others? What else could explain his choice than the future role computers play in applied economics? Was there no other device, which, according to some thinkers of the 1930s and 1940s, had the potential to reform economics? This book suggests how Michael Polanyi, another famous Hungarian, imagined transforming economics with the unlikely help of another device, the film projector. Despite the considerable reliance on the use of a device, Polanyi's economics was anything but mechanical. This brings us to another debatable point in

Mirowski's account. He argued that in the 1930–50s "it was a taboo to speculate about mind, and all marched proudly under the banner of behaviourism, and society was thought to spring fully formed from the brow of an isolated economic man".[22] The following chapters will show that several intellectuals were actually occupied with thinking about the relation between the individual and society. Some of them even thought that revisiting this relationship was the only way out from the economic, moral, and disciplinary crisis they perceived. A couple of them, including Polanyi, sought to find answers by focusing on the mind. For Polanyi, the process of knowing, an inherent process of the mind, resided at the very heart of his germinating postmodern economics. Intellectuals were indeed exchanging ideas, publishing articles and giving radio speeches (using another technological device having a notable role in the economics of the 1930–40s) about their non-behaviourist ideas. This suggests that it was not so much a taboo to do so, only a road which was generally considered to be strange or too risky to take and not worth the trouble if one wanted to build a career in economics. But such disciplinary conventions and commonly held beliefs were less likely to stop mavericks like Polanyi, who came from a different background and was just entering the social sciences.

Mirowski pointed out that there was a second wave of immigrant natural scientists coming from Europe and finding sanctuary in the American economics of the 1930s. Others, like Frank, focused on a specific group of Continental emigrants, Jewish-Hungarian professionals who left Hungary in a "double exile", first to Germany, and then to England and the United States.[23] The two narratives meet at a somewhat unlikely place: an informal economics discussion group in Berlin with participants like Leo Szilard, John von Neumann, Eugene Wigner and others. Mirowski portrayed the seminar as an early incubator for cyborg economics, articulating the first steps in economics of figures who later played a pivotal role in the transformation of economic machine dreams by pushing these imaginations from mechanical and towards mathematical realms. He did not mention here a participant and later organizer of these meetings who was present at such a crucial early episode of cyborg economics but who took a very different path, Michael Polanyi. Perhaps, from what has been noted so far, one might argue that Polanyi's postmodern economics can either be seen as 'unmachinistic' (even anti-machinistic) and 'otherwise machinistic' (unlike both *economic protoenergetics* and cyborg economics), based on what importance one attributes to a device, the film projector, in his related thought. But, as the following chapters will explore, Polanyi's postmodern economics was immensely personal and only used the film projector to spread knowledge and a new concept of knowing without making any kind of machine-performativity inherent to its content. What Mirowski excavated from the archival sources in his *More Heat than Light* (1989) and *Machine Dreams* (2002), and he did an excellent job, was how two different kinds of 'machineness'-es penetrated into how certain economists and non-economists in general think about economics. Polanyi, despite witnessing the dawn of what later become seen as cyborg economics, and despite being in close relationship with the most notable cyborg-assemblers, banished machineness from the core of his economic thought. He was developing an economics of men, not of machines.

Machines, unlike men, seemed to be capable of doing similarly well in democratic and dictatorial régimes, being unaffected by moral dilemmas or chains restraining their free will. Polanyi's rescue mission to save liberalism, democracy and Western civilization through a new kind of economics disseminated through an economics film, although not technophobic, intended to leave behind technological devices. Machines, for Polanyi, were rather immoral techno-mercenaries than tireless and selfless myrmidons of those building democratic futures. They offer their services to whoever operates them, and they do not care about the consequences, even if taking the job brings closer the end of their shining world of cogs and wheels. Polanyi and some of his correspondents claimed to find machinistic traits as a fundamental common denominator in the dictatorial régimes of the Soviet Union and Nazi Germany. Traits, which, as the following chapters will show, Polanyi aimed to avoid and thus greatly influenced him in imagining and making his postmodern economics. He put his hope in men who, in contrast with machines, have a moral compass. One might argue that if somebody's moral compass is not in line with what one does, she can either change what she is doing or the moral compass she is using to judge her behaviour, thus human morality is nothing more than stories we tell to ourselves. Indeed, people have done terrible things by following their moral compass. Polanyi and his contemporaries were aware of this, as they had experienced at first hand some of the most extreme cases of human brutality feeding on a twisted, perverse kind of morality. But being able to modify either one's moral compass or what one does is not equal to not having a compass at all. People feel frustration if there is a perceived difference between what they do and what they think they should do. Machines do not feel frustration or anything else. Hope, love, faith, attachment is outside of their barren, insentient world. According to Polanyi and a handful of his intellectual friends, the multifaceted crisis of the West, having essentially moral origins, could and should also be addressed by a grand-scale project of moral revitalization – an endeavour which rests on the shoulders (and variable moral compasses) of men and not on the immutable amorality of heartless, iron-bred devices.

So far, literature on Polanyi and machines has been mostly concerned about whether and in what sense recent discussion about the relation of machines and knowledge can benefit from later Polanyian philosophy.[24] These accounts, having closer ties to philosophy of technology than to philosophy of science, were focused on whether and in what sense machines can understand, and were less concerned about other Polanyian aspects of knowing. Whether machines can believe and belong to a group of believers according to Polanyi has, so far, not been studied in detail. Studying these other aspects of knowing, however, might reveal asymmetries between human and nonhuman (pseudo)subjects of Polanyian knowing. If machines cannot feel, then they are unable to believe and to belong to a group of believers, meaning that they cannot embrace the two aspects of Polanyian knowing which makes personal knowledge personal. And because Polanyi did not define any other kind of knowing, machines, for Polanyi, are not knowing subjects. However, this book is more concerned about tracking machineness in Polanyi's literary practices in economic realms in the 1930s and 1940s and is less concerned about his other kind of machine practices in the period or his later philosophy, which was more fine-grained about machines but having only weak or no ties at all to economics. Even though tracking this specific kind of machineness is not the primary aim of this book it is necessary for at least two reasons. First, because previous literature on the history of economics described the period as quite homogeneously dominated by machine economics[25] without portraying contemporary rivals possibly deconstructing such a simplified view. This is not to call into question the claimed influence of natural sciences on economics. It is to draw attention to other kinds of influences and to balance accounts of the history of economics accordingly. And second, because Polanyi and his correspondents, though most of them were not developing economic protoenergetics or cyborg economics, used machinistic tropes in their discourses about economic and social realms.

Besides a few early accounts, most studies focusing on the economic thought of Michael Polanyi are of a relatively new breed. At the very beginning of my doctoral programme in 2014, I was encouraged by Phil Mullins, Eduardo Beira, Marta Feher and Tihamer Margitay, prominent members of the two Polanyi societies, to pursue studies of the economics of Polanyi, a field they considered promising but saw as quite uncultivated. During the years of writing my dissertation, Polanyi scholars have started to develop an increased interest in Polanyi's economics. Two international workshops were organized in recent years to discuss ongoing research on Polanyi's *Unemployment and Money: The Principles Involved* (1940) and his economic magnum opus, *Full Employment and Free Trade* (1945): the first was *Michael Polanyi's Unemployment and Money – 75* in Budapest (2015), the second, *Trade, Employment, and Public Policy: Polanyi Then and Now* in Boston (2017). Scholarly accounts have analysed the correspondence between Hayek and Polanyi,[26] studied the visual presentation of social matters in Polanyi,[27] contrasted the visual methods of Polanyi and Otto Neurath,[28] pursued whether Polanyi's economics can be seen as evolutionary,[29] and compared the economic thought of the two brothers, Michael and Karl Polanyi.[30] This book gives an inside view of Polanyi's personal journey towards the social sciences by exploring the story of how he was crafting a heart for postmodern economics.

The first chapter shows that Polanyi, in his early economic writings, was drawing boundaries towards both extreme liberalism and socialist planning. The perception of being in crossfire encouraged him to search for commonalities in the two extremes which he eventually found by delving into not only non-fictional literary realms but fictional ones of utopian and dystopian flavour. What he found was hard to notice but easy to grasp. Perhaps, because both orthodox laissez-faire liberalism and economic collectivism were successful not only in making certain things visible but also in making other things invisible. What Polanyi found had lain, quite unnoticed, in the common section of these manufactured invisibilities: mechanicality. It was something he eventually learnt not to unsee, something which became an antithesis not only to his practices aimed at crafting a postmodern economics but also to his later philosophy of science. But, being more than a scholarly insight, this epiphany also encouraged him to step forward, and to take action by writing and speaking to versatile audiences and publics in multiple forms about his non-mechanical third way.

The second chapter follows the thread of how Polanyi was using one of these forms with his *Unemployment and Money: The Principles Involved* (1940), which was the first educational film to portray not the working of the economy but a certain kind of economics. Polanyi cultivated a grandiose sociotechnical vision about how his film, carrying the seeds of a postmodern economics, could save democracy and Western civilization. But most people who came into contact with his film did not embrace his vision of "democracy by enlightenment through the film".[31] Some saw it as an interesting piece of visual art, some as economics coming in a strange package, others as part of their everyday to-do list or a threat to their beloved expertise from which they make a living. The chapter explores how Polanyi's film was acting as a *boundary object*[32] by bridging the social worlds of economists, film experts, managers, economics tutors and others, connecting such diverse groups and their manifold perceptions and satisfying the information needs of members of each group. By taking an ecological approach, focusing less on the process of *interessement* and the making of *obligatory passage points*, and more on mapping as many characteristic points of view as possible,[33] my aim is to explore the diverse habitat of socially crafted eyes and hands in which Polanyi's film needed to prove its fitness if it was to survive.

The third chapter analyses the social micro-cosmos of economic expertises in the 1930s and 1940s through the eyes of Polanyi and his correspondents. Recently found economic discourses in archival materials suggest that this period in the history of economic thought should be described as having a heterogeneous disciplinary milieu of rival traditions rather than as a univocal transition from economic protoenergetics to cyborg economics. Some of the intellectuals in Polanyi's network saw the increasing mathematization of social sciences in general as a symptom of authority- and success-mongering by following the time-tested suit of natural sciences, without noticing that the latter had already started to cast its still-celebrated enlightenment-tinted methodological skin. Others discussed the transformation of what counts as mainstream economics with Polanyi. One of the leading economists even asked him for private coaching in advanced mathematics, a field which he considered to be his weakness but perceived to be on the rise in the community of economists. Of course these people were not detached excavators of some objective economic reality. They had interests, dreams, feelings, hopes, fears, political convictions, religious beliefs, tastes and personalities which all put their stamp on the evolution of their economic expertise.

The fourth chapter examines the origins and the novelty of Polanyi's visual method and found possible influences in unexpected places, including a proto-Monopoly game of a Nobel Peace prize laureate economist, a Rockefeller-funded project of the president of General Motors Overseas developing physical apparatuses to represent the working of the economy, and Neurath's all-embracing international mass education experiment, ISOTYPE. Although a few commonalities can be found between these visual methods and Polanyi's, the latter seems to take a unique shape fitting more to the philosophy of economics it aims to represent than to the prevailing conventions of visualizing social matters. The chapter shows that Polanyi's visual method was as similarly innovative as the ideas constituting the very heart of his postmodern economics, and ends by sketching some overarching traits of Polanyi's visualization both present in his early work in physical chemistry and his later contributions to economics.

The fifth chapter explores the notion that, for some intellectuals, scientific and spiritual realms were not separated but connected. Without attempting to deconstruct the widely held historiographical topos of a mechanical view of science which would lay outside the scope of this book, this chapter dares only to offer several spiritually inclined views of science from Polanyi and his correspondents. Some argued for subordinating science to religious faith. Others, including Polanyi, warned that the rise of materialism and scepticism in the modern era has resulted in the expulsion of the spiritual from the realms of science. According to them, traditions, morals and faith are not something to be purged from the sacred grounds of science and economics. These are immanent parts of how people perceive the world around them, therefore explaining traditions should take them into account. They saw the roots of their contemporary economic and moral crisis in losing touch with personal, humane and moral aspects of life, and the solution in reintroducing these into scientific discourses.

The sixth chapter portrays what certain of Polanyi's interlocutors considered to be the cause of economic evil. Connecting mechanicality and evil was quite common in their accounts, but while some saw this machineness in the "evil titanism"[34] of the state, others discerned it in the "satanic mill of the market".[35] Polanyi was not satisfied with either of these mappings and traced the evil even further, eventually finding it in how economic theories of both laissez-faire liberalism and socialist planning handle man. Both treated people as fitters of pre-made economic schemes. Socialist planning viewed people as identical implementers of multi-annual plans having only the traits necessary for them to realize economic plans coming from above. Laissez-faire liberalism viewed people as having only the traits necessary for them to conform to economic models of economists. Polanyi was interested in how to avoid the unconditional surrender either to state authority or to the market mechanism in making economic theories addressing our everyday economic endeavours. His proposed solution might be seen as a postmodern alternative of *homo oeconomicus*, the concept which is still generally considered to be one of the theoretical cornerstones of economic science.

Notes

1 Hilgartner 2015.
2 The term 'postmodern' is being used in this book to denote what should come after 'modern' in Polanyi's view. He argued that modern science, economics and society have gone too far on the road of scepticism and utilitarianism which lead to the moral and economic crisis of his time. The postmodern economics he proposed is gradually unfolded in the upcoming chapters, which perhaps, makes this account the first book on postmodern economics. Polanyian postmodernism is being compared to other postmodern views in Chapter 5.
3 Jasanoff 2004.
4 Preda 2009, 18.
5 Ibid.
6 Jasanoff and Kim 2015, 15.
7 Ibid., 18.
8 Ibid., 4.
9 Latour 1990.
10 Ibid.
11 Jasanoff and Kim 2015.
12 Ibid., 4.
13 Ibid.
14 Shapin 2010.
15 Ibid.
16 Mirowski 1989, 1990, 2002; Hands and Mirowski 1998, 1999; Weintraub and Mirowski 1994.
17 Mirowski 2002, 522.
18 Ibid., 7–8.
19 Ibid., 521.
20 Ibid., 520.
21 Ibid., 521.
22 Ibid., 6–7.
23 Frank 2009.
24 Héder and Paksi 2012.
25 Mirowski 1989, 2002.
26 Jacobs and Mullins 2016.
27 Beira 2014; Mullins 2014.
28 Bíró 2017a, 2017b; Jacobs 2017.
29 Festré and Garrouste 2015; Festré 2017; Bíró 2018.
30 Gulick 2010, 2017.
31 Polanyi 1935c, 1.
32 Star and Griesemer 1989.
33 Ibid.
34 Editorial note in *The Listener* 1 June 1944.
35 Karl Polanyi 1944.

1 Polanyi's work against extreme liberalism and socialist planning

Polanyi started to mould his economic thought in the 1930s when the struggle between liberalism and socialism hit an unprecedented scale. He feared that Western civilization would be devoured by the growing influence of the dictatorial régimes coming from Nazi Germany and Soviet Russia. This put him on a mission to stop the proliferation of the related ideological and scientific monstrosities. The easy way to do so was to join the anti-dictatorial ranks of mainstream liberals and to sing their old hymns about the good, the bad and the democratic. But Polanyi did not agree with them either. And he sought to fight for what is best for society, even if this meant to fight against socialist and fascist dictatorship and their conventional counterpoint, liberal orthodoxy, at the same time. He wanted to have both the right aim and the right way. As a Central European who had fled from Hungary (1919), and then from Berlin (1933), he witnessed the destruction extreme ideologies brought to the democratic power structures of a nation and to the everyday life of its enlightened citizens. But he also witnessed how these ideologies successfully fired up the masses with clear-cut messages and passionate speeches about what should be done right here and right now. Meanwhile liberalism had lost its charm for the common layman due to its sophisticated narratives of why knowing and doing nothing is the best method possible in times of economic hardship. Polanyi was aware that, for saving liberalism, and eventually Western civilization, he needed a better message, and a better way of conveying that message to the masses.

Polanyi was a liberal, but he was also a maverick. By being critical about mainstream liberalism, which was widely considered to be the only antidote to extreme ideologies and dictatorial régimes, he risked being labelled as a blindfolded stranger from illiberal soil. He had no degree in economics or in any other social sciences, and only started to build his network of economists in 1928, five years before he crossed the English Channel to work at the University of Manchester as a well-known physical chemist. Paying no heed to this considerable risk, he sought to map the weaknesses of extreme liberalism in order to be able to develop and disseminate a better liberalism. Such 'betterness' was thought to be based on the elimination of fallacies and the capacity to raise the social consciousness of the general public more effectively than socialist planning. Polanyi realized that during the Great Depression the outcome of ideological and disciplinary rivalry in economic realms would be primarily decided by which camp's knowledge-claims were more plausible to the masses on one defining question: how can we end the economic downturn without inducing collateral damage on freedom and democracy?

Polanyi launched a new kind of liberalism clustering around answering this question. He did this by drawing rhetorical boundaries between his revamped liberalism and extreme liberalism and socialist planning respectively. The aim of these boundary drawing practices was to preserve and enlarge material and symbolic resources for economists cultivating this stream, and to defend their professional authority and expertise from those promoting extreme liberalism or socialist planning. Polanyi was heightening the contrast between his Keynes-inspired economic thought and the "two most pernicious extremes",[1] and made efforts to monopolize both the expertise of putting an end to the economic crisis and the authority to be able to plausibly claim to do so. Since the opposing streams had more resources, supporters and established practices in the scholarly and non-scholarly worlds, only an assertive campaign could breach their supremacy.

Being a liberal did not prevent Polanyi from condemning what he called "extreme",[2] "crude",[3] "orthodox"[4] liberalism based on "classical Free Trade doctrine"[5] and "complete laissez-faire".[6] He acknowledged that even this kind of liberalism could be, in a sense, a source of "material and moral blessings"[7] when it was being used to wipe out collectivist patterns. These patterns, in his view, had started to corrupt even the poster countries of economic freedom through the increasing number of regulations and trade restrictions. Polanyi wanted liberalism to return "with the fervour of its early intransigence"[8] but without its "superstitious fear"[9] hindering any kind of state intervention on principle – and without its self-imposed epistemic void drifting towards "extremism"[10] and "barbarous anarchy".[11] In one of his early economic writings, *On Popular Education in Economics*,[12] Polanyi identified four mistakes of the utilitarians whom he considered promoters of orthodox economic liberalism.

The first of these mistakes was that utilitarians failed to see that the just reward of the factors of production does not lead to the just reward of the people disposing the factors of production.[13] Such an idea might be seen connected to certain contemporary discourses. In a letter of 1935, Oscar Jaszi (another Hungarian liberal emigré) directed Polanyi's attention to Franz Oppenheimer's *Mehrwert* (added value) theory.[14] According to Oppenheimer, similarly to other geoists (or Georgists), people should own the value they produce or add during the process of production, and the added value coming from land should be distributed equally between each and every member of the society. This advice to check Oppenheimer's added value theory was given just in the time to influence Polanyi's economic awakening. But it did not, at least not significantly. We cannot be sure whether he checked Oppenheimer's related theory and the radical economic philosophy of geoism as

Jaszi advised him, but his first claimed mistake of the utilitarians suggests that he was aware of the political thorn in the eye of liberal economics usually referred to as the problem of added value.

According to Polanyi, the utilitarians' second mistake was their belief that the idea of the free market is applicable to all human relations. He thought this to be an overstatement. Moreover, he wittily noted that orthodox liberals had a 'magical belief' that the market takes revenge on anyone who dares to interfere with its inherent mechanism by raising the level of unemployment. Polanyi thought that interference with the market mechanism is not bad in principle. He emphasized that the alternative to economic planning is not some system of absolute and unconditional laissez-faire in which the state is "supposed to wither away"[15] as supporters of orthodox liberalism frequently proclaimed, but "freedom under law and custom" established and amended "by the State and public opinion".[16] He stressed the limits of both the power of the state and the market and proposed an intelligent third way.

The utilitarians' third mistake, in Polanyi's view, was their inability to explain trade cycles. He thought that Keynes, and his own Keynesian-inspired economic thought, was capable of such a feat, and, therefore more adequate to influence economic policies than laissez-faire liberalism. This mistake was particularly important because people wanted to get out of the economic downturn and they first needed an explanation about why this situation had occurred. Economic liberalism lacked a good explanation which threatened the very future of liberalism. Polanyi conceived that basically doing nothing except telling people that it will be better with time is not enough when millions live desperate and hopeless lives. Something should be proposed, and this should be properly communicated to the masses. This leads to what Polanyi called the fourth mistake of the utilitarians.

Polanyi thought that not just the "mechanism of the trade cycle",[17] but the whole "economic machinery"[18] should be readdressed in a way in which it would be "accessible to a wide popular discussion".[19] His third way was intelligent because raising the social consciousness of the "common layman" was central to his economic thought. Polanyi considered this social consciousness to be a "historic force more fundamental for the present [twentieth] century than even the national idea", and was convinced that "the struggle for it will dominate public life until it has found reasonable satisfaction".[20] The power of buying and selling was touched by the power of knowing. Although Polanyi conceived this general demand for social consciousness, this need of individuals to know how their everyday doings contribute to the 'big picture', to be quite new, he saw multiple contemporary "attempts" to achieve such consciousness in Soviet planning, German fascism and Roosevelt's New Deal.

But Polanyi's criticism of extreme liberalism did not end with the identification of these four mistakes. He pointed out that certain economic phenomena have different meaning and value for the individual and the community. According to Polanyi, laissez-faire supporters failed to address this issue, unlike Keynesians who kept it in mind when developing their related ideas. He contends that "the possession of money is not of the same, or even remotely similar, value to a nation as it is to the individual".[21] But he did not think that Keynesians were the only ones tinkering with non-individual schemes of economic value.

Polanyi recognized a correlation between the perceived economic situation and the general faith in the prevailing economic system. He was worried about the liberal economic system, which he thought would be severely threatened by an additional wave of unemployment bringing an additional wave of discontent. Polanyi saw that such discontent is an opportunity for fascist and Communist régimes to spread their influence. The power-mongering march of these extremes was not only likely to destroy democratic political settings, but also Western civilization, including its cultural products, e.g. liberal economics. Fascism and communism were ideological parasites leeching on the faith of people who hoped for a better tomorrow. But, instead of working on how to lead these people towards a brighter future, they imperceptibly made them first builders then slaves of a hopelessly blind and miserable one. Similarly to these dictatorial régimes, Polanyi devoted an important role to the masses. But in his vision, people are consciously working towards a vision of which they are not only executives but also co-dreamers. This probably sounds nothing like orthodox liberalism and its doctrine of the invisible hand either. Moreover, it might be tempting to view Polanyi's related endeavours as practices to make the invisible hand visible for the masses. But Polanyi did not think that such a hand could be made completely visible, or, in other words, that such complexity can be grasped by either the experts or the (re)educated masses. Was this a symptom of an internal contradiction or an inconsistency at the very heart of Polanyi's economic liberalism?

The doctrine of the *invisible hand* was used by Adam Smith to show that society is, in most cases, better off when individual economic agents seek their own gains and not some presumed social interest when making economic decisions. In Smith's account, finding out what is and what is not in the interest of the society is generally beyond the epistemic grasp of the individual. Every economic agent is best in making decisions based on her self-interest in her specific socioeconomic niche. The invisible hand is a real-life economic mechanism relying on the swarm of individual transactions but which is detached from the mind of the people making those transactions. Polanyi's interpretation of the invisible hand is different. He considered it a vision, residing not out there in the economy, but inside the mind of the people who have faith in it, and carrying it forward. Polanyi thought that orthodox liberals turned this vision into its own travesty by overextending its scope and claiming that it is the main guiding principle not only in the economy but in the entire social sphere. He considered the original a "great vision of harmonious human cooperation",[22] which, by so ambitiously claiming to have an increasing influence in various realms, lost something very important in the process.

Polanyi pointed out that orthodox liberalism was, in its original form, value-laden. It fought against feudal shackles, undeserved privileges and hereditary advantages. It was a source of moral blessings. It was a conscious endeavour for all those working for a new world and having faith in realizing a specific vision. In Polanyi's view, "it was perverse, therefore, to describe the capitalist system as a mere machine of interlocking appetites; as a cruel and inexorable robot".[23] Liberalism had spirit. Values, which provided the personal relation with all those believing in the vision and consciously developing it further. The plausibility of liberalism was not supported by its depersonalized, unfathomable, unchangeable, machinistic nature. It was provided by the personal belief of millions to make a change in their daily lives based on a common vision. What then, Polanyi asked, had led liberalism into this dead end?

A kind of scientific hubris. Polanyi presented several examples, from how Bentham intended to provide scientific grounds for the desires of man to build a good society, to how Ricardo and Malthus defined society itself "in terms of greed and mathematically progressive breeding".[24] According to Polanyi, these attempts were milestones in the "scientific travesty of society"[25] and contributed to the mechanization and dehumanization of liberalism. Mercy was banished from liberalism due to its "unscientific" nature, sympathy due to its perception as "the true enemy of welfare".[26] Polanyi enriched his description of such a hollow kind of liberalism by borrowing two Dickensian characters, Thomas Gradgrind and Josiah Bounderby. Gradgrind is a man of science who is "ready to weigh and measure any parcel of human nature, and tell you what it comes to".[27] In his world, everything is quantifiable, measurable and calculable. He named his two youngest children after Thomas Malthus and Adam Smith, two prominent political economists of classical liberalism. What seems worthy to note here is the character development of Gradgrind in *Hard Times*. Towards the end, he became a more humble and wise man, leaving the road of pure rationality and making "his facts and figures subservient to Faith, Hope and Charity".[28] It would, perhaps, be an exaggeration to say that Polanyi proposed a Dickensian turn of liberalism, but the parallel between the character development of Gradgrind and Polanyi's anti–utilitarian reimagining of liberalism have, undoubtedly, a lot in common.

The other character Polanyi referred to, Josiah Bounderby, constructed a mendacious narrative about himself as a self-made man who, from deep poverty and desolation, had risen to be a factory owner and financial expert. His story, in this context, offers an insight that economic realms are inhabited by both true and false beliefs, and who neglects this realization might face grave consequences. By uncovering the real story behind Bounderby, Dickens showed that there was a difference between how the ideal and the personality traits and behavioural patterns of the self-made man spread. Bounderby was not a self-made man, but wanted to be seen as one. He was a cruel capitalist, a man of wealth and power; someone who only believes in himself, and who lives from the faith of others. He was a figure opposing the role of blood and parentage in social relations. Bounderby found pleasure in the story of his own prevail due to his self-made man qualities and the story of Mrs. Sparsit, remnant of an old world, an aristocrat who became his house-keeper. He was too busy manufacturing his own egocentric world to care about anything else. For Polanyi, Bounderby was another example of how dehumanized orthodox liberalism could distort personality. Gradgrind is a caricature of science-mongering, Bounderby is a caricature of profit-mongering. As Dickens portrayed these two characters as best friends, Polanyi produced a view of classical liberalism which explains how these two principles tend to embrace each other.

According to Polanyi, orthodox liberalism fostered a mechanistic view by calling into question and trying to rule out everything which goes against economic necessity. Practices of knowing what is economic necessity and what is not (Gradgrind's profession), and of conducting business accordingly (Bounderby's profession) became primal. In Polanyi's view, "the market is a machine and an indispensable machine, but this machine need not overrule respect for humanity and social justice".[29] Polanyi wanted to break these inhuman "shackles of laissez faire"[30] to free the personal, social and value-laden qualities of liberalism. It seems adequate to examine which Dickensian characters correspond to this sentimental reimagination of liberalism in *Hard Times*, if any. Two characters seem to be the most fitting. The first, Cecelia Jupe, is a contrast, a foil to Louisa, daughter of Gradgrind. While Louisa was raised under the rigid charm of rationality and self-interest of her father and grew to be very much like him, Cecelia was all about sentiments and imagination. She was doing not-so-well in Mr. Gradgrind's and Mr. McChoakum-child's classes because she found it uneasy to see the life and death of people or animals as "a mere question of figures, a case of simple arithmetic".[31] She withstood against the irrational worship of rationality, and was a sober, sentimental and humane voice in a cruel, industrial and mechanical world. The second, Stephen Blackpool, was portrayed as a man of integrity and moral, who eventually died because of the corruption of his environment. Blackpool had a hard life, but he had a star in the sky on which he could rely in times of great sorrow. His personal relation to this star and its light, his unbreakable belief in what it represented for him in this otherwise decayed realm provided him spiritual relief, even in his last minutes at the bottom of a mine shaft. Polanyi's leading light was not a star but a vision of a kind of economic liberalism based on social consciousness, and his radiating light was economics enlightenment. However, he did not want to be a sole believer but one among many working together against the moral and epistemic decline of Western civilization.

Polanyi warned that the hollow, mechanical worldview goes hand in hand with moral scepticism and with the prevailing, modern view of science. He pointed out that university teachers write and speak in a non-imaginative and "timid"[32] manner, and their writings "do not stand by the acts of their imagination but merely put them forward as provisional pointers which should lead to demonstrable truth". Academic statements are often "slow", "cumbersome" and not as "expressive" as their less prosaic counterparts in fictional or business literature. In Polanyi's view, "universities are not places where either works of imagination are composed, or important action undertaken, or a personal faith professed".[33] They are places where university teachers make observations, draw inferences and phrase statements which they believe to be true. Teachers are not acting like "prophets"[34] guiding their people out of moral and epistemic crises. But they are not simply "scribes" either, disseminating pure 'facts' in the way that Gradgrind perceived his inhuman mission in *Hard Times*. Polanyi thought that there is a personal and moral message which could and should be disseminated by academic minds which, despite seeming to "work mechanically", would be capable of developing "immense powers".

Polanyi pointed out that what seem to be "stale" or "placid" "intellectual pools"[35] have capacity to generate power, "there lies dormant a mighty torrent"[36] at universities. According to Polanyi, contemporary academics are only concerned with what fits into their specific system of thought. He stressed that even the "heavens may fall without disturbing the peace of the academic mind, provided they fall by some accident which does not affect any major principles of academic thought".[37] Academics, as experts, are looking for discoveries which might have overall influence on their expertise. They are doing this in pre-existing systems of thought which have limitations. Polanyi argued that such academic blindness has a disciplinary and a social face. The first can explain the power of academic orthodoxy in relation to the knowledge-claim of an individual scholar and the general opinion of the scientific community; the second can explain why this blindness is also of great social concern. For demonstrating the latter, Polanyi relied on the example of how mass unemployment was addressed in discourses of classical economic liberalism. He explained how Smithian ideas "grew into a complex speculative structure of great beauty and analytical power",[38] and by doing so, lost their relation to economic experience. Believers of the Aristotelian cosmos did not see the birth and death of stars, because for them the heavens were, by definition, a perfect and unchanging realm. Similarly, mass unemployment remained unseen by followers of classical economic liberalism because, for them, it was axiomatically impossible.

Followers of classical economic liberalism, therefore, condemned other voices as "complete nonsense"[39] disseminating the "most primitive elements of economic science".[40,41] They framed their own blindness as adherence to the most developed elements of economic science against unscientific common nonsense and "truisms",[42] on the one hand, and as efforts to defend capitalism from the threat of socialism, on the other. Polanyi showed that the "overbearingly rejected"[43] idea of mass unemployment became widely taught in British universities with the triumph of Keynesian economics. Previously, mass unemployment "was the kind of thing nobody could help seeing straight away unless he had been specially trained in academic economics to explain it away" or had such a blind faith in his professors which overwrote "evidence of his own common sense". Polanyi warned that the systematic thought of the academic world does not guarantee the soundness of its knowledge-claims, or that scholars produce the best knowledge possible. And when academic speculation, in the form of manufacturing and disseminating demonstrable facts, clashes with sound common sense, the latter often has only little chance against the influence of academic discourses.

Polanyi pointed out that, when a new demand for social justice appeared in the nineteenth century fostering wide-scale social reforms for workers, it met a "theoretical opposition"[44] based on the ideas of Adam Smith and other laissez-faire supporters. Professors of political economy were spreading the "'inexorable laws' of economic science"[45] at universities and elsewhere enlightening or corrupting (depending on whom we are asking) the mind of the intelligentsia. Self-interest became the 'guiding light' against the clueless and uneducated proposals, e.g. to ban extensive child labour in mines. Claims of struggling from economic exploitation, arbitrariness and corporate social irresponsibility became unfounded in the moment they were said out loud or put down to paper because these phenomena were considered to be, by definition, non-existent. Liberal economics was made to be perfect, immutable and untouched by human fallibility – a kind of academic heaven. As Polanyi pointed out, academic obtuseness came across a natural ally in all those interested in maintaining the economic status quo. Certain patterns of academic and lay epistemologies found each other, just as Gradgrind and Bounderby became best friends in Dickens' *Hard Times*. These epistemologies have been increasingly intertwined and so have the plausibility of their knowledge-claims. The "most burning"[46] social and economic problems are of "immediate academic significance".[47]

A cloister-like academic world is particularly dangerous because non-democratic forces often aim to seize these distinguished epistemic terrains to strengthen their power. Seeing science as the "highest authority"[48] threatens overwriting everything non-scientific, even common sense. Polanyi showed that while the West portrayed both the Nazis and the socialists as having insufficient education, they were, in fact, thoroughly educated. The problem was not so much an epistemic void. It was having a bad education based on speculative academic excesses. These examples show that, when this kind of academic system meets a political movement with an 'all or nothing' attitude, the consequences can be disastrous. But it can also be very harmful when it is embedded in a country with a democratic political life. Polanyi thought that the excesses of utilitarian idealism and laissez-faire theory made an inhuman milieu in the economic science of the United Kingdom by fostering a kind of mechanistic liberalism. He thought that the academic reimagining of economic liberalism should be realized by taking on some axioms from outside. Academia should be more open to other arenas of civic life and more critical to its own disciplinarity.

The "crystallising and re-crystallising"[49] of scholarly consensus has to be more responsive to what is happening outside the academy. Science, this fascinating combination of "rigorous discipline"[50] and "fruitful flexibility"[51] has to cultivate a feeling for what is outside its ever converging realms of systematic academic thought. Economic liberalism went astray because it rejected everything it could not fit into its mechanistic, value-neutral and dehumanized perspective. Polanyi pointed out that building further this axiomatic structure became an end in itself. Thinkers of laissez-faire liberalism were rather led by their self-interest to craft elegant orthodox theories (perhaps to obtain academic credit, perhaps from the urge to act convention-ally) instead of crafting non-orthodox ones more compatible with economic experience. Polanyi's solution was to cultivate a kind of social sensitivity in liberal economics. He seemed to be suggesting that not only does humanity need knowledge, but knowledge, as well, needs humanity.

Polanyi stated that the socialists claimed to establish a common scheme of economic value which was in fact "far from being able to summarise the essence of an economic situation independently of the autonomous exchanges"[52] and to "replace their operations by a comprehensive scheme of its own".[53] According to Polanyi, eventually the Soviet Government should recognize such a failure to substitute the numerous individual valuations arising from the exchanges of economic agents. Going into the details, Polanyi reflected on some of the findings of Colin Clark's *A Critique of Russian Statistics* (1939). Clark's book had revealed "anomalies of Russian valuation which even within one group of articles of consumption amount to more than tenfold distortions of relative values".[54] Polanyi wanted to show the inadequacy of such economic valuation with the following simile:

> the compilation of statistics on objects consumed, comprising the number of handkerchiefs, spectacles, prayer books, and countless other kinds of merchandise, are as meaningless from this point of view as would be the valuation of the National Gallery by square yards of canvas or pounds of paint.[55]

He claimed that socialist economic theory propagated the "just reward of the people"[56] in its rhetoric similarly to orthodox liberalism. However, in this system, unlike liberalism, such 'justice' was not seen coming from an idea of market but from an idea of equality.

Another weakness of socialist planning was its inability or unwillingness to develop an idea about the economic role of prices and profit. The central direction of prices and the elimination of profit dominated the ideology and the respective theories. However, as Polanyi pointed out, even though the influence of the "evil powers of the market"[57] was officially denied in this régime, it reappeared in unexpected forms to take an increasing effect. Profit became camouflaged as "planned surplus"[58] or "director's fund",[59] and took effect in the realms of state enterprises and multi-year economic plans. But disguise is needed when there is something to hide. And, in most of the cases, as Polanyi showed us, it was not only the outcrop of the profit principle.

Dictatorial régimes with centralized power structures tend to embrace "political gangsterism",[60] "arbitrary privileges"[61] and "favouritisms".[62] Surrogates for profit were mainly pseudo-currencies to reward loyal subordinates and to forge political capital. Corruption and oppression grew strong, without anything in its way and, sometimes, without anybody noticing it.

According to Polanyi, proponents of socialist planning recognized the existence of trade cycles, and claimed that a centralized direction of economic life could and should fight these in favour of the people. The state had annexed the entire media, so getting reliable information about how economic policies perform was an exceptionally burdensome if not impossible task. For many, the only choice left was believing or not believing the propaganda without making further inquiries themselves. For a few, peeking behind the veil of official news meant flirting with epistemic freedom and political consciousness. But such flirting held no great promise.

Socialist planning was seen as trying to develop a kind of social consciousness which crude liberalism lacked. Polanyi did not elaborate on his opinion of the motives of the promoters of such consciousness. Did hatchers of these ideas believe in them or did they have more pragmatic reasons for developing and disseminating these narratives? Polanyi seemed to treat these ideas more as fallacious beliefs and misconceptions of not-so-well-informed people rather than a maleficent memento of the political manoeuvres of Machiavellian actors. Although Polanyi considered this kind of economic consciousness fallacious, he acknowledged that socialists had successfully developed a "socially purposeful"[63] view of economic life which could strengthen the demand for other, more accurate kinds of social consciousness.

Polanyi also acknowledged the success of these consciousness-building attempts of socialism to reach out to the masses, but warned that this kind of consciousness did not come without its side effects on freedom. He thought that "democracy can satisfy this craving for economic consciousness"[64] too by "creating a popular understanding of economic matters". He saw this as "the only way to obtain economic consciousness while preserving freedom of thought"[65] by other means than the "dictatorial regimentation"[66] of socialist and fascist régimes. His approach was "to elaborate the new economic ideas and at the same time to simplify their outline so as to make them comprehensible to the intelligent layman".[67] He thought that by doing this one can raise social consciousness without limiting freedom or without amplifying non-democratic patterns of social life.

Polanyi thought that central direction of the economy is impossible for various reasons. To illustrate what cannot be managed in the economy and why, he constructed three examples (or thought experiments) of imaginary economies.[68] The first, *atmospheric economy*, is about what happens when the market mechanism ceases to exist because there is only one good, which, no matter what, has to be produced and consumed.[69] That is a hypothetical economy in which neither the producers nor the consumers have a word in what counts as a good and what constitutes a market. Unmanageability comes from the absence of the dollar-voting phenomenon, the feedback mechanism of making consumer choices between multiple commodities. The second example, *economy of smells and noises*, is about what would happen if the costs of production in factories were negligible and the production externalities would be disproportionately high.[70] What is unmanageable here, according to Polanyi, is how to minimize the overall amount of externalities in a situation in which bargaining about social costs is not an option for factories. The third, *clockwork economy*, is about an economy which works like one big machine producing all the goods the society needs but consisting of perfectly unique parts, each with only one producer capable of creating it, and only one consumer needing it for further production.[71]

These imaginary economies were critiques showing that, whatever socialist propaganda says, economies could and should not be planned. They were thought experiments exploring the hidden implications of taking the road of 'planners', and showing the economic consequences of pretending to know what could not be known in the long run. In the first thought experiment, the *atmospheric economy*, there is only one commodity, which is a kind of atmosphere providing satisfaction for every kind of human need. Atmosphere is produced in every factory, and it is consumed by everyone. Being the only commodity, it has no substitute and complementary products. Every consumption is atmosphere-consumption. Even though there are several producers and consumers, there will be no competition between them. There is no point in making additional money or investments. There is no place for mutual adjustments. There are no incentives and feedback mechanisms of an economic nature. Business coagulates into mere bureaucracy.

The second thought experiment, the *economy of smells and noises*, explains what could go wrong in the economy when basically there are no production costs, but there are production externalities of great extent. In this imaginary economy, individual producers are not so much interested in curtailing production costs any further, and neither individual producers nor individual consumers are very much interested in reducing production externalities. There is a trade-off between maximizing individual satisfaction and minimizing externalities, but there is no good solution. There is no conceivable rational solution by central direction either because of the great number of individual producers and consumers. Nor can it be solved by bargaining because individual producers are not interested in reducing their externalities and those of others. This second thought experiment shows what would happen if fundamentally there were no production costs and the 'tragedy of the commons' became the new normal. Business turns into a corrupted race for preserving corporate social irresponsibility or, again, coagulates into mere bureaucracy.

The last thought experiment, the *clockwork economy*, explores the consequences of having absolutely no competition between producers. It is about having one extremely complex machine which consists of about 30,000 parts, each made by a distinct factory. Once the machine is being put together, it satisfies every kind of need, but it satisfies none until it is completely finished. How, then, should the resources be distributed between the factories? Parts of the machine are like perfectly complementary products. There is no economic reason to prefer one part or factory over another. There is one seller of each part, and only one buyer in the whole economy. Factories can set any price they want. There is no good way of allocating the resources (or to define a picking order) between the factories or of establishing the price of each part. It would lead either to chaos or to an arbitrarily fixed allocation of resources by the state, the latter being, once again, a way business coagulates into mere bureaucracy.

These thought experiments are, of course, not free of errors. The *atmospheric economy* is not a good example to explore what happens with economic incentives by fixing what could and should be produced and consumed because such an atmosphere, being a metaphorical bundle of all goods and services, cannot leave by definition any need unsatisfied. If this first imaginary economy is to show where the central direction of production and consumption leads, it would be better to differentiate between satisfied and unsatisfied needs of people and explore how the fixation of one need affects anything else in the economy. In a nutshell, by having both only one completely homogenous market (a_1) and a good (also a market) not defined by the dollar votes of customers (a_2), we cannot be completely sure which of these two fixed points induce the unwanted outcome. Perhaps, having only one of them, and thus taking the road of ceteris paribus, would result in a better thought experiment.

The second thought experiment also has its flaws. If more production means more externality, and, if consumers do want products but do not want externalities, less externality and therefore production could become a product in itself. Non-production becomes a kind of production having its own product, market, supply and demand. For example, if I move to the suburbs for a healthier environment I must pay the additional price for not having extreme air and noise pollution nearby. Polanyi did not seem to recognize this mechanism. He assumed that, in his example, there are only two solutions, both impossible: having the factories bargaining about reducing externalities and having the state decide on reducing externalities. However, if producers are led by profit-seeking, and, in this imaginary economy, they are, it seems that there is a third solution: the consumers who, after satisfying their needs to a certain extent, value non-production more than additional production, become the driving force of decreasing production externalities by having effective demand for non-production. Because externalities in the example affect large areas around the factories, non-production seeking customers and their sellers induce a spatial restructuring in the economy. The more externality-sensitive costumers (or those having effective demand for less externality) are gradually separating from the less sensitive ones, and eventually, ghettoization prevails. Production, and therefore production externalities, do not increase infinitely. There is a break, even if we presume purely self-interest seeking economic agents without a grain of concern for their hypothetical planet of smells and noises.

Perhaps the third thought experiment, *clockwork economy*, is the most flawed. If the only way to satisfy needs is through a machine which consists of 30,000 parts and each requires its own factory, how could these factories be built and operated by people? They have no needs until the last part is installed into the machine and it starts functioning? If so, why are they doing anything? If they do have needs, how do they satisfy these (e.g. eat, sleep) if there is no other way of meeting needs, due to the axioms, besides using the machine? Why are people not supposed to die in the process of making parts of this machine in factories? In this imaginary economy, people are being treated as small wheels themselves until the machine is finished and then they all of a sudden become consumers with preferences, tastes and decision-making capabilities, which is rather inconsistent. Polanyi thought that in this imaginary realm factories can define the price of their unique machine-parts; the only thing they have to consider is the minimum substinence of all other economic agents. There are, at least, two problems with this statement. First, in this system, there are only machine-parts in the economy until the great machine is finished and one part-producing factory is not interested in having the part of the other factory, therefore there are no economic transactions and there is no use of money. How, then, do factories define the price of their machine-parts, and for whom? Second, if people are just wheels until the machine is completed, they have no cost of subsistence (they do have perhaps maintenance costs but that is to be covered by the factory using them). If there is no subsistence level, it cannot act as a guide in price-setting or in anything else. This thought experiment has serious inconsistencies. If Polanyi's aim was to construct a thought experiment showing what becomes unmanageable in the economy when there is no competition, perhaps he should have hypothesized an economy which consisted of perfectly unique products satisfying perfectly unique needs and left other factors untouched.

Besides demonstrating why central planning of the economy is unmanageable, it was equally important for Polanyi to show that it implies radicalism. One of his examples was *Soviet Communism: A New Civilisation?* (1936) by Sidney and Beatrice Webb (founders of the London School of Economics and the periodical *New Statesman*) in which the authors argued that communism is more than a political ideology, it is a new civilization which will eventually replace Western civilization. Although the Webbs were Fabian socialists having a strong commitment to gradual and democratic change through social reform towards Communism, their ultimate purpose, the 'big picture' they had in mind was, no doubt, radical. Their Brobdingnagian book of more than 1200 pages is a thoroughgoing manifesto and, perhaps, a guide-book about how to lay down the foundations of this new civilization. But, for Polanyi and many others, democratic means were seen here justifying undemocratic ends. In *The New Machiavelli* (1911) H.G. Wells caricatured Sidney and Beatrice Webb as Oscar and Altiora Bailey. A couple having a "bony"[72] soul and an irresistible desire to bring what they consider order and perfection to the world. No matter what. And whether the world wants it or not. They were on a mission to classify and rationalize everything but their omniscience lacked any kind of metaphysical and social sensibility. They were, in their social insensibility, quite similar to Dickens' Gradgrind and Bounderby. However, Oscar and Altiora Bailey, unlike their Dickensian counterparts, were not content with living a life which corresponds to their peremptory ideals. They were eager to get entangled with the strings of the world, and to become rather puppeteers than puppets on its stage.

Wells wrote his novel in the first person, telling his story through the eyes of Richard Remington, a high-achiever at Cambridge who had robust enthusiasm for "statecraft"[73] and politics. Remington's late discovery of love and women brought disaster both to his predictable personal life and to his career, similarly to how falling stars shook the belief in the supralunar sphere of Aristotelian cosmology. First, Wells portrayed Machiavelli himself as a foil to his protagonist, then he used the Baileys for the same purpose. For them, love and sentiments were not related to their grand-scale, universal explanation of society. Remington learnt through his love affair with Isabel Rivers that the separation of sentiments from knowledge and social progress is artificial, and makes way for a model which might be inherently consistent but has serious explanatory defects. Wells warned, similarly to Dickens and Polanyi, that the humane side of our world is not to be ignored. Even working towards a humane vision could be inhuman itself. And reformers taking such a road might easily find themselves turning into the nemesis of their own ideal. Social reformers always have a personal story inextricable from their endeavours to reimagine and reshape society. This book also follows, in this sense, a Wellsian narrative, because it aims to explore both the personal journey and the sociotechnical vision of Polanyi in the relevant two decades.

Whether Wells portrayed Sidney and Beatrice Webb properly or not in *The New Machiavelli*, their *Soviet Communism: A New Civilisation?* was, indeed, more of a propagandistic declaration than an impartial discussion paper. They seemed to have relied mostly on official Soviet records and pronouncements, and bothered little to gather information from the flesh and blood residents already living under Soviet Communism. Polanyi had corresponded with his Russian friends (Alexander Frumkin, Nicolai Semenoff) for years, and even visited the Soviet Union a few times. Having been raised in Hungary, he had experience with multiple shades of socialism, including the radical ideology of the Hungarian Soviet Republic, which made him flee the country and seek refuge in the rapidly industrializing and open Weimar Republic. Polanyi published his own account of Soviet Russia, *U.S.S.R. Economics – Fundamental Data, System, and Spirit* in 1935, one year before the Webbs' book hit the shelves. His account pointed out that there was a huge gap between Soviet propaganda and the real economic performance of the Soviet Union. Polanyi argued that most of the people in the USSR were poor, and that the Soviet practices of frequent (re)planning, as well as the methods of commensurating multiple kinds of commodities, made socialist accounts about winning the economic race less plausible.[74] In his view, economic planning necessarily forces a set of moral convictions on society in a non-democratic way. The Webbs' book was radical in this sense. They might have been fostering only gradual social reforms and not a great and reckless leap towards Communism, but they had not considered any other viable option and did not draw the attention of their readers to the possibility that there might be any. Their depersonalized and insensitive way of doing things was in deep contrast with the Polanyian perspective.

For Polanyi, another example of the radicalism of planning was F.H. Knight's stance on economic control. In his review of *Modern Economic Society* by Sumner H. Slichter (1931), Knight argued that the control of economic activity became a religious ultimate.[75] Asking who controls what, how and by what means in the economy was increasingly seen as betraying the common aim of easing economic hardship. Enemies of this perspective and school were framed as enemies of the people. In this system, there was no place for intelligent discussion or critical inquiries. There was no place for *unarmed bohemians*. There was a dominant view which has to be held by everyone on the side of Truth with a capital T, and it was believed that all other views would eventually fall one way or another. Economics education turned into an engine of propaganda spreading such 'untainted' belief in economic control to the masses. Even universities embraced salesmanship of ideas over groping towards truth, regardless of the prevailing popular conceptions of truth, objectivity and progress. Polanyi perceived this threat of economic collectivism to the culture of discussion quite similarly to Knight. He argued that the spread of such a religious ultimate would lead to the polarization of society, and would eventually divide it into "irreconcilable camps"[76] which could only be governed by violent means and dictatorship. Polanyi argued this undesirable process should be reversed by fostering the voluntarily dissolution of conflicting groups. He pointed out that, in a free society, there are always a plethora of dissentions and conflicts. The "unending task"[77] of the man of liberty is, therefore, to seek for harmonious, non-violent solutions, and to teach this culture of finding and solving problems to the general public. Knight was rather pessimistic about the chances of stopping this religious ultimate from taking over because he thought that it had already triumphed or was very close to victory. Polanyi believed that the process could be stopped and reversed, and took on this mission of saving liberty himself.

Knight claimed economics education to be a transmitter of propaganda. But it became a vehicle for saving liberalism, democracy and Western civilization in Polanyi's account. By establishing centres of economics education demonstrating and discussing his film and economics, Polanyi hoped that a "calm light"[78] of epistemic and affective qualities would radiate throughout the entire society, and would put an end to the dauntless march of the lapdog ideologies of dictatorial régimes. He did not consider either the content or the method of his agenda to be set in stone and was open to the ideas of others. His economic liberalism was also tempered in this sense. It was not an enemy but a friend of the culture of discussion. Polanyi corresponded with many intellectuals, some with considerably different convictions. He did not fire his arrows from a well-guarded ivory tower of liberal thought. Rather he went to the agora to discuss economic matters with scholars promoting the planning of science and economy. One example of these adventures was his exchange of letters with Lancelot Hogben about economic planning. Polanyi carefully mapped the issues on which they were on the same page. They both refused to accept Robbins' orthodox liberalism; they both considered an unsatisfied need for social conscience to be the cause of the spread of socialism in the realms of the intelligentsia, and beyond. And, more importantly, they both considered arenas of education a defining site of the battle between socialism and liberalism. Although they disagreed about basically everything else, including whether economics of the plenty is an option, Polanyi made Hogben feel that they agreed "far more closely"[79] than Hogben agreed with other leading socialist scientists such as Hyman Levy and J.B.S. Haldane. In light of the radical and exclusive manner of the planning movement, this was quite an achievement.

Polanyi conceived that "errors both of Classical Free Trade doctrine and of socialist teachings have done a great deal to confuse people and to undermine their confidence in modern society".[80] He also pointed out that a common point in their rhetorics was the implication that there is no third way for handling or ordering economic affairs. He proposed that "instead of accepting this joint view [seeing each other as the sole alternative] of orthodox liberals and collectivists",[81] a new kind of liberalism with social consciousness should be developed and disseminated. He thought that by opposing each other

> the social and individual interests of man seems to have separated two essentially connected elements and formed a pair of evil principles which tend to disintegrate society by pulling in the economic collectivism on the one side and of blind self interest on the other.[82]

Polanyi pointed out that orthodox liberals embraced the implication that there is a "logical system of complete laissez-faire, the only rational alternative to which is collectivism".[83] He claimed to find precisely the same position in the collectivists' view suggesting that "none of the evils of the market can be alleviated except by destroying the whole institution root and branch".[84] He was sure that the choice is not between just these two, but several options. But what are these options then and how to choose between them? Polanyi thought that the essentially Keynesian economic thought he proposed was compatible with multiple "standards of economic justice",[85] and that the economy can operate in conformity to any such standard. The task ahead is then to clarify what does our society mean by 'economic justice', and to establish an agreement on one of the imaginable options. Polanyi said little about the process of establishing such social agreement. But it did not seem to be simple either. Establishing such agreement requires a prior agreement on the method, otherwise it is being established in a non-democratic way. But how to agree on the method of establishing a social agreement? With an even earlier agreement. And so on. Without claiming that it is impossible to establish a social agreement on the standards of economic justice, this is only to point out that the conventional solution even contemporary constitutional democracies use to cut through this infinite regress disguises non-democratic elements.

Polanyi thought that a form of Keynesianism, the third way besides these two extremes, could "restore the decency and vitality of the capitalist system".[86] In order to be able to do this, more focus should be given to the social implications of Keynesian theory to facilitate the dissemination of its "vital message" through a "wider circulation".[87] He emphasized that there are multiple methods of ordering human affairs. He proposed 'supervision' which he described as "almost the opposite of planning"[88] because it recognizes individual initiative and relies heavily on them unlike planning which would subordinate initiatives to a central will. Supervision was different from the orthodox liberal way of ordering human affairs, as well. Extreme liberals, in Polanyi's view, believed that order emerges from chaos in a natural way, and every individual and collective effort which tries to influence how human affairs are being ordered is unnatural, and therefore does more harm than good. Polanyi took the middle ground. He thought that the public was perplexed by both the memories of the Great Depression and the seductive offer of totalitarian régimes to "ensure full employment"[89] with economic control.

The battle between extreme liberalism and socialist planning was not so much a unique phenomenon in Polanyi's view, but a single instance in a never ending war of social patterns. Polanyi thought that there is a "permanent rivalry between the individualist and collectivist patterns of social life, and the balance between them is ever shifting to and fro".[90] His historical account was compatible with the essence of both the strain and the interest theories of ideology. He believed that social structure affects patterns of social life (see his argument against dictatorship), and that the social structure could also be altered by changing these practices (see his project on economics education). The excess of individualist patterns of social life threatens with barbarous anarchy; the surplus of collective patterns fosters tendencies towards dictatorship. According to Polanyi, the most important political problem was to find the middle ground

> between these two most pernicious extremes, to draw correctly the line which divides those cases in which it is the duty of the State to interfere, from those cases in which it is the duty of the State to abstain from interference.[91]

Such boundary-drawing was no assignment for single reformers, but a task which needed extensive social (re)conciliation.

Polanyi pointed out that the justification for the inequalities in income is basically the same in the two system. He wrote that in a planned economy "If a manager gets the income of thirty workers, it is only because his work is thirty-times more valuable. Therefore, there is no: exploitation. But this is exactly the same reason which liberal economy gives for inequality of incomes."[92] In the first, the difference in the income should be just, because every unjust difference in the income would be exploitation which is non-existent. In the second, the difference should be just, because the market mechanism abolishes every unjust difference. Polanyi showed that neither of these arguments was convincing, and that they were similar in a non-convincing way. He did not completely unpack but clearly tinkered with deductive matters, or more precisely, with the problem of axioms. What is even more unsettling here than the discretionary nature of deductive arguments is how this trait remains hidden from most of the general public. Polanyi warned that "the extent of social injustice could become about equal in both systems"[93] and that even the "system of capitalistic enterprise can be made to conform to any standard of social justice on which society is sufficiently agreed".[94] How could one build democracy in a democratic way, then? By properly informing members of the general public about economic ideas. Polanyi imagined that an enlightened public would be capable of reaching an agreement on standards of social justice without being misguided by fallacious economic theories and power-mongering politicians.

Polanyi thought that both socialist planning and extreme liberalism failed to produce an idea about the limits of buying and selling. But unlike orthodox liberals who deemed its power limitless, promoters of socialist teachings thought buying and selling does not have power at all. Both caused much trouble for their supporters. Polanyi pointed out that while the Soviets' baseline was state-driven production they "have, out of necessity, submitted more and more to the guidance of prices and profits".[95] He claimed to find an opposing tendency in the Western countries. While these insist on conducting business life on the traditional principles of prices and profits, they "have, out of necessity, admitted a wide range of restrictions and subsidies by the State".[96] Polanyi believed in the power of buying and selling, but thought that it is necessary to establish limits by the state through public opinion. What are these limits and how these limits are being established depend on social agreement on the standards of economic justice.

One could argue that the social agreement Polanyi proposed was nothing more than revisiting the social contract theories of the seventeenth–nineteenth centuries. I think it was closely related to these ideas but had something which makes it very different, and perhaps even more advanced. Classical social contract theories were created to provide political legitimacy for the state and for those exercising power in its name. The explicit aim of these social contracts was to defend the people from each other, who were imagined to be essentially peccable, immoral, brutish and uneducated, by avoiding the situation of *bellum omnium contra omnes*. Social contracts were non-democratic tools in social and political warfare. They were not so much engines of democratic reforms or revolutions but confessions of the 'sins' of the people towards the omnipotent state asking for its inscrutable advice. The main question here is how can fundamentally flawed, savage and uncooperative people consciously and responsibly make a decision about establishing a social contract which they are by definition unable to grasp? If people can establish such a contract, they are nothing like their characterization. If their characterization is right and they can make such a decision, it would not be a conscious and responsible decision. Although Polanyi did not expound a similar argument about social contracts, he seemed to work hard on this inconsistency lying in the very heart of the Enlightenment heritage.

Polanyi's social agreement was focused around a kind of epistemic empowerment. He had a rather optimistic attitude towards the masses and thought that people could and should be educated in order to be able to make a better social agreement. Knowledge and the related responsibility to use knowledge was not attributed to the state, but to the people. It was not a manifesto about why the epistemic sovereignty of the state should be acknowledged, but a manifesto about why and how the epistemic empowerment of the general public is necessary for democracy. It could be seen as a readdress of the earlier social contract theories, but it was rather a more sophisticated remake than a simple revisit. Furthermore, Polanyi's social agreement was dynamic. It was imagined to be modifiable at any time and to any degree, by public opinion following the tides of the struggle between the individualist and collective patterns of social life. It was not something setting a specific status quo into stone for a longer period, rather a temporary arrangement of a consenting society in a state of permanent evolution. As the balance between these social forces is "ever shifting to and fro"[97] so does the social agreement which is similarly "never at rest, and every historical force, all rival interests and ideas deflect its position in one way or another".[98]

Polanyi believed that a "correct Keynesian policy should regenerate free competition and re-establish capitalism on renewed foundations"[99] as a middle road between the two extremes. At the end of his *Full Employment and Free Trade* (1948), he made it clear that "in the controversy between Laissez Faire and Planning [his] outlook leans distinctly towards the former",[100] but also noted that he is aware many of his readers might consider some of the provisions he proposed to be planning. By going into details, he stressed that he "wholeheartedly accept[s] the guidance of the 'invisible hand' for the mutual adjustments of productive units" and "repudiate[s] the mood of millenist planning",[101] but he also reminded his readers that the Keynesian theory revealed that "tariffs and price agreements do not create mass unemployment [per se], and that their abolition [ceteris paribus] would not restore Full Employment"[102] either. Polanyi thought that freedom of competition is beneficial for the economy, but acknowledged that it needs certain foundations or frames in order to be able to flourish.

According to Polanyi, the lack of social consciousness was the "greatest deficiency"[103] of the prevailing economic system of crude liberalism. He also noticed that cultivating a kind of consciousness or at least pseudo-consciousness was one of the greatest assets of socialist planning in the battle between the two extremes. This is the reason why developing a kind of social consciousness became central to his mission to save liberalism and Western civilization. He wanted to improve public understanding of economic ideas to establish an "enlightened public"[104] which is capable of ordering its own economic life in a conscious and responsible way without imposing unnecessary constraints on freedom. By doing this, Polanyi drew boundaries between both extreme liberalism, which had freedom without consciousness, and socialist planning, which had consciousness without freedom.

In Polanyi's view, both extreme liberalism and socialist planning had a mechanical view of man and science. In these schemes, there is no place for personal, sentimental or, more generally, metaphysical elements, which cannot be grasped by mathematical or statistical means, and therefore cannot be inserted into fancy mathematical formulae. Carriers of these ideas either embrace self-seeking or social purpose but not both, and believe that one, having no other option, has to choose from these two extremes. In the case of orthodox liberals, their aim can be to express their admiration of abstract beauty and to celebrate their own cognitive capabilities to face such taintless perfection (Gradgrind), or to construct and self-justify their business success as achievements of a self-made man (Bounderby). In the case of planners, their aim can be to cut off every unpleasant irregularity of economic life and to replace it with an apodictic economic system (Oscar and Altiora Bailey) or to lead society on the one and only righteous path towards Communism, no matter what the others say. People are treated as numbers on a spreadsheet or as an undistinguishable hand in the million working to satisfy the needs of the common head. Both of these streams embrace the culture of measuring, quantifying and counting, and their fate lies with that of this culture. This mechanistic heaven might resist the high-minded charge of the best and brightest academic virtuosi, but if Polanyi was right, it can be shaken by the smallest deeds and sentiments of ordinary men.

A little academic excess can go a very long way. Polanyi showed that greater ones can go a long way too. By separating the individual and collective interests of man, and by fostering one without taking care of the other, both extreme liberalism and socialist planning set out on a road which would disintegrate society. Their radicality lay in their conviction that there is one best solution to economic problems without shades or interpretative flexibility, and that a wider social debate about its principles would be either pointless or harmful, or both. The non-radicality of Polanyi's third way might be best grasped as an attempt to contribute to the (re)balancing of the individual and collective patterns of social life and by suggesting that there is a social agreement on standards of social justice whether we acknowledge it or not through which a democratic mechanism could and should affect the economy. There are multiple standards of social justice, multiple concepts of economic fairness and righteousness which enlightened people, not exclusively experts or policy-makers, have to choose from. This important role of the public in the constant (re)making of economic realms is unlike anything in the accounts of extreme liberalism and socialist planning. But it must not be confused with completely democratizing (or decommissioning) the expertise of economists. In Polanyi's economic thought, both common laypeople and economists have a pivotal role in making and remaking economic knowledge. He embraced a democratic view of expertise instead of the elitist view espoused by orthodox liberalism and socialist planning.

Polanyi was using rhetoric to heighten the contrast between his tempered liberalism and the two extremes, orthodox liberalism and socialist planning. His attempts to monopolize the expertise of putting an end to the economic recession without unnecessarily curtailing freedom, and the authority to be able to plausibly claim to do so were, first and foremost, feats to convince the masses. Polanyi did not think that the opinion of economists was not important, but conceived that most of them misinterpreted the social role of their field as well as their own responsibility towards society. He was quite critical about these experts and made suggestions himself on how to reshape their expertise even though he was not one of them. He primarily aimed to convince non-experts about the adequacy of his third way. The following chapters will show that he turned to economists mainly to get feedback on his drafts or to use their authority to get into the spotlight. This is not to accuse Polanyi of being unfair with economists. It is to acknowledge his skills for properly assessing his situation. Despite being a non-economist, and being unknown to most economists, he proposed a value-laden remake of economics, including normative statements about what economists should do and how. He would have had little or no prospect of realizing his agenda if his primary target group had been the expert community of economists. He seemed to be aware of this and turned to the general public instead.

But the usual tools and methods for promoting economic ideas were mostly established to accommodate expert-to-expert accounts, and not expert-to-layperson accounts. Journal articles, academic books and conference presentations are very good for building a professional network of experts, but are not so good for reaching many different people without this expertise. Thus, Polanyi needed to find new ways to reach out to the public at large. The next chapter shows one of these ways by exploring how Polanyi's economic film connected the social worlds of economists, film experts, economics tutors and others.

Notes

1 Polanyi 1943w, 4.
2 Polanyi 1940i, 24.
3 Ibid.
4 Ibid., 26.

5 Polanyi undateda, 2.
6 Polanyi 1940i, 26.
7 Ibid., 24.
8 Ibid.
9 Ibid., 26.
10 Ibid., 25.
11 Ibid.
12 Polanyi 1937b.
13 Ibid., 4.
14 Polanyi 1935b.
15 Polanyi 1940i, 26.
16 Ibid.
17 Polanyi undatedc, 1–2.
18 Ibid., 1.
19 Ibid., 2.
20 Polanyi 1937c, 32.
21 Polanyi 1948a, 1.
22 Polanyi 1946c, 8.
23 Ibid.
24 Ibid., 8–9.
25 Ibid., 9.
26 Ibid.
27 Dickens 2005, 4.
28 Ibid., 316.
29 Polanyi 1946c, 14.
30 Ibid.
31 Dickens 2005, 4.
32 Polanyi 1947a, 1.
33 Ibid.
34 Ibid., 2.
35 Ibid.
36 Ibid, 3.
37 Ibid.
38 Ibid., 13.
39 Ibid., 15.
40 Ibid.
41 Polanyi quoted agreeingly from Gustav Cassel's "Neuere monopolistische Tendenzen in Industrie und Handel. Eine Untersuchung über die Natur und die Ursachen der Armut der Nationen". Memorandum für die Weltwirtschaftsconferenz in Gent, 1927.
42 Polanyi 1947a, 15.
43 Ibid., 16.
44 Ibid.
45 Ibid., 17.
46 Ibid., 30.
47 Ibid.
48 Ibid., 18.
49 Ibid., 7.
50 Ibid., 11.
51 Ibid.
52 Polanyi 1940i, 20.
53 Ibid., 21.
54 Ibid., 20.
55 Ibid.

56 Polanyi 1937b, 4.
57 Polanyi 1940i, 26.
58 Polanyi 1946m, 4.
59 Ibid.
60 Polanyi 1943d, 10.
61 Polanyi 1942h, 16.
62 Ibid.
63 Polanyi 1937c, 31.
64 Polanyi 1937b, 11.
65 Ibid.
66 Ibid., 10.
67 Ibid., 12.
68 Polanyi 1948b.
69 Ibid., 106–8.
70 Ibid., 108–9.
71 Ibid., 110–11.
72 Wells 1911, 206.
73 Ibid., 367.
74 Polanyi 1935a.
75 Knight 1932.
76 Polanyi 1947c, 8.
77 Ibid.
78 Polanyi 1936a, 4.
79 Polanyi 1939c, 1.
80 Polanyi undateda, 2.
81 Polanyi 1940i, 26.
82 Polanyi undatedb, 1.
83 Polanyi 1940i, 26.
84 Ibid.
85 Polanyi 1948a, 146.
86 Polanyi 1941f, 2.
87 Ibid.
88 Polanyi 1940i, 3.
89 Polanyi 1941f, 3.
90 Ibid., 7–8.
91 Polanyi 1943w, 4.
92 Polanyi 1937c, 28.
93 Ibid., 29.
94 Polanyi 1946m, 8.
95 Polanyi 1937c, 29.
96 Ibid.
97 Polanyi 1941f, 8.
98 Ibid.
99 Polanyi 1948a, xvi.
100 Ibid., 149.
101 Ibid.
102 Ibid., 148.
103 Polanyi 1937b, 11.
104 Ibid., 12.

2 The first economics film

Polanyi had the idea of making an economics film by the end of the 1920s. He released a version of his film titled *An Outline of the Working of Money* in 1938, and then the final version in 1940 titled *Unemployment and Money: The Principles Involved*. This chapter seeks to explore how his film, as a *boundary object*,[1] acted as an "anchor" or "bridge" connecting different social worlds of economists, film experts, managers, economics tutors and others, satisfying the information needs of each. Actors in these diverse social worlds had a range of disparate visions of Polanyi's film. In other words, his film inhabited multiple social worlds. By carefully analysing the correspondence between Polanyi and his allies, one can get a glimpse into the richness of these social worlds, ranging from artistic to scientific, educational and administrative realms.

Polanyi developed a sociotechnical vision around his film, which he succinctly summarized as "democracy by enlightenment through the film".[2] The aim of his vision was to remake economic liberalism with a kind of social consciousness needed to save democracy and Western civilization. To achieve this, he started to develop – and urged others to join him in developing – new ways of increasing public understanding of economic ideas. He referred to one of Ivan Pavlov's experiments which resulted in developing neurosis in a dog by making it increasingly difficult for it to differentiate between a circle and an ellipse (by gradually modifying the ratio of the semi-axes of the ellipse) and inducing a conflict between the two responses of salivating and non-salivating.[3] After becoming neurotic, the dog was unable to discriminate even between the very dissimilar symbols it had been easily capable of discriminating earlier. Polanyi drew a parallel between the neurosis of Pavlov's dog and the contemporary perplexity of common laymen about economic ideas.[4] He thought that the symbols of the economy were not comprehensible enough for the laymen, similarly to the 'too circlish ellipse' for Pavlov's dog. His proposed solution was to develop a new set of symbols which would embody certain economic elements, and would be capable of carrying their meaning for the masses.

From the three main sets of symbols (verbal, mathematical, visual), Polanyi advocated a visual set, more precisely, a visual method, using diagrammatic motion picture technology to make the economy visible. He recalled how Francis Bacon's "mechanical contrivances"[5] fostered large-scale "mechanical progress",[6] and suggested an analogously grand endeavour, but this time based on tools of the mind and not tools of the hand. He envisioned this timely proposal to pick up where the Enlightenment had left off. His emphasis was on the progress of the mind – an epistemic empowerment of the masses, a cultivation of a social consciousness to fight against economic misconceptions and false beliefs. Polanyi sought to introduce the new graphical method through centres of economics education. First, he imagined his "calm light"[7] to enlighten a core of educated people, then a somewhat wider stratum and, eventually, if things went well, the whole society. Acquisition of the new understanding of economic matters would save democracy and our civilization by fostering the interpenetration of this social consciousness to domains of our everyday social life. Human minds carrying economic ideas were the main building blocks in the Polanyian view of the economy.[8] Therefore, one can plausibly claim, yet in a quite anachronistic manner, that Polanyi's early economic accounts were evolutionary economics in the making. However, 'knowing' has quite a different meaning for Polanyi than for evolutionary economists in general. This issue will be further discussed, due to its importance, in Chapter 3.

How did Polanyi imagine including the somewhat, but not completely, dog-like humans in his experiments of economics education? After all, Pavlov's dog had no other choice than to participate in the experiment, but people had many choices. Polanyi needed powerful allies who could help him reach out to the public at large. Without them, there was no hope of getting the motor of his social agenda running and reaching all those imagined desirable societal effects. The Workers' Educational Association (hereafter W.E.A.) seemed to provide an adequate niche for experimentation. It had several tutors and students, and it was already concerned with the education of the public. Harold Shearman, an officer of the W.E.A., made arrangements to show Polanyi's film at their annual meeting, organized experimental courses with various economics tutors using the film, and summarized and forwarded the feedback for Polanyi's consideration.

Polanyi's film project was almost completely financed by the Rockefeller Foundation (hereafter the Foundation). He mostly corresponded with Charles V. Sale, Tracy B. Kittredge and Ruth Pedersen, who became deeply involved in Polanyi's film project. In one of his letters to Kittredge, Polanyi explained why he had to pursue his vision despite the fact that neither projectors nor competent staff were available at most schools due to wartime conditions. He believed that his method could help to establish an "enlightened post-war opinion",[9] which would take intelligent steps rather than ardent and reckless ones, sacrificing even what was left of freedom after the war. In the war, extreme steps were taken to find a way out from the labyrinth of economic hardship. This was undoubtedly an outcry for conscious and calm economic policy-making. But it was also something more. Polanyi wrote to Patrick

Blackett that there was "little tradition left of sober and considerate agreement, and only the desire left to deal a blow".[10] He likely referred to the decline of the culture of discussion and the rise of the culture of destruction.

A similar situation occurred during the Paris Peace Conference in 1919, which led John Maynard Keynes to resign in frustration from his position as an economic advisor to the British Government. Keynes wrote about his unpleasant experience in the witty but bittersweet *The Economic Consequences of the Peace* (1919). Keynes argued for a more "enlightened order"[11] solving the international economic turmoil instead of the brute force solution of the Allied Powers, which eventually became accepted, formulated and signed. He warned that crushing and oppressing Germany would be harmful for the whole European economy, not just the Central Powers, and would probably lead to another war in 20 years. Sadly, he was right, but nobody listened to him among the key players in European politics. Twenty years later, World War II broke out, and 23 years later Polanyi started to think that even if this war was won, something immanent to Western civilization would be lost. Polanyi's sociotechnical vision aimed at epistemic empowerment of the masses, perhaps, in part, to cool down and counterbalance the heat of macro-political power-mongering.

Polanyi knew that, as an outsider, he had to be very careful in making statements with political implications. His sociotechnical vision of "democracy by enlightenment through the film"[12] was a reimagination of democracy. But it did not claim to be so, or at least not in a simple, clear-cut manner. It could be seen as a manifesto and a guidebook to establish a (post)modern democracy based on better knowing and being, even if it was framed in a humble, low-keyed tone. Perhaps it was too humble to be noticed and taken up by revolutionary forces. Polanyi was proposing calm and peaceful methods, but his ideas could have been picked up by overheated political activists. But they were not picked up by anyone, overheated or otherwise, perhaps because of his careful framing practices, perhaps because of the complexity of his vision – maybe both.

The key to Polanyi's (post)modern democracy was the reimagination of *knowing*. For Polanyi, even in his early years, knowing was not universal. It was personal. It was a compound of *understanding, believing* and *belonging*. It had three "indissolubly connected"[13] aspects: a theoretical, a confessional and a social aspect.[14] For Polanyi, knowing was not simply passing over universal, abstract packages of facts from one mind to another. Believing in certain suppositions, and belonging to a group sharing these suppositions were inseparable from knowing. Polanyi argued that "it is this social aspect which principally determines, which knowledge is true, and which is false".[15] Perhaps it would be anachronistic to consider these Polanyian ideas postpositivist, or a precursor to the Strong Programme. But it seems adequate to note here that they are from 1947, 15 years before Kuhn's *The Structure of Scientific Revolutions* (1962) first hit the shelves, and one year even before Kuhn started to teach a course in history of science at Harvard and turned his interest towards historical and social explanations of science. These new findings reinforce Mary Jo Nye's illuminating insights about Polanyi's involvement in the social turn of philosophy of science, and about the underlying economic, political and cultural drives[16] by providing additional archival evidence.

All of these three aspects can be traced in Polanyi's sociotechnical vision. As Phil Mullins and Charles McCoy pointed out, Polanyi was a Platonist about matters for whom knowing the good leads to doing the good.[17] Polanyi was on a mission to change what and how is known about economic realms. Because economic knowledge is carried in the minds of the people, and what people do in economic settings is driven by their minds, their practices can be changed through changing their mindsets. Better knowing leads to better being. Knowing economic ideas, like any other kind of knowing, was three-fold for Polanyi. Laymen were expected to go to centres of economics education, to watch the film, and, to discuss it with fellow students and tutors. They were expected to understand the represented economic ideas (theoretical aspect), to believe their suppositions or axioms (confessional aspect) and to belong to a community sharing this understanding and belief (social aspect). In a sense, people were expected to change their practices (e.g. by going to education centres, watching films) in order to change their mindsets. Thus, to a certain extent, better being also leads to better knowing in the early economic thought of Polanyi.

Polanyi saw his film crucial for moving towards the realization of his sociotechnical vision of "democracy by enlightenment through the film".[18] For him, it represented hope in a (post)modern democracy which, due to a kind of epistemic empowerment, would function based on a continuous (re)forming of a considerate social agreement between knowers, instead of being the barren scene of never-ending clashes of irreconcilable political camps. He intended to extend the culture of discussion and to abridge the culture of destruction by cooling "the superheated modern mind".[19] Polanyi took a stand against the mechanical view of man, science and society and committed himself to a personal, sensible and social worldview. The film was imagined to be the engine of disseminating his new kind of economic liberalism with social consciousness, which he hoped would influence not only economic but other social realms, and by doing this, eventually, save democracy and Western civilization.

Administrators of the Foundation primarily treated Polanyi's film as part of their to-do lists. Although Sale, Kittredge and Pedersen were involved in the core of the project, they seemed to show little or no interest in Polanyi's sociotechnical vision of "democracy by enlightenment through the film".[20] They were busy connecting Polanyi with the potential concerned parties, informing him about parallel projects running at the Foundation, giving him feedback on the progress of his own project and advising him on how to proceed further. Kittredge called Polanyi's attention to Spencer Pollard (Educational Film Institute) and Donald Slesinger (American Film Center) and suggested ways of contacting them. Pollard was the founder of the New

York University (NYU) Educational Film Institute with the US Department of Commerce and the Sloan Foundation in 1939. The aim of the institute was to provide training for teachers and film technicians, so it could have seen as a suitable intermediary step in the dissemination of Polanyi's economics film. Moreover, one of their first films, *Valley Town: A Study of Machines and Men* (1940) by Spencer Pollard and Willard Van Dyke defined itself as "the first in a series of films on national economic issues",[21] which suggested that there would be more to come, and possibly Polanyi could have fitted in to the series with his film.

But *Valley Town* (1940) was not like Polanyi's *Unemployment and Money* (1940). It was a sociographical documentary exploring the economic and social effects of deploying a new technology in a Pennsylvania steel town. It was characterized by Jay Ruby as "possibly the first postmodern film".[22] By taking a critical stance towards steel companies and by calling attention to their corporate social irresponsibility, makers of the film achieved two things: a well-received, successful premiere at the Steel Workers' Organizing Committee convention in 1940, and an intense break-up with the Sloan Foundation, primary funder of the NYU Educational Film Institute and a non-profit philanthropic organization established by Alfred P. Sloan, president and CEO of General Motors. The Sloan Foundation stopped the release of the three completed films, and rereleased two of them (*And So They Live* (1940), *The Children Must Learn* (1940)) later with minor changes, but not *Valley Town*. *Valley Town* was reworked to such a degree, according to William Alexander, that "The film's carefully crafted structure was destroyed in order to present the viewer with a different perspective."[23] The original cut was distributed by the Museum of Modern Art Film Library in New York City. The same library eventually became the home for Polanyi's film in the United States. Perhaps this seems to be a minor detour from our main topic, but it is not, for at least two different reasons. First, because Kittredge suggested that Polanyi contact Spencer Pollard of the Educational Film Institute in relation to his economics film. And second, because the fate of *Valley Town* showed how an educational film could be drawn into social and political battles.

While commercial filmmaking had strong traditions in the US, and perhaps even had a trend-setting role for the rapidly globalizing industry, American non-commercial filmmaking was two steps behind its British counterpart. The Foundation itself was experimenting with educational films and played a pivotal role in establishing the related organizational, informational and financial niche from the mid-1930s. After making the diagnosis that "unquestionably the film is among the most powerful influences in the cultural life of the world today",[24] the Foundation sought to influence the public taste for and through educational films and to improve the equipment needed for educational purposes.[25] It seems worthy to note here that the General Education Board had only launched exploratory projects with an intention to map the realm of educational films in June 1935. As Ramírez pointed out, these resulted in foundational texts like *Educational Film Catalog*

(1936), *Teaching with Motion Pictures: Handbook of Administrative Practice* (1937) and *Motion Pictures in Education* (1937). One might wonder how the perception of Polanyi's film might have been affected if he had released it a few years earlier, so that the film could have been included in these compilations. Donald Slesinger, the second person Kittredge suggested Polanyi contact, became the first director of the American Film Center. While the Center was functioning from 1938, it did not receive the funding it needed to be in full operation until 1939, the year in which Slesinger travelled to Hollywood to study filmmaking, distribution and the job of the producer.[26] By this time, Polanyi's film project had progressed beyond its early phase, thus the support the Center could have provided him in terms of script-writing, editing, reviewing and budgeting was too little too late. Notwithstanding, the help of Slesinger would have been undoubtedly useful in the dissemination of his completed motion picture due to Slesinger's newly acquired producer skills and, perhaps, recently made acquaintances.

Officers of the Foundation had to advise Polanyi on how to progress with his film in such a shaping, uncertain environment to challenge and conquer a sub-industry (non-commercial educational films) in the making. Rival interests formed diverse ideas about how the scene of non-commercial educational films should look. Officers had to be particularly careful about what advice they gave and how, or they could easily find themselves without a significant role in the process of making and circulating such films, and maybe even without a job. Commercial filmmakers, politicians, social reformers, artists and generous philanthropic funders all wanted to have a decisive voice in how to nurture the nascent field. Officers, like other interested parties, probably thought that going down one road too far would curb opportunities to take others later. There was no direct sign of pressure echoing any of these voices towards either the content or the format of Polanyi's film in his correspondence with officers of the Foundation. The officers confined themselves to suggesting steps with little risk. They primarily suggested contacting institutions established specifically to be the vehicle for developing, collecting and disseminating educational films but not the related (sociotechnical) visions.

Dissemination of Polanyi's film was hampered by the low number of available copies. There was only one copy of the film in the US at the disposal of the Foundation, a copy which they lent to professors and tutors all around the country to use in their courses. If the copy was not being used, it was stored at the Film Library of the Museum of Modern Art. When Jacob Marschak inquired about whether he could use the film in his monetary policy course the next semester, Ruth Pedersen regretfully informed him that the one and only copy was being shipped to Condliffe in the next few days. He was also told that "there is, however, a negative of the film which might be developed at a future date when a definite policy has been determined as to the methods of putting it to wider use".[27] Laura Polanyi-Striker, sister of Michael Polanyi, also informed her brother about "the 'policy' of the foundation in a concrete case when a Professor at a university … wants to base his semester on the film".[28] Perhaps the dissemination in the US started slowly, but it soon improved. In a 1942 letter, Kittredge wrote to Polanyi that "I am sorry that circumstances during the past year have made it almost impossible for teachers of economics in this country who may have been interested in your film to do any constructive experimentation with it."[29] But he also informed him about six screenings during the previous six or eight months in important American higher education institutions, including Princeton University (Prof. Oskar Morgenstern), Yale University (Prof. Kenneth Spang) and the University of California (Prof. J.B. Condliffe).

People at the Foundation primarily saw Polanyi's film as one of their ongoing projects. They were engaged in giving a financial grant to Polanyi, in monitoring his progress and in finding and informing as many stakeholders as they could. It was mostly a mundane to-do list for them consisting of sub-tasks of financial, legal, communicational and organizational nature. They did not seem to internalize nor completely understand the social implications of Polanyi's film. For them, the film was not a mindful sequel to the enlighten-ment heritage, nor a means of melting the heart of economic liberalism, and certainly not a way of saving democracy and Western civilization. They did not seem to share Polanyi's enthusiasm and ideas; they were just doing their job as officers of the Foundation. Educational films on economics, money and, most of all, unemployment were few. The eleventh edition of the *Educa-tional Film Guide* (1953) indexed 11,000 16mm films for educational use, but listed only 15 under the subject 'Economics', 7 under 'Money' and 3 under 'Unemployed'. Polanyi's *Unemployment and Money: The Principles Involved* was the only one included in all of these groups, sharing the latter with *Valley Town* and *Howard Street*.

For film experts, the film inhabited another social world. In a letter of 1938, Richard Stanton Lambert from the British Film Institute provided an account of one of the earliest screenings on English soil:

> Everyone was exceedingly interested in the experiment, the original nature of which was much appreciated. In the main, the audience was inclined to be critical of the slow movement of the film, not perhaps realising that, had this been accompanied by a lecturer, they would not have noticed the repetition of the movement of the figures, etc. I noticed that although the audience seemed to find the film slow, they did not observe some of the finer points of the film, which I think justifies you in your method of repetition, to drive home points. Several keen film enthusiasts seemed to think – and I rather agree with them – that from the technical point of view G.B.I. [Gaumont British Instructional] did not acquit itself very well: the movement of the model figures might have been less jerky, and the lettering was not always photographed distinctly. Mr. Beales, of the London School of Economics (who was in the Chair) and I were greatly impressed with the way in which you built

up your theme from a simple beginning, to a complicated yet lucid climax. For myself, I think the latter part of the film is most effective – i.e. the parts which we had not time to show.[30]

Figures, lettering and slowness were the key points in Lambert's account. He was a founder and board member of the British Film Institute who had an unpleasant public encounter related to Gef the talking mongoose,[31] which had almost cost him his career a few years earlier. Lambert was not an economist or a student of economics. He treated Polanyi's film as an application of film technology, as an artefact which was to be seen in terms of standards of contemporary film technology. Techniques of making the film (not photographed distinctly, less jerky movement of model figures) and the mode of the storytelling (slowness, repetition, complicated yet lucid climax) dominated his account from a "technical point of view".[32] Lambert said nothing at all about the adequacy of the economic content or about how the audience attempted to understand the elaborated economic ideas and what difficulties they had, if any. The screening was held at the London Film School, so probably the audience here was also more concerned with the film as an instance of using film technology for educational purposes than as a way of visually representing Keynesian ideas. A similar account was provided by Oliver Bell, the Director of the British Film Institute who saw the film more as a "visual notation"[33] supporting the audience in understanding economic ideas. He emphasized that as students in adult education are not the most "accustomed" to "verbal or numerical notation", they would probably "benefit considerably" from a visual one. Bell primarily treated Polanyi's film as a new method of teaching which should be used "in association with the more customary methods of teaching".[34]

Film experts in the US also offered a few comments on *Unemployment and Money*. In the June 1940 issue of *Documentary News Letter*, a brief analysis had been published on the film titled *Economics on the Screen*. The review, which was written by an unnamed London University Extension lecturer (economics), contained critical remarks both from the social world of economists and of film experts. The reviewer acknowledged Polanyi's pioneering work using films in teaching economics. Indeed, there were a few films about the economy and certain economic mechanisms in the era, but none of them was framed as visualizing a specific economic theory rather than the economy – except Polanyi's readdressing of Keynesian economics titled *Unemployment and Money*. The reviewer wrongly stated that Polanyi only included one type of income, wage, in his film and forgot about the others. Perhaps it is not easy to notice, but Polanyi did not restrict himself to representing "where people have their jobs".[35] He was also concerned about where they "look after their property".[36] From the context, it seems rather plausible to think that by "property" he meant land, capital and perhaps entrepreneurial skills yielding in succession rent, interest and profit. It would have made Polanyi's model extremely complex from the beginning of the film if he had gone into the details of the four different types of resources and their related income types. Such complexity would have been contradictory to Polanyi's efforts to bring the message of Keynesian economics to the masses as simply as possible.

The reviewer was not pleased by the abstract diagrams and "monotonous geometrical symbols",[37] and called for more "concrete", "vivid and realistic pictures" of everyday economic life. He or she argued that the lack of vividness is a great problem with the Polanyi method because vividness is often equal to (or seen as equal to) the power of conviction. Presentation of a boring, lifeless economic drama would not draw the attention of the common layman. And Polanyi needed this attention to realize his sociotechnical vision. The reviewer noted that Polanyi's diagrammatic exposition was inferior to the chalk and board method of teaching due to its lower level of adaptability to learners, and emphasized that such a trait makes it more fitting for serious classwork than for ad hoc popular usage. A competent teacher could split the film into separate intelligible sections, complement its narrative with her own explanation and drive the class discussion towards a better understanding. A screening without careful support of an expert would probably leave an unskilled audience confused about certain economic matters, perhaps more confused than they were before the showing.[38]

Polanyi made his repost in the August issue of *Documentary News Letter*, two months later. His response was anything but moderate. He argued that the "main documentary approach to economic life represents a technocratic view of production which is essentially collectivist".[39] What was needed instead, according to Polanyi, is a commercial view of economic life. This view focuses on the division of labour, the "grand circle of exchanges" and the "gyrating money belt" which cannot be grasp by any photograph. These are fundamental for the explanation of the commercial mechanism. Polanyi drew a parallel between how maps represent the island nature of Britain by a closed curve along its coastline, and how his film represents the monetary circulation by the motion symbol of circulation with "a rotating belt of definite width and rate of gyration".[40] Both are diagrams, making otherwise invisible things visible. For Polanyi, diagrams explain, guide the reason, while photographs (and documentary films primarily using photographs) illustrate, appeal to the senses. Both explaining and appealing are crucial for conveying the message. What Polanyi was tinkering with here might remind us of contemporary discourses on the hybridity of visual representations, their mixed nature coming from their dual origin in scientific and artistic realms. But such anachronistic bridge will not be built. Polanyi wanted to explain the commercial mechanism to the masses with his visual scheme mirrored in his economic film. A mechanism which cannot be illustrated by any documentary film. These films might be capable of showing the results or a microscopic fragment of the commercial mechanism but not the mechanism itself. From the documentarist's point of view, the abstract visual scheme of *Unemployment and Money* was a weakness, a deficiency putting "a severe strain on the faculty of attention".[41] From Polanyi's point of view, it was a strength, a trait providing him unprecedented explanatory power to guide the reason of the common layman to otherwise invisible and incomprehensible realms.

Economics tutors focused in their accounts on the usability of the film. Polanyi corresponded with some of the tutors directly, but he mainly received their feedback through Harold Shearman, an educational officer of the W.E.A. Polanyi gave three silent copies and lent one "sound copy" (i.e. copy with synchronized sound) to the latter institution in order to be able to conduct educational experiments with it. The W.E.A. testing began in November 1941, which was too late to properly include the film in the syllabuses of the semester, thereby causing trouble both for tutors and students. Eventually, nine tutors and Polanyi used the film in the framework of the W.E.A. experiment. There were a couple of common strands in their accounts which might help us to explore what social world Polanyi's economics film inhabited for these tutors. First, the undesirable effects of the sound of the film (if a sound copy was being used): sound diminished their role as teachers and their expertise as economics tutors. The "sound version"[42] or the "talkie method"[43] was usually not considered to be completely compatible with classwork. This type of verbal exposition was often seen by the tutors as limiting their power and freedom in terms of what they taught and how. Regardless of the type of the copy used, some of the tutors thought that the film made certain conventional teaching methods (e.g. blackboard work) unnecessary; others argued that this method made it even more necessary to use these more traditional ways of exposition. This was the first economics film and the first systematic experiment to explore whether this method could be used on a larger scale. If it succeeded, it would have probably reformed economics education and the expertise needed to do such work. If it failed, it would have left the status quo in economics education untouched. This is only to argue that, for tutors, the stakes were higher than participating in the W.E.A. experiment. It was about whether they would contribute to the transformation (or the decommissioning) of their own expertise. One might wonder how this realization affected their participation and feedback.

Second were the technical difficulties related to projector devices and screenings. One of the tutors, Mr. H. Dawes, wrote in his account that, in a small village, it took three-quarters of an hour for the operator to obtain a properly focused picture on the screen.[44] Other notable hitches included a blackout, an improvised screen, and a small and stuffy classroom. Projectors and film copies, the scarcest resources needed for the experiment, were provided by the association. Projectors, especially sound projectors, were very expensive – so expensive that small village schools could hardly afford to buy one. In the United States, school representatives and manufacturers of the film industry agreed on a price reduction of projecting devices to foster the widespread usage of educational films at the end of the 1930s, after a survey of the General Education Board showed that it was badly needed.[45] In the United Kingdom, the film industry took another road. Non-commercial filmmaking had strong traditions, but weak ties to education authorities. And shortly, when the Board of Education finally decided to pay half of the cost of the projecting devices purchased in the next four years (1938–42) by schools and universities, World War II broke out, rewriting the previous grand plans for gearing up British education. Film copies of *Unemployment and Money* were less expensive than projecting devices but harder to get because they were only produced on-demand, at least in this early phase of distribution.

Third, most of the tutors noted that the film was most useful for intermediate students for clarifying their ideas. The film was too complicated for beginners without prior knowledge of economics. And it was unsatisfactory for advanced students addressing complex questions and seeking complex answers. Some claimed that, for elementary students, the film was "rather disappointing",[46] "almost incomprehensible"[47] and "disastrous".[48] Others emphasized the film's merits in conveying a "helpful sense of lucidity"[49] in the related economic ideas, describing it as being "very valuable",[50] "extremely useful",[51] "invaluable",[52] and the "most valuable aid"[53] to the Keynesian exposition of monetary circulation and trade cycle. Accounts mentioned that students enjoyed the film and were stimulated to pursue further studies of related economic ideas. Several tutors (and Polanyi) stated that the content of the first three reels were generally easier to grasp than the rest of the film. For students without previous training in economics, demonstration of these three reels, having a slower narrative and a less abstract notation, was the best if accompanied with class discussion. There was no point in moving on to the later reels with them, at least not at this time. Tutors moving on to the later reels with elementary students usually claimed that it shortly "became too complicated"[54] for them to follow, leading the novices to puzzlement and "hurried and wrong conclusions",[55] and in doing so, perhaps, threatening even their general interest in economics.

Fourth, the Keynesian ideas included in the film were of a controversial nature, wrong or were presented in a rough-grained manner. Some of the tutors criticized the way Polanyi portrayed managerial decisions regarding aging and renewals, and pointed out the lack of the specific effects of monopoly conditions to corporate policies, as well as the missing representation of the own "volition"[56] of the banking system and its influence on the trade cycle. Others showed terminological incompatibilities with contemporary economic discourses, an oversimplified depiction of the effects of investment, and claimed that there was a fallacious belief in the film, notably, that booms come to an end because every employable person is being employed. One of the tutors suggested developing an additional reel or reels about the banking system in order to be able to portray how changes in the credit issuing practices and interest rates of banks affect the economy. But were these flaws of the model or reasonable limitations to fit its purpose? One of the tutors, H. Dawes, noted that "the film was to be regarded as a model presenting a set of basic ideas needing amplification and modification".[57] But how, and on what basis, could someone properly draw the boundaries between the crudeness and the adjustability of such a pioneering model, first of its kind? Even tutors and economists disagreed, not to mention non-experts. That is why the official document of the W.E.A. (*The Film in Economics Classes: A W.E.A. Experiment*) about the first demonstrations by economics tutors was particularly important for both the future of Polanyi's film and that of the nascent modelling genre.

Unemployment and Money took some of the British press by storm. Insightful articles praised how its visual method broke with the convention of showing the "size, weight and shape of economic organs",[58] and focused on their "functions"[59] instead. Others appreciated that the emphasis was not on showing the "results"[60] of economic activity, but the underlying "principles",[61] and was gradually building a "sustained reasoning about facts"[62] instead of piling up additional economy-related "encyclopaedic knowledge".[63] Polanyi found allies arguing that photographs, still or stationary diagrams and documentary films are not able to grasp the "most essential characteristics of economic life"[64] which are "adaptability" and "instability".[65] The film has been acknowledged as "a new mental tool"[66] to foster clearer popular thinking about economic realms, and, to fight against public confusion and propaganda. The *Financial Times* and *To-Day's Cinema* explicitly called it (correctly) the first film on economics. A few other papers conveyed this message less explicitly, mostly by giving a title which hinted at this feature (*Economics by Film,*[67] *Economics on the Film*[68]), or by emphasizing the newness of representing economic ideas rather than the economy itself by using motion picture technology. Another recurring element in these accounts was that *Unemployment and Money* was the first instructional film sponsored (at least partly) by a British university. Sadly, the high hopes shortly met with serious obstacles.

Five years after the premiere of Polanyi's *Unemployment and Money: The Principles Involved*, Harold Shearman, an officer of the W.E.A., a middleman between Polanyi and the economics tutors, shared his thoughts with Polanyi about why his film had still not been used extensively. Shearman identified two main causes, one related to the expert community of tutors, the other to general economic and political conditions. First, he noted that "generally speaking our tutors, and the profession in general in this country has not yet become interested in visual aids to any important extent".[69] It was not framed as a critique against *Unemployment and Money*, or against using film technology in economics education, but as a symptom of a general resistance against using any kind of visual notation. Unfortunately, Shearman did not provide further explanation about why he thought that tutors preferred non-visual kind of notation. Interestingly, available accounts of tutors experimenting with the film were, on the contrary, rather favourable towards using visual aid in classes. Second, he remarked that wartime conditions made it much more difficult than usual to get the necessary equipment. Surely, during World War II, there were things of higher priority than how to get projecting devices. Shearman ends his letter by stating that he recently saw a few experimental instructional films in the US, which were using a very different technique than Polanyi's, one "more related to the Disney Cartoon".[70] This closing remark might lead us to wonder: How, and in what sense, did "the art of a new Walt Disney"[71] become 'undisneyian' in the seven years between 1938 and 1945?

The answer might lie in the account of another tutor, G.D.H. Cole, who provided insightful feedback years after the preliminary W.E.A. experiments. Cole was against any kind of standardization in economics teaching that provided pre-made arguments for tutors in controversial topics.[72] He thought that tutors, after getting "past the novelty of [Polanyi's] experiment"[73] would mostly agree with him, and would also refuse to accept such constraints on their freedom. In 1938, the Walt Disney[74] metaphor was meant to convey the message of novelty and the pioneering nature of Polanyi's art. His economics film was rather seen as exploring unknown and unoccupied realms. It was mainly considered as a fundamentally new add-on to economics teaching. But during the mentioned seven years, the 'disneyness' of Polanyi's art changed significantly. *Unemployment and Money* has became seen more as a conqueror of already inhabited and, perhaps, flourishing realms than as an explorer of educational terra incognita. The film was less and less seen as an add-on and more and more as a surrogate for traditional ways of teaching. Polanyi's art transformed from disneyian to undisneyian as its newness turned into otherness. Pre-made argument and standardization became counterpoints to individually crafted arguments and adaptive teaching methods. It was no longer seen as a tool helping tutors extending their expertise, but as one curtailing their freedom and authority with "its very closely-knit structure".[75]

A few years after the premiere, Polanyi realized that his film project had begun to lose its charm and he started to work on backup plans in order to be able to realize and extend his sociotechnical vision. One of his backup projects was his Keynesian popularizing book, *Full Employment and Free Trade*, first published in 1945. In a letter to Shearman, Polanyi made it clear that he intended to promote his film through the new book, which he hoped, "may possibly reopen the issue of a wider use of the film for economic teaching as distinct for the use as a background for elementary talks".[76] He used the symbolism of the film in the illustrations of his book and referred to the film, and to his own demonstrations, to "nearly a hundred popular audiences in the last six years".[77] Another backup plan was to adapt the film, or a version of it, for the Army programme of the British Ministry of Information. Polanyi and his correspondents were not on the same page about what to expect from the Army.

Polanyi was not suspicious about cooperation with the Ministry of Information. He wrote to John Jewkes that "I would be delighted to assist the Government in using my film or a new film based on a similar technique to explain its intentions for the prevention of general unemployment."[78] He went into detail, stating that "there is a standard size sound print available in London which could be shown at the theatre of the Ministry of Information and I would be delighted to come down to London and take part in the discussion". Polanyi even noted that some of his ideas about "a new version based on the first three reels, but considerably simplifying and abbreviating the material" could be produced. Moreover, he suggested that the "technique could be touched up to a somewhat higher degree of potency, for example by the introduction of colour which is now quite commonly used for cartoon films" to reach out for theatrical audiences. Polanyi would have also been pleased to include "a demonstration of Governmental intervention"[79] which was absent from the available version. He seemed to be open to adapt both the content and the format of his film.

In a 1942 letter, Basil A. Yeaxlee, a prominent figure in British adult education, wrote to Shearman about the recent conversations he had at the War Office which made him think that the Ministry of Information (operating between 1939 and 1946) might be interested in a simpler form of Polanyi's film. Arthur Koestler, Polanyi's childhood friend, jumped in the discussion and established contact between Shearman and Arthur Calder-Marshall of the Ministry of Information's Film Division. At this time, Koestler was working for the ministry writing scripts for propaganda purposes (broadcasts and films). Shearman noted that the ministry might be open for "filming the White paper",[80] but expressed his worries about the film's likely transformation into "propaganda for their policy".[81] Such worries were, perhaps, not completely unfounded. George Orwell, author of *Animal Farm* (1945) and *Nineteen Eighty-Four* (1948) also worked for the ministry during the war[82] and this influenced his anti-totalitarian literary efforts. The Ministry of Information inspired the Ministry of Truth; the initials of the first man of the ministry, Brendan Bracken,[83] the *Big Brother* in Orwell's *Nineteen Eighty-Four*.[84] Koestler and Orwell were both anti-totalitarians working on propaganda, using one of the enemy's most powerful weapons against itself. Desperate times call for desperate measures, for sure, but does such an end, winning the war, justify such means, manipulating our own people? Perhaps, such an unsettling dissonance between what they believed and what they did, whether putative or substantive, motivated these two intellectuals to commit their careers to promoting democracy through building fictional and non-fictional literary realms. For most of Polanyi's allies, the cooperation with the ministry would have been about whether either to keep calm or to carry on, but not both.[85] Polanyi himself was not so suspicious about cooperation with such an Orwellian ministry. He did not seem to worry about his sociotechnical vision of "democracy by enlightenment through the film"[86] or the emergence of another competing sociotechnical vision based on his film.

The line was, and will always be, quite blurred between disseminating knowledge about economic ideas to uneducated masses, and, of doing propaganda for economic policies. What counts as spreading propaganda for one person can be seen as democratizing expertise for another. Where can laypeople, who are not capable of or willing to understand all the details, turn for authoritative guidance? To scientific and scholarly communities of experts. Not because experts are untainted by interests and biases, but because they are, unlike members of most other social groups, constrained by organized scepticism. Polanyi correctly realized that the majority opinion of a specific expert community, the community of economists, was particularly important for the future of his sociotechnical vision. He knew that he needed "authoritative backing"[87] of powerful allies from the social world of economists, and who could be more powerful in economics during World War II than John Maynard Keynes?

Interestingly, although Polanyi intended to convert Keynesian ideas into "a matter of common sense"[88] from the very first days of his film project in the 1930s, he only contacted Keynes directly when *Unemployment and Money* was almost completely finished in 1940. In this first letter to Keynes, Polanyi emphasized that the aim of his film was to enlighten the general public by using "a novel and striking illustration of elementary monetary facts".[89] He did not write to Keynes that he aimed to transform Keynesian ideas for the masses, and he did not mention his related sociotechnical vision either. Polanyi asked Keynes' advice and offered him an opportunity to watch the earlier (1938) version at Cambridge, or to come to the studio in London to watch and discuss the newest version,[90] still in the making. The answer from King's College was short and straightforward: "I have much else to do and I must, therefore, regretfully reply to your letter that I cannot spare the time to take an interest in your film."[91] Keynes might later have realized the insensitivity of his harsh fragment because, 11 days later, he wrote a kinder follow-up: "Though I was not able to take an interest in your film, may I say how much I liked your recent letter to the New Statesman."[92,93] Polanyi's first attempt to get Keynes involved with his film project did not work out so well. They exchanged some letters, but there was no discussion about economics or about visual presentation of economic ideas. Fortunately, Keynes was not the only economist Polanyi could get in touch with.

Most of the economists who had seen Polanyi's film in the early years participated in screenings in Manchester, Paris (Walter Lippman Conference, 1938) and New York (Loewe screening, 1940). Manchester University, as Polanyi's home institution and co-financier of his film, became a place of experimental screenings with expert audiences. John Jewkes, head of the Department of Economics, played a pivotal role in revising the content of the film, and members of his department were among the first economists to see it. Jewkes and Polanyi became friends soon after Polanyi's arrival in the British Isles, and Jewkes shortly became a guide to Polanyi in his quite reckless journeys into the realms of economics, still unknown to the Hungarian-born physical chemist. One of their earliest letters was about Polanyi returning a copy of the already mentioned *Soviet Communism: A New Civilisation?* (1936) by Sidney and Beatrice Webb to Jewkes and expressing his indignation that the book was considered to be a classic. Polanyi struck an unconventional tone in this letter, defining the Webb's book as a "wrangling which is posing as impartiality",[94] and as "a series of inconsistencies thinly covering its dishonesty".[95] Polanyi expressed how glad he was that, as a non-economist, he could pass on reviewing the book and, at the end of the letter, reflected on the general state of the progressive movement: "How horribly sad! On what dark days has the 'progressive' spirit fallen to produce this book, and after having produced it not to rally the power even to criticize it. Please accept my sympathy."[96] A few days later, Jewkes suggested Polanyi write about Webbs' book for the Manchester School or, perhaps, for the *Manchester Guardian*. Moreover, he declared that he would not review the book anywhere before Polanyi did. Their strange competition for not-reviewing Webbs' book might help us understand the professional reasons behind their unlikely alliance. Polanyi was not an economist, therefore he was less constrained by the disciplinarity of economics which enabled him to leave the beaten paths, but threatened him with not being taken seriously. Jewkes was an established economist with a considerable degree of authority, but a plethora of written and unwritten rules to follow if he hoped to preserve his authority. Perhaps, and this is highly speculative, they realized that they could help each other. Polanyi could deliver a novel, unconventional account, Jewkes could deliver authoritative backing and theoretical background.

In a letter of December 1936, Polanyi gave feedback to Jewkes on one of his manuscripts (perhaps on what later became his "Ordeal by Planning") and informed him about reading Robbins' book on the meaning of economics which he found "very entertaining"[97] and "fine".[98] He did not write anything about whether he agreed or disagreed with Robbins' argument in the book, but he stated that, after reading it, he better understood why Jewkes disagreed with Robbins. Even though Polanyi did not include the title of the book in his letter, it seems highly probable that this book was *An Essay on the Nature and Significance of Economic Science* (1932). In this book, Robbins was drawing boundaries between economic science and applied economics. He framed economic science, by following the footsteps of Menger and Mises, as a realm of pure theory which "studies human behaviour as a relationship between ends and scarce means which have alternative uses".[99] According to Robbins, other aspects of human behaviour or human non-behaviour belong to other disciplines and arts, similarly to technical elements of production which threatens with letting in "incredible banalities"[100] into this honourable sanctuary of the purest of pure theories. What makes Robbins' account relevant in this respect was his argument for the complete separation of economic policy (applied economics) from economics (economic science). This was a discrimination which frustrated many, including Polanyi and Jewkes, who treated these two subjects together and, perhaps, as inseparable from each other.

Most of the economists who saw Polanyi's film or read the related (manu)script were not moved by it to a considerable degree. They mostly approved the general outline of the film, criticized certain details and sometimes warned Polanyi about the dangers of oversimplifying complex economic discourses. Only a few of them, including Condliffe and Marschak, showed serious interest in the film and wanted to implement it immediately in their economics courses. Others treated it more as a matter of curiosity and less as a novelty with a potential to greatly reform how economists teach economics and reach their publics. Their criticism, in general, focused on the adequacy of the portrayal of Keynesian ideas and the way Polanyi's film portrayed them. For economists, the film was more like an "animated text-book"[101] than a work of art, a kind of to-do list, or a visual signpost moving towards the realization of some starry-eyed sociotechnical vision. They saw the film as a *diagrammatic carrier*[102] of Keynesian ideas and they were particularly concerned with comparing it to other kinds of carriers. Some seemed to rule out even the possibility of a trade-off between the comprehensibility and the accuracy of economic representations. Others seemed to be considering that there could be, and perhaps there is always, such a trade-off, and that the related scaling should primarily follow the characteristics of the audience to whom the economist intends to speak or write. The latter group was divided between those who thought that Polanyi had found the 'right' balance and those who believed that he had sacrificed too much accuracy for comprehensibility.

Polanyi made the second attempt to get Keynes involved with his film project in relation to one of his backup plans, his popularizing book of Keynesian ideas, *Full Employment and Free Trade*. He aimed to breathe new life into his sociotechnical vision through this book, and reached out to Keynes once again to get one of the most powerful allies who could help him revitalize his vision. In the preface to *Full Employment and Free Trade*, Polanyi drew a parallel between Keynesian economics, his own contributions and the atomic theory of chemistry of John Dalton (1809) and the work of Cannizzaro (1858), who "set out the whole matter once again – without any important addition – in a new, more straightforward fashion".[103] Polanyi claimed he gave a similar treatment to Keynesian ideas. And, not least, he wanted to be considered as doing so. In a letter of 20 December 1945, Polanyi wrote to Keynes himself about this "slight attempt at expanding economic and social policy on the basis of your work",[104] and added that as his recent book is "too obvious" for Keynes, the latter should only read the "chapter on Russia and [of course] the story of John Dalton and Cannizzaro in the Preface".[105] While Keynes should have been happy about such a grand parallel with the acknowledged natural scientists, he refused to see himself as the Dalton of economics and did not embrace his parallel Cannizzaro either.

Polanyi's tour with his film had a stop at a local Rotarian club. After the screening, one of the organizers, Peter Thomason, wrote a letter to Polanyi articulating a vision of the film similar to Polanyi's own. He framed the film as a means for "bearing the betterment of the individual, the community, and the nations",[106] and this was in line with the overall aim of the Rotarians. For both Polanyi and the Rotarians, doing the good requires knowing the good. Thomason pointed out that the good done by the Polanyi film does not stop at the day of screening; it will foster related discussions and draw people to pursue further studies in economics. Such enlightenment was seen as particularly needed in the upcoming era of Reconstruction after World War II. Although no general conclusion can be drawn from a single letter, it seems safe to say that Polanyi's sociotechnical vision of "democracy by enlightenment through the film"[107] and the social mission of the Rotarians were rather compatible.

Unemployment and Money rang bells for some and left others untouched, but few saw it in a darker tone than Polanyi's wife, Magda. In the quite intimate realm mirrored in the correspondence between husband and wife, Magda portrayed the film as a threat to Polanyi's physicochemical professorship and, consequently, to the financial status of the family and all those who depended on Polanyi. Patrick Blackett, during one of his visits, asked Magda whether "Misi [nickname of Mihaly, the Hungarian counterpart of Michael] is not really interested in chemistry any more?"[108] Magda informed Michael about Blackett's unsettling question and expressed her worries to her husband in a very direct way by stating that "I'm afraid I have to better keep an eye on you in the future, so that you will not lose your job."[109] Elsewhere, she made an even more tongue-in-cheek report to her husband suggesting that "he [Blackett] thinks that political activity is the most important – even more important than the film".[110]

Notes

1 Star and Griesemer 1989.
2 Polanyi 1935c, 1.
3 Polanyi 1937d, 2–4.
4 Ibid., 9.
5 Ibid., 10.
6 Ibid.
7 Polanyi 1936a, 4.
8 Bíró 2018.
9 Polanyi 1942a, 3.
10 Polanyi 1941d, 1.
11 Stevenson 2004, 417.
12 Polanyi 1935c, 1.
13 Polanyi 1947b, 6.
14 Ibid.
15 Ibid., 12.
16 Nye 2011.
17 Plato 352 BCE.
18 Polanyi 1935c, 1.
19 Mullins 2017, 1.
20 Polanyi 1935c, 1.
21 Pollard and Dyke 1940.
22 Hennig 2002.
23 Alexander 1981.
24 Ramírez 2009, 2.
25 Ramírez 2009.
26 Ibid.
27 Polanyi 1940l, 1.
28 Polanyi 1940m, 1.

29 Polanyi 1942c, 1.
30 Polanyi 1938a, 1.
31 R.S. Lambert and Harry Price made inquiries into the hypothetically paranormal case of Gef, the 86-year-old talking ghostly mongoose, on the Isle of Man and wrote a book about their pursuits titled *The Haunting of Cashen's Gap* (1936). Consequently, Lambert was charged by Sir Cecil Levita for being unfit for his job at the British Film Institute. Lambert brought a legal action for slander (the "Mongoose Case", 1937), and eventually won the case against Levita.
32 Polanyi 1938a, 1.
33 Polanyi 1938d, 2.
34 Ibid.
35 Polanyi 1940a.
36 Ibid.
37 "Economics on the Screen", 6.
38 Ibid.
39 Polanyi 1940j, 6.
40 Ibid.
41 "Economics on the Screen", 6.
42 Polanyi 1943f, 1.
43 WEA 1942, 10.
44 Ibid., 6.
45 Ramírez 2013.
46 WEA 1942, 10.
47 Ibid., 9.
48 Ibid., 8.
49 Ibid., 6.
50 Ibid., 7.
51 Ibid., 6.
52 Ibid., 8.
53 Ibid., 13.
54 Ibid., 10.
55 Ibid., 6.
56 Ibid., 7.
57 Ibid.
58 "Economics Taught by Film", 1.
59 Ibid.
60 Williams 1941, 1.
61 Ibid.
62 Ibid., 2.
63 Ibid.
64 "Economics Taught by Film", 1.
65 Ibid.
66 Ibid., 3.
67 *Yorkshire Post* 26 April 1940.
68 *Times Educational Supplement* 11 May 1940.
69 Polanyi 1945h, 1.
70 Ibid., 2.
71 "Money is Star of this Film", 1.
72 He emphasized that very few economic questions are non-controversial "in the sense that competent tutors would agree about the substance of what needed saying". One might recall here the anecdote attributed to Winston Churchill: "If you put two economists in a room, you get two opinions, unless one of them is Lord Keynes, in which case you get three opinions."
73 Polanyi 1943f, 1.

74 Walt Disney and his studio were pioneers in developing synchronized sound, full-colour three-strip Technicolor feature films from the late 1930s. *Snow White and the Seven Dwarfs* (1937), *Fantasia* (1940), *Pinocchio* (1940), *Dumbo* (1941) and *Bambi* (1942) came shortly after each other, revolutionizing the industry of cartoon films in the period which became known as the Golden Age of Animation (1937–42).

75 Polanyi 1945i, 1.

76 Polanyi 1945k, 1.

77 Polanyi 1948a, xvi.

78 Polanyi 1944a, 1.

79 Ibid.

80 Polanyi 1945i, 2.

81 Ibid.

82 As well as Orwell's wife, Eileen O'Shaughnessy (Censorship Department), and Koestler's close attachment and intellectual companion, Daphne Hardy (Photographic Archive).

83 Bracken was, among other things, the founder of the *Financial Times*.

84 Reisz 2013.

85 *Keep Calm and Carry on* was a British propaganda slogan at the beginning of World War II (1939) with the primary aim of raising the public morale against the continuous threat of German air attacks on British cities by recalling and promoting a stoic, 'stiff upper lip' mentality of Victorian origins.

86 Polanyi 1935c, 1.

87 Polanyi 1943u, 1.

88 Polanyi 1948a, v.

89 Polanyi 1940b, 1.

90 Polanyi 1940a.

91 Polanyi 1940c, 1.

92 Polanyi 1940g, 1.

93 The letter Keynes referred to was Polanyi's "Science in the U.S.S.R.", published in *New Statesman and Nation*, 19 (10 February 1940), p. 174.

94 Polanyi 1936b, 1.

95 Ibid.

96 Ibid., 2.

97 Polanyi 1936c, 1.

98 Ibid.

99 Robbins 1932, 15.

100 Ibid., 65.

101 "A Monetary Movie", 1.

102 Zemplén 2017.

103 Polanyi 1948a, v.

104 Polanyi 1945r, 1.

105 Ibid.

106 Polanyi 1943g, 1.

107 Polanyi 1935c, 1.

108 Polanyi 1938b, 2.

109 Polanyi 1938b, 2–3.

110 Polanyi 1938c, 4.

3 Rival schools of thought in the 1930s and 1940s

Polanyi believed that, in order to be able to realize his sociotechnical vision, he needed to reimagine economics through its social face. His attempts to reinvigorate democracy and liberalism by economics enlightenment were entering a heterogeneous disciplinary milieu of rival schools of thought. His immensely rich correspondence offers a glimpse into these incompatible and rather hostile landscapings, and could be used to explore various contemporary imaginations of the desirable economic discipline. One can witness Robbins' laborious struggles to build a purest of pure abstract castle of economic science untainted by any kind of political and social mundaneness, Hogben's backstreet quarrel with economists to protect and extend the authority of political arithmetic (and his wife), the making of a Keynesian compound of economic theory and economic policy, the deeply contextualized and socialized accounts of the Hammonds embracing political activism, the Webbs' theoretical monstrosity of 1200 pages on how to kick-start communism, and Polanyi's renegade mission to bring the chessboard of economics to the agora. One might discover not only visions of desirable and undesirable economic discipline(s) in these letters but also that of societies, the two often inseparably linked to each other. Certain imaginaries of economic disciplines were promoting certain social visions and vice versa.

Never wrestle with a pig-philosopher. You get dirty and, besides, he likes it. An advice Robbins seemed to be completely unaware of. Nevertheless, one of the most influential of contemporary economic landscapings was Robbins' mission to purge what he considered to be metaphysical nonsense from the terrain of economic science. He was determined to completely remove the economic conception of the end from the "realms of the metaphysical",[1] to drive economic analysis away from moral ultimates and to push it towards action-driven individual objectives.[2] He even criticized economists' talk about "economic satisfactions"[3] because he considered satisfaction an end-product of economic activity, and not part of the activity itself. Robbins admitted that it would be undoubtedly an exaggeration to say that an economic analysis cannot grasp economic satisfaction at all. It can, according to Robbins, grasp some aspects of satisfaction deriving from the scarcity of means, but it cannot handle aspects of an entirely subjective nature. What follows for Robbins was that we should leave out satisfaction altogether from our economic analysis, because it does not fit certain implications of our definition. Such self-imposed hollowness came handy to Robbins in his argument against the "neurotic critics of Economic Science",[4] including Ruskin and Carlyle. Robbins stated that it does not matter for an economic analysis whether the demands to analyse are of material or immaterial nature. Economic science is concerned only with the relationships between ends and means, not their content. Thus "poor Carlyle's"[5] pig-philosophy happened to be "all-embracing"[6] and was not limited to tinkering with swinish pleasures and pains of muddy mundaneness. Robbins accused Ruskin and Carlyle of not putting enough intellectual effort into their pursuits of economic science and with criticizing it unjustly in its embryonic state of scientific self-consciousness. Quite an assault from an economist who, a few paragraphs earlier, ruled out the consideration of satisfaction from economic science simply because it was not in harmony with some implications of his own definition.

Another strand in Robbins' grand exposé of what is and what is not economic science was a defence against those considering economics no more and no less than the study of material welfare. While accounts of socialist and communist economic theories tended to weave the economic and the material inextricably together (subordinating their duo to some non-material social aim), there is, surprisingly, no direct mention of these theories in this part of Robbins' narrative. He used the term 'communist' only four times and 'socialist' only once. He referred to the communist economy as an example of Crusoe-economy or closed economy, and described economic analysis as having most utility in exchange economies, but as being unnecessary in isolated economies and "debarred"[7] in a communist society. Thus he chose to frame economic analysis as less useful in communist contexts instead of criticizing communist conditions as hampering the same economic forces he claimed to be able to grasp with his economic science in exchange economies. Should we rather consider this rhetoric as an example of playing safe and 'staying clean' in an age of unseen political and disciplinary turmoil, or was he not so much critical of leftist economic concepts as it would have been expected from one of the leading liberal economists of the 1930s? Or, perhaps, he thought that taking a more critical stand towards communism would have undermined his argument for a morally neutral economic science? Possibly not only one but more of these factors played a role in his rather passive depiction of the communist economy.

When he wrote *An Essay on the Nature and Significance of Economic Science* (1932), Robbins was still a young scholar who had studied Fabian socialism with figures like Edwin Cannan, Harold Laski and Hugh Dalton. Moreover, he worked at a university established by leading Fabian socialists such as Sidney and Beatrice Webb and George Bernard Shaw. At this time, gradual and conscious progress towards communism was not generally considered to be nonsense, impossible or harmful to society. On the contrary, it became, from a progressive ideological flame, a widely held view in certain circles of the British intelligentsia. Perhaps, and this is highly speculative, Robbins thought that showing the fallacies of socialist economic theory would have made both his life and his efforts to establish economic science harder than it should be. This would explain why Robbins did not criticize communism himself in his related book, but put a tremendous amount of work to support others who were doing so, including Polanyi. Just as Hayek became Robbins' fierceful combatant against Keynesian economics, Polanyi became his ally against socialist economic theories. Robbins managed to occupy a niche which provided him access to all these more dangerous roads, but waited to take these and sent others first instead, perhaps to minimalize his personal risks. Although Robbins helped Polanyi by revising his economic writings, he had a considerably different view of science (not just economic science) than did Polanyi.

Robbins considered economics to be a positive science. Like members of the Vienna Circle, he intended to purge all metaphysics from scientific realms. He labelled the engagement with materialistic reductionism as "sheer metaphysics",[8] calling it either a "pseudo-Hegelian twaddle" or a "profound insight", but not science at the moment. Robbins identified an undesirable popular fallacy enmeshing materialist and economic interpretations of history and stated that economic science lends no support to materialist doctrines, thus materialism "must stand or fall by itself".[9] He argued that the "causes influencing taste and so on"[10] are not technical in nature but, interestingly, he considered it important to state that this implies neither the denial nor the acceptance of metaphysical materialism. Did he pull punches for pragmatic reasons? Or did he simply avoid paying too much attention to non-science in his scientific account? In any case, Robbins was viciously fighting to earn a place for economic science in the hall of positive sciences. Meanwhile Polanyi was reimagining both science and economics from a non-positivistic perspective embracing metaphysics.

Polanyi corresponded with fellow liberal intellectuals about studies of the economy. But he also exchanged letters with their main ideological antagonists, socialist planners, including Bernal Hogben. Polanyi wrote to Hogben that he also objected to Robbins' orthodoxy and suggested discussing economic matters starting with Hogben's own objections to Robbins' liberalism. Hogben was inclined to join Polanyi's efforts to reach a common ground concerning economic problems and started to feel that they differ "mainly on emphasis"[11] and agree "far more closely"[12] than Hogben did with Levy, Haldane and others. Hogben did not answer all the points Polanyi raised. Instead, he focused on the main deal-breaker between them. And that was how to view the satisfaction of the population. Hogben promoted a social perspective. He believed that the bad distribution of population makes us falsely believe that we are in severe need of certain commodities. And this distribution could and should be re-engineered based on common agreement of the people. Hogben scornfully noted that he does not positively "regard the greatest good of the greatest number or the greatest number of advertisable goods which the greatest number of people can purchase".[13] He argued that using scientific planning to revise the habit of procreation is much more important than chasing higher and higher levels of production because the population "forfeited its capacity to perpetuate itself".[14] In Hogben's view, the number and distribution of consumers has to become the most important element in economic discourses. Reading his bitter lines on the increasing number of commodities and the decreasing number of people, it is not hard to imagine an anti-Malthusian future with a handful of overly satisfied people sitting on the hilltop of unused commodities which eventually will bury them underneath.

Although their correspondence showed a promising start, soon an avalanche followed. Polanyi sent an article of Jewkes to Hogben which, according to him, "throws considerable doubt"[15] on the basis of Hogben's attitude concerning population. Hogben answered with thunder and lightning, giving a verbal beating to economists and their discipline. He noted that he was the director of the only department in Britain which was conducting "patient and unambitious research"[16] into the population problem, and more precisely, the analysis of differential fertility. He describes the latter as not being part of economics but requiring more statistical ingenuity than most branches of economics and "more biological common sense than any economists whom I have met possess". Hogben made it clear that he is "not in the least interested in what Harrod, Jewkes or any other economists" say because they are not familiar with the relevant literature and rely on his "wife's publications in their occasional excursions into the realm of fact"[17] without conducting intensive studies themselves. In his view, political arithmetic explains economy better than economics, and it should be treated so. At the end of his letter, Hogben was wondering whether Polanyi's intention was to insult him or it was unintentional.

This debate between Hogben and the economists is more than a quarrel between conflicting disciplinary groups drawing boundaries in interwar Britain. It is also a microscopic cutting of the centuries old fissure between political arithmetic and economics. The term "political arithmetic" was coined by William Petty in the seventeenth century, which made it older than "economics". The field was, from the beginning, the study of economic and demographic statistics concerning the state. It preserved this strong empirical perspective, sometimes against abstract economic science. Hogben deemed it important to draw attention both to the age and the empirical nature of his field. In his *Political Arithmetic: A Symposium of Population Studies* (1938) he noted that Petty, one of the three fathers of the field, was among the earliest members of the Invisible College, "the parent body of the Royal Society",[18] the intellectual home of Boyle and Hooke, which held one of its earliest meetings at Petty's rooms in Oxford. The importance of experience over scholarly nuance was stressed even in the three epigraphs in his book. Hogben quoted the preface of Petty's *Political Arithmitic* (1691) which framed the field as a "very mean science" with ordinary rules. He also quoted William Harvey's ars poetica of learning and teaching anatomy not from books and positions of philosophers but from dissections and the fabric of nature. Last but not least, Hogben quoted Lord William Beveridge's philosophy which affirmed learning and teaching economics, politics and sociology not from books and positions of philosophers but from observation and from the "conduct of mankind".[19] Hogben interpreted these quotations as scaffoldings for his argument against abstract theoretical science, and supporting his efforts to remake science as a more popular enterprise. His related efforts were embodied in his books *Mathematics for the Million* (1936) and *Science for the Citizen* (1938).

Polanyi realized that the language of his letter was indeed unfortunate, and softened his wording by writing that Jewkes' article only attempted to throw doubts (rather than actually throwing doubts) on Hogben's results. He apologized to Hogben, admitting that he was not "familiar with this field of statistics",[20] suggested that the discussion of the population problem, having "immense public importance", should be more widely discussed, and should not remain in the "extremely small circle of experts"[21] of political arithmetic. Polanyi urged Hogben to reply to Jewkes' criticism in public. Hogben answered that he did not want to spend half of his life replying to "noodles"[22] unfamiliar with the subject on which they are writing and suggested that Polanyi would be "equally irritated"[23] if Hogben sent him "a half baked essay from the Christian Science Monitor about your research in physics written by someone who'd never been in a physical laboratory".[24] Drawing such a parallel suggests that, according to Hogben, economics has little to do with explaining and addressing economic problems, and that economists are claiming to build their theories on empirical foundations which they do not completely understand. Hogben noted that he is up to his neck again and that he has "given up trying to induce a British university to undertake realistic Social Studies".[25] Thus, in Hogben's account, economics was among the unrealistic social studies losing touch with empirical reality. Polanyi thanked Hogben for the batch of books he had sent him and noted that if he had further questions about the subject of population he would write to Hogben's wife (fortunately, he did not write that he would consult with his wife on the subject of fertility).

The Polanyi–Hogben correspondence was a missed opportunity. Both men were critical of orthodox liberal theories and were working to bring science to the masses. But it would be delusionary day-dreaming to think that they could have worked together if that 'real or imagined' insult had never happened. Another strand in Polanyi's correspondence, his exchange of ideas with John Lawrence Hammond and Barbara Hammond, social historians, authors of *The Labour Trilogy*, might explain why. Polanyi got in touch with the Hammonds in the 1930s and read at least one of their books in the summer of 1939. After the literary experience of reading the book, which was a kind gift from the Hammonds, Polanyi let John Lawrence Hammond know that the book "had a profound impression on me, showing me how the advance of human conscience can victoriously struggle against fierce vested interests, supported by deeply engrained errors of economic science".[26] His succinct reminder about the epistemic aspects of the struggle and, particularly, about the undesirable social effects of fallacies of economic science was in line with Polanyi's ambitious endeavours to reform liberal economics. Noticing the maleficent social effects of false beliefs was not limited to liberal accounts. Socialists alike were concerned about bad knowing. But knowing did not mean the same to socialists, including Hogben, and to Polanyi.

One might recall the famous American cartoon caricature (a remake of an earlier Russian one), called the *Pyramid of Capitalist System* (1911). Next to one of the depicted classes, clergy, the artist put the text "We fool you", suggesting that this class rules by having power over the knowledge of the working class and dishonestly weave labour epistemologies. What most socialist accounts offered, in this respect, was either bringing down knowledge to the masses from the ivory tower of the elitist victors of class struggle or annihilating knowledge-claims by labelling it pseudo-knowledge of the leisure class conceived in the impure, interest-laden niche of the messy establishment. For these socialist accounts, including Hogben's, knowledge can and should be democratized. But for Polanyi, it is knowing, not knowledge, which can and should be democratized. Knowing is a compound of understanding, believing and belonging. Its three aspects, namely, the theoretical, the confessional and the social are inseparable from each other, which makes knowing an utterly personal phenomenon. For Hogben, democratizing expertise was about how to make knowledge more understandable. For Polanyi, it was also about how to make people believe in certain assumptions and how to make them belong to a group sharing these assumptions. No wonder Hogben was starting to write popular science to reach the public through the bookshelves, while Polanyi was venturing into an economics film project to foster the understanding of Keynesian ideas, the believing in certain related assumptions and the belonging to a group sharing these assumptions, with several experimental screenings to small audiences.

Polanyi also stated to John Lawrence Hammond about the book that "it is a warning never to wander in social matters too far away from the guidance of our human instincts".[27] For Polanyi, knowing, e.g. knowing the economy in a certain way, was always already social and personal. The latter aspects were immanent to the fabric of economic knowing, and resided at the very heart of his economics. The Hammonds became Polanyi's allies in his pioneering inquiries exploring these yet unknown realms. Barbara reminded Polanyi that there is much in common between the propaganda conducted by the "heavy hand of the state"[28] and the commercial advertisements being made by producers for the greatest satisfaction of consumers. She noted that

Hammond may make an excellent mouth wash and have a well established business, but Polanyi can sweep his customers away and destroy his business livelihood by producing a far inferior article and covering the hoardings with Polanyi's Paste Prevents Pyorrhoea.[29]

This example not only suggests similarities between propaganda and advertisements but, perhaps, indicates that from the perspective of the consumer, there is no hard distinction between the real and the non-real attributes of articles. Advertisements weave beliefs in the same way that propaganda does. The most efficient tool of totalitarian régimes is being used by capitalist enterprises on a daily basis widely and effectively, even in liberal economic systems. Where, then, does the inhumanity, the machineness of modern economic life originate if not from the ideological veneer of the system?

According to one of Polanyi's correspondents, Max Born, it has nothing to do with the system being capitalist, socialist or liberal. Born warned Polanyi that by reading Dickens one can witness how liberal capitalism, when "flourishing unhampered"[30] creates "just as many cruelties" as its totalitarian counterpart. Born emphasized that he is "not a socialist, as [he does] not believe in definite economic theories", but he admitted that he is "decidedly" "anti-capitalistic" as well as "anti-liberal" if by liberal one means the right of businessmen to seek for unencumbered profit. Despite not believing in economic theories, Born was generally convinced by the propagandistic economic accounts of Russia, and argued that, after its successes, "it is impossible to continue describing her as inefficient". Born seemed unable to grasp that there are no distinct boundaries between economic theories and economic propaganda and, perhaps, more importantly, between an economy and an economic theory that seeks to explain it. He thought that Polanyi, Crowther and the others missed "our ideals with the very non-ideal purposes of business affairs"[31] and should take a closer look at the Scandinavian countries living and flourishing under a system of reasonable socialism for a considerable time. Born did not discern that the hollow, inhuman laissez-faire liberalism he described was not an ideal for Polanyi but an adversary to surpass, similarly to socialist planning. He was convinced that Polanyi had a disposition against the Russians which impeded him from seeing their economic successes. He warned Polanyi that he and his fellows took a dangerous road by coupling ideal freedom with the "practical liberty of capitalism",[32] which exploits the labour of others and destroys competition. The popular view of the industrial corporation of the Victorian era, mostly its depiction of Dickensian flavour, becomes a recurring topos in Born's letters, framing "child labour and other dreadful cruelties" as a *sine qua non* of the liberal economic system.

Born remarked that he does not, in the least, believe in the "economic laws" developed by "liberal" economists, and that the time has come to "try a little reason, cooperation, planning, combined with education for service and collective spirit" instead of the "egoistic motives"[33] governing prevailing liberal systems. He even urged the restriction of science to an extent by making it impossible to exploit scientific ideas for private profit.

Unfortunately, he did not write anything about how to put a price on scientific ideas, or how to draw the line correctly between fair and unfair incomes paid for certain scientific activities. Although Born identified himself as a non-socialist, he seemed to be taking the role of an apologist for socialist economic thinking. Polanyi assured Born that he was very much concerned about the social conditions, but "do[es] not believe that they can be improved without definite economic theories".[34] He also pointed out that the differences between them "originate in the intellectual, not in the moral or emotional field" and that he shares Born's sympathies for the poor as well as his exasperation about the "squalor of industrial settlements". Polanyi emphasized that he has no intention to go back to extreme laissez-faire, and that he "strongly emphasized the contrary",[35] although not in his last paper. Polanyi saw little connection between the economic measures of the Swedish Government between 1932 and 1939 and Soviet economic policies, which suggests that the two had different concepts on what counts as economic planning. Planning, indeed, was easy to spot but hard to define in contemporary economic discourses.

Another correspondent of Polanyi, Franz Borkenau, author of *The Totalitarian Enemy* (1940) shed some light on the problem in one of his letters to Polanyi. Borkenau evoked an example from the story of Thomas Mann's *Buddenbrooks* (1901) which elaborated the revolution of 1848 in Lübeck through the life of a wealthy merchant family. Borkenau recalls that in this book, the excited workers pressed the senator to refuse many things in order to be able to proclaim a republic, while, as the senator points out, Lübeck was already a republic without complying with their demands. According to Borkenau, the Soviets failed to see that science has always been planned and "they wanted to plan it a second time, just as the Lübeck workers wanted a second republic on top of the one they had already".[36] For Borkenau, planning of science means planning the expenditures of science, allocating and (re)distributing resources, but not the planning of scientific output. He warns Polanyi that science was mostly a "state-owned and state-financed affair",[37] thus an anti-planning attitude in science might not just contrast with the Soviets 'second planning' but also with the older, non-Soviet traditions of scientific management and finance. Borkenau called absolute planning nonsense, but propagated planning when the results of free trade are undesirable. And he hurriedly added that they are "nearly always undesirable".[38] His explanation refers to the monopolistic tendencies of modern capitalistic economies which tend to smile upon the already strong and to make life harder for others. Borkenau considered his view unorthodox in relation to both liberal and socialist points of view. He promoted mild doses of planning (i.e. tariffs, controlled currencies, anti-immigration laws), to slow down economic progress; on one hand, to inhibit excessive economic concentration, and on the other, to slow down the process of economic equalization. Borkenau called it unscientific to discuss free trade and planning in the abstract and urged for empirical studies about why liberalism declined. According to him, the main reason for such a decline was that the industrializing countries could not keep up with the increasingly intolerable international competition and have lost faith in liberalism. Borkenau tried to involve Lionel Robbins in this discussion, but the economist did not reply. One can only speculate how Robbins might have defended his pure economic science from such policy-oriented social excursions.

Thomas Mann's *Buddenbrooks* offers another interesting strand to the discussion which Borkenau did not expound. Mann's first longer novel was not only a fictional, stylized, yet reality-laden account of the author's early family life in Lübeck; it was also an incidental portrayal of the general decline of Hanseatic commerce in the mid-nineteenth century. As Borkenau argued that the economic, social and legal macro-processes have a definite role in how agents get along in their economic micro-cosmos, he could have used such a general lesson from *Buddenbrooks* to scaffold his argument about why we should focus more on real processes than on abstract philosophy when giving economic accounts. He did not. Interestingly, at the time of writing, not even Mann realized that he was depicting the dusk of an era, the fall of the Hanseatic bourgeoisie in a rapidly industrializing Germany. Mann's book was about the tragedy of the Buddenbrook grain merchant family, the story of how their insistence on their old way of life and ideals was slowly but surely suffocating and destroying their family. This was a painful reminder that none can escape from the hard burden of constantly adapting to ever-shifting economic conditions. Borkenau could have also mentioned the deep economic and social changes leading to the unification of Germany in 1871, and eventually to the German Revolution of 1918–19 and the establishment of the Weimar Republic (1919–33). He might have emphasized the inter-penetrating macro-effects mirroring Mann's micro-events to support his argument. He did not, and therefore his insistence on sticking to real social processes instead of doing abstract theoretizing might be considered a bit underdeveloped.

Elsewhere, for example in *The Totalitarian Enemy* (1940), which impressed Polanyi, Borkenau provides a more socializing account about the nature of fascism. Orwell's review of the book published in *Time and Tide* emphasizes that both left-wingers and right-wingers failed to understand the true nature of fascism. As Orwell puts it, according to the mainstream, "Hitler was a dummy with Thyssen pulling the strings",[39] and Hitler was generally seen as the leader of a derailed, but fundamentally capitalistic nation – a nation which will protect the propertied against Bolshevism. Orwell depicts what he considered to be a deadly delusion of his age, seeing Bolshevism and fascism as completely antagonistic forces without any kind of family resemblance. But after the "scum of the earth" and the "blood-stained butcher of the workers" established their alliance, with the Russo-German pact making their unexpected friendship "cemented in blood", the Strachey-Blimp thesis, he argues, became "untenable". The shock of witnessing the approach of a grim fate to all those who value liberty, Orwell implied, could have been prevented by noticing the trends in the two totalitarian régimes both converging towards the same system of "oligarchical collectivism". Orwell claimed, based on Borkenau's fine-grained socioeconomic analysis, that the Nazis, under the surface, did not care much about ideologies or values. The only thing they cared about was power. And there were no rules about how to "keep the ruling clique in power". They would be Reds, Whites, anti-Marxists, anti-capitalists, whatever it took to preserve and extend their power. The hate campaigns of such totalitarian régimes were fuelled by their limitless greed for power, and anyone "can figure as Public Enemy No. 1" at terrifyingly short notice. Orwell realized that such hatred, once stirred up, "can be turned to any direction" quite easily, "like a plumber's blow-flame". Borkenau promoted, as Orwell interprets him, a milder version of collectivism with increasing economic efficiency but without the terrible 'side-effects'. Orwell closes his review by stating that "nearly all books on current politics have been compounded of lies, or folly, or both, his has been one of the few sane voices heard in the land, and long may it continue".[40] Borkenau pointed out that beyond the human brutality of extreme ideologies there are crude economic interests.

What made it particularly hard to reach a common ground between Polanyi and his correspondents about the effectiveness of the economic theories and policies of totalitarian régimes was that they, in some cases, even disagreed about the economic performance of these countries. After Patrick Blackett, Polanyi's long-time acquaintance, voiced his rejection of his friend's reading of Soviet economics, Polanyi felt it important to share some additional information with Blackett which never got into the published materials. One item related to Colin Clark, another scholar studying the Russian economy. Polanyi informed Blackett that he had corresponded with Colin Clark about the subject, who had read his *Soviet Economics* (1935) four times and found its "internal evidence right".[41] Polanyi admitted that later Clark discovered some errors in his *Critique of Russian Statistics* (1939), but, based on his correspondence with Clark, shed some new light on how that book was written and why it could be important to this discussion. Clark wrote to Polanyi that his book started as "a few notes designed to controvert your conclusion", but during his voyage from England to Australia he realized that the more he went into the details the more he found himself "in agreement with your conclusions". Clark revealed that the quotation on the front page of his book was from Hugh Dalton (Chancellor of Exchequer between 1945 and 1947) who said it in 1932 after returning from Russia. Clark reckoned that although Dalton "would not let his name be attached to the quotation" earlier, "perhaps now he would not mind if it had been". Polanyi did not think that he could convince Blackett and his friends about how to pursue the truth about the Soviet experiment because, as Polanyi perceived, "there seems to be little tradition left of sober and considerate agreement, and only the desire left to deal a blow".[42]

In his answer to Polanyi, Blackett accused his friend of having a "very hostile attitude"[43] against the Soviets and of cherishing "progressive obsessions". He expressed his hope that, some day, Polanyi would be able to convince him that he is not one of those "leading anti-soviet intellectuals".[44] Blackett wrote to Polanyi that, "you speak as if it is always a duty to publish the 'truth' "[45]and denoted that if he wrote down everything he knew about English war efforts he would have probably been locked up. Blackett seemed unable or unwilling to differentiate between knowing the truth but not publishing it because of concerns of national security, and knowingly publishing false or misleading accounts because of concerns of international politics. His admiration for the Soviets holding their ground against both Germany and Japan, with a population four times greater than England and only half of the English national income was, perhaps, rather a Machiavellian political manoeuvre than a bona fide recognition of the ingenuity of Soviet economic experts. This was not only disturbing because it suggested that macro-political interests penetrated into the evaluation of economic performance, economic policy and theory, but also because they were starting to construct a narrative of 'so-what?' similar to how the Nazis established their economic power in Orwell's account.

Polanyi and Orwell were not alone in seeing common patterns in the economic and political régime of the Soviet Union and fascist Germany. Perhaps another correspondent of Polanyi, Archibald Vivian Hill, Secretary of the Royal Society, Keynes' brother-in-law, was the most outspoken of all. Polanyi shared the minutiae of his critique of the Soviets with Hill. He wrote to him that Soviet terror found a "ring of hush hushers in the West"[46] and described the example of how it was intentionally left out of the papers that the Soviets did not let Pyotr Kapitsa back to the United Kingdom after he went to Russia to visit his parents in 1934. In his letter to Hill, Polanyi accused the Communists who became members of the Council for Intellectual Freedom and "Crowther of the Manchester Guardian" with connivance. He told a story to Hill about how even the "infinitely earnest" Bohr has been taken in by such narratives and "harangued a circle of scientists about their magnificent opportunities in the new civilisation". Polanyi was primarily blaming British left-wingers, and stated that "we must insist that our left wing colleagues should now tell the truth".[47] He made efforts to organize action to counter propaganda, together with Hill. Haldane and other left-wingers emphasized that such denunciations of the Soviet Union risked embroiling Britain in war with that country. This suggests that they were quite ready to subordinate their intellectual efforts to perceived momentary macro-political interests. Hill wrote *The Faith of St. Ribbentrop* (also known as *The Creed of Saint Ribbentrop*), a memento of the joint attack of the USSR and Germany on Poland and a purposely outrageous reimagination of the *Athanasian Creed* with fascism, Communism and Hitler, intended to show people their eldritch future revolving around only one axis, the axis of Communist faith.

Although Polanyi agreed with Hill that Haldane and his fellows were dangerous, he did not paint with a broad brush. He seemed to realize that while arguing against the USSR could be useful for defending Western civilization (he was doing it himself strenuously), it would probably not help (or harm) Kapitsa in his case. Polanyi contended that he is not "annoyed by Haldane and his crowd, but seriously alarmed by the movement they represent – in view of the weakness and the off-hand manner of our liberal defence",[48] emphasizing that liberty is not strong enough to give such advantage to its enemies. Hill pointed out that there are similarities between how the Soviets differentiated between proletarian and bourgeoisie cosmology in Russia, and how the Nazis differentiated between aryan and non-aryan physics in Germany.[49]

As noted earlier, Polanyi regularly exchanged ideas with Oscar Jaszi about liberal economics. Jaszi appreciated Polanyi's early essay on Soviet economic planning, but warned him that it did not address "how far and to what extent the free market could or should be regulated",[50] and was thus similar to Walter Lippmann's *The Good Society*. Jaszi drew Polanyi's attention to Henry Bamford Parks' *Marxism, An Autopsy* (1939) which he considered to be the best criticism ever written on Marxist philosophy, and a book coming near to Polanyi's conclusions. Jaszi was an advocate of world government and an opposer of American isolationism during World War II. In a letter of 1940, he wrote to Polanyi that "in our practical proposals we should not stress the Streit Plan"[51] because the "isolationist feeling is so strong in America that the North Atlantic Federation seems to be utopian for the near future". Jaszi said that they should better focus on Europe, but thought that changing totalitarian régimes on the continent is "almost a super-human task if the Weltgeist does not come to our aid". He wrote that a friend, Prof. Salvemini, was "working on a highly illuminating memorandum [probably on his contribution which later became *The City of Men* (1940)] which envisages the future in the most realistic terms".[52] One might wonder whether Polanyi's personal economics was, in a sense, an initiative aiming to move the Weltgeist in what he considered to be the desirable direction.

In another letter, Jaszi praised Polanyi's *The Social Message of Science* and expressed his displeasure about the "inhumanity of the whole outlook"[53] of Mannheim's new book on planning, which Jaszi perceived as mirroring Nazi and Bolshevik structures of thought despite its claim to explain democratic ways of planning. Jaszi's democratic liberal revival had an international, anti-state character. However, Polanyi considered it "remote"[54] and "dangerous" to replace the historically established state-based system with a new, "yet rather undeveloped" international organization. For Polanyi, statehood was a constitutional and political tradition, a pattern of 'social crystallisation' safeguarding democracy by providing people with a political instrument they knew how to handle. Polanyi thought that by replacing this system one would lose or at least devalue what modern societies had gradually learnt through the centuries of legal and political development about social cohabitation. Thus it would be better to amend the functions of the already existing units rather than to throw in a surrogate lacking any kind of social embeddedness. Polanyi considered a planetary electoral campaign an "utter farce" favouring those who are the ablest to manipulate its "mammoth machinery". According to Polanyi, world representation could only be effective if it is formed similarly to the "motley crowd" of the early British Parliament, as a coagulation of rather organic, informal but influential gatherings. A constitutional and political system cannot be alien to a society it intends to regulate and from which it requires regulation. Having a more "comprehensive machinery" such as the planetary régime Jaszi suggested, would either result in the "collective impotence of all" or "become a mere pretence, setting a rubber stamp of approval to decisions made without its machinery". Instead, Polanyi preferred a mechanism of mutual adjustments between the policies of different states, each relying heavily on the public opinion of their own people.

Jaszi and Polanyi both saw weaknesses in *The City of Man* (1940) related to economic aims. Polanyi thought that these might be "partly due to the lack of appreciation of the theoretical position", and added that British economists developed "mutual agreement to a new level" led by his friend, John Jewkes, who currently worked for the Secretariat of the War Cabinet. Polanyi also noted that he sent "what is foremost in my mind regarding the unemployment problem"[55] to Jewkes and his colleagues. Jaszi welcomed Polanyi's endeavours to reform economics because he was "convinced that any form of thoroughgoing planned system of economics must lead to semi-fascist systems"[56] and thought that Polanyi's relevant efforts are leading in another direction. Jaszi saw a great danger in socialism and he was also sceptical about certain conservative counter-campaigns, such as the International of the World, which he thought to be backed by both monopolistic capitalism and the Roman Catholic Church which had a very clear but not necessarily democratic view about what to accomplish through the organization. Jaszi and Polanyi saw a threat in the Central-Eastern European politics of the United Kingdom and the United States. They were afraid that these beacons of the West would not find powerful allies in the popular forces of these countries which are "not desirous to be harnessed to the Soviet Leviathan".[57] Instead, they would work for making a change from outside. Polanyi recalled that there was a tradition of tolerance and freedom in the Danubian countries until 1914, a tradition which is not dead at all but which lay dormant waiting for its awakening from the delusionary dream of Soviet Communism. Polanyi urged Jaszi to try to affect British understanding of Eastern Europe. He perceived a confusion to a great extent and a lack of "solid faits accomplis"[58] in these matters on British soil, which prevented the "crystallisation of any definite policy for Eastern Europe".[59]

Jaszi asked Polanyi about whether he read the *London Economist*? He noted that Justice Felix Frankfurter[60] "drew my attention to it, and he was right in saying how superior this old magazine is compared with the radical leftist press".[61] Jaszi thought that his public activity in England would not be welcomed by those who believed that the Soviet experiment is of a democratic nature and who followed "a policy of uncritical enthusiasm concerning

Russia".[62] In the matter of Central-Eastern Europe, and especially Hungary, Jaszi warned that it was important to think realistically, "undisturbed by [both] conservative pessimists and Soviet fellow-travellers".[63] Jaszi predicted in July 1944 that Germany would shortly fall and he was afraid that "the coup de grace will be given, almost symbolically, by Russia, instead of a collective action". He shared a speech of a colleague, Andrew Bongiorno, with Polanyi about the contemporary moral crisis and the idea that "without a standard of values we build our state and politics on sand".[64] Bongiorno himself became a correspondent of Polanyi. From their letters, it seems that they understood the nature of the moral crisis of their age quite similarly. Bongiorno thought that the people of America "have been saved from moral and political disaster by moral and political prejudice, but one cannot help fearing that prejudice will grow weaker as it gets farther and farther away from philosophy and religion".[65] He was worried about the spread of nihilism in academic circles and pointed out that the majority of those loudly championing freedom were, in fact, "busy undermining its metaphysical and religious foundations".[66] Bongiorno and Polanyi did not see metaphysics as something which could and should be cast out from scientific heaven. For them, it was the source of intellectual vitality, the realm from which, they hoped, help would soon come to reinvigorate the moral foundations of science.

Jaszi was pessimistic regarding the Hungarian situation in July 1945. "That most of the Moscow emigrants are at home, but Karolyi is still in London and Vambery is in New York, is a very characteristic symptom."[67] Extending his scope, he noted that democracies, in general, are astonishingly "aimless" and "barren of ideas". Polanyi, Bongiorno and Jaszi realized that democracies, similarly to science, need a vital force, a metaphysical or moral pointer which does not necessarily show where we are but where we are heading to, and how we believe we could get there. They missed this vitality from many contemporary democracies and found its perverse counterpart in dictatorial régimes, the latter having a metaphysical compass but without providing individuals the freedom to decide in democratic ways. Jaszi borrowed the concept of diminishing returns from economics to describe his state of mind but also blamed the "terribly gloomy"[68] situation in Hungary, and in the world, for sapping his energy. Jaszi thought that there was "no real doctrine"[69] and "no real leader", thus they would be "crushed by the ruthless dictatorship of Stalin who with his false messianistic doctrine and unrestricted Machiavellianism will ultimately swallow the masses".[70] Jaszi supported Polanyi's economic work because he thought that this could contribute to raising such a vital force. As he noted, "there is a great need for a new and clear-cut synthesis".[71] Polanyi saw epistemic empowerment through economics enlightenment as a means to fight against anti-democratic political tendencies. Reforming economics, for him, was a way to defend Western civilization, liberalism and democracy. It remains unclear what Jaszi meant by synthesis. Perhaps he meant, and this is highly speculative, the need to moderate the battles of diverging interpretations in the expert community of economists. Some[72] have recently claimed that Polanyi made a Keynesian-monetarist synthesis two or three decades earlier than any economist. Whatever we think about this statement, there is no evidence that Jaszi viewed Polanyi's economics as making such a synthesis or that Polanyi was thinking about his own economic work as doing so.

Perhaps the one with whom Polanyi agreed the most about how to view economics was the German economic journalist and economist Toni Stolper. They first met in Germany during the 1920s, quickly became friends, and regularly exchanged ideas for decades. Stolper, like Polanyi, realized that the greatest accomplishment of the Russian method, and the greatest threat it constituted to the Western world, was not economic or social but of an epistemic nature. Stolper thought that the Bolshevik method of complete secrecy kept "the minds in the state of a clean panel for whatever propaganda is to be inscribed or wiped off at a sign from on high",[73] an achievement which the Nazis tried to copy but failed to do so. She also claimed to notice how this corruption of the public mind grows in the West due to "unashamedly crude and silly Russian propaganda". She posed the two following rhetorical questions to Polanyi: "Shall we not even notice what they are doing to us by their masterly secrecy? Shall we let them spread their veil further and further until the world becomes an unknown Mars to us?" Stolper thought that England lacked the "wisdom to cure" the troubles, or "to make them less virulent", and noted that it is increasingly seen that America will have to deal with the problem which lies at the heart of European conflicts. She noted that American minds are "tragically unprepared"[74] for this task and was afraid that the "knowledge and the intensity of groping for it may simply not be there",[75] similarly to their rather instinctive intervention in World War I, which was essential to win the war but was quite insensitive in handling the underlying conflicts. This is not to say that Stolper had an anti-American attitude. She did not. She just warned, similarly to Polanyi, that legal and political systems are embedded in societies which developed them, therefore they cannot be changed *ad libitum* from outside without taking these societies into account.

Stolper saw a great danger in English Vansittartism, which was a radical political-ideological stream based on the work of Robert Vansittart,[76] primarily on his *Black Record: Germans Past and Present* (1941). In this book, Vansittart argued that German people are aggressive and militaristic, and that Nazism is only one instance of the several large-scale manifestations of this personality trait which has had a crucial effect on the history of Germans from Roman times. He supported violent military action to win the war and the re-education of upcoming German generations by the United Nations. He gave voice to his conviction that there is no point in differentiating between Germans as "they are all alike".[77] Such extreme racist statements were unsettling and outrageous, not just for Germans but for everyone having a strong moral sense and a cool head. But a cool head is a scarce resource in wartime. People are looking for theories to justify terrible deeds, and the more terrible their own or their enemies' deeds are, the more radical the theories they embrace to explain what is happening. Vansittart was accused by promoting aggression against Germany in the late 1930s by historian Harry Elmer Barnes. Barnes thought that Germany and the Austro-Hungarian Monarchy were the victims and France and Russia were the aggressors of the July Crisis leading to World War I. He made literary efforts to legitimize Germany's overthrow of the unfair and morally wrong Versailles Treaty and promoted American non-interventionism. While Barnes turned out to be a German apologist, he had also become increasingly anti-Semitic. The parallel development of Vansittart's anti-German and Barnes anti-Jewish rhetoric crossed each other when Barnes accused Vansittart of agitating against Germany; consequently Vansittart sued Barnes for libel in 1939. Various extreme interpretations were on the table and were discussed publicly. Stolper, Polanyi and many other intellectuals recognized that these could easily influence the uneducated and heated public opinion to a dangerous degree. They also realized that, against these radical narratives, only comprehensible accounts could stand up effectively.

Stolper, similarly to Polanyi, saw serious epistemic problems, but unlike her British-Hungarian friend, she focused more on those coming from the West. According to Stolper, the West, "believing that automatically, sooner or later, the world would necessarily fall into line with Western life, got completely out of touch with everyone outside their own narrowing sphere".[78] Stolper claimed to identify economic and ideological disturbances radiating from the West. For the first type of disturbances, she gave an example of what she called the "silly theory of capitalistic" "'imperialism'", for the second type, the "Western idea of nationalism and national sovereignty", which was "perfectly suited to the West, but necessarily creating chaos or domination elsewhere".[79] Stolper's critique of the implicit presumption that Western economic, political and legal ideas are of universal applicability seems to echo Polanyi's argument about why Jaszi's concept of world representation would not work. Ideas, including economic ones, are not necessarily compatible with every sociopolitical milieu. Ideas are, whether we acknowledge it or not, embedded in a certain social niche, and cannot be considered as universal and necessary steps in the historical development of every state. Stolper asked Polanyi about how upset the liberal morale was on British soil, and brought up the topic of India to the discussion. In Stolper's view, Gandhi was "clearly speculating on the West's downfall",[80] and Nehru was combining his solicitude for Russia with his wish to "unseat the West in Asia".[81] Stolper agreed with Churchill that 'Congress-India' was working for the enemy. Churchill said that leaders of the Indian National Congress are "Brahmins who mouth and patter principles of Western Liberalism",[82] which implied that the forces working for an independent India were quite homogenous in their political and economic rhetoric. But Gandhi and Nehru, the most prominent leaders of the nascent nation, had starkly different visions of the future of India and the most desirable economic model to follow. On the one hand, Gandhi promoted a bottom-up approach focusing on reaching the "greatest good for all"[83] in a non-violent way and emphasized that individual freedoms should not be denied by anything, even majority vote of a democratic system. Nehru, on the other, supported rapid and extensive industrialization and a planned economy from a top-down perspective, adopting the Soviet model. After Gandhi's death, Nehru's model became dominant in the Indian state embracing socialism.

One might wonder whether there were any similarities between how Polanyi and Gandhi argued against the socialist economic model. Gandhi criticized both capitalism and communism because they embraced a materialistic view of man. Instead, he argued for a spiritualistic view, emphasizing the spiritual and social needs of man which should not be neglected by the economic system. Gandhi and Polanyi both stressed the importance of having roots in tradition and both thought that we should not think separately about a legal-political system and its socioeconomic niche. For Polanyi, the "motley crowd"[84] nature of the British parliamentary system was a positive example because it simply provided an ex post justification for a rather organic and informal constitutional development. For Gandhi, the conviction that every child must learn Sanskrit because the local historical and spiritual texts are written in this language suggests similar lines of thought. Also, British rule was undesirable because it forced an alien power structure on the people of India. Gandhi's "ordered anarchy",[85] *swaraj* (self rule), and his concept that learning individuals gradually change their society are akin to Polanyi's ideas about *dynamic order* and his approach to *knowing* in terms of the three interrelated aspects of understanding, believing and belonging. Both Gandhi and Polanyi were greatly influenced by Leo Tolstoy. Gandhi considered himself a disciple of Tolstoy, and even exchanged a few letters with him between 1908 and 1910. He agreed with him in opposing strong state authority, colonialism and in promoting non-violence.[86] Polanyi admitted to Mannheim that, between 1915 and 1920, he was a "completely converted Christian on the lines of Tolstoy's confession of faith"[87] by which he most probably meant a personal, non-dogmatic faith in God and a spiritual attachment to life. Similarly to Tolstoy and Gandhi, Polanyi favoured individual freedom over state authority. However, there were also significant differences between them. While Gandhi called for direct political involvement, Tolstoy and Polanyi did not call for it, but intentionally abstained from it. Gandhi and Polanyi considered nationalism a rather positive spiritual force, however, for very different reasons. For Gandhi, nationalism was a positive force because, in the Indian case, it could be used to pull together very diverse people as one against the British rule and, eventually, lead to independence. For Polanyi, nationalism was a rather positive force, because it relied on the traditions mirroring the historical development of the state, helping individuals to cultivate a social consciousness, a bond with their history, nation and society. Unlike Gandhi and Polanyi, Tolstoy did not support any form of nationalism because he considered it to be impossible to differentiate between good and bad patriotism in a satisfactory way.

Although Polanyi did not address Stolper's remarks about the Indian situation, he did write to her, in a couple of letters, about how he thought faith affects economy and politics. In a letter of October 1943, Polanyi noted that "Germany may breach now almost any day"[88] which would fit the forecast of Toni Stolper's husband, Gustav. Polanyi found rays of hope in desperate times: "it may be only lethargy, or real tolerance, but there is undoubtedly more feeling of community among the underground population in Europe than there was a long time past in the same regions".[89] He mentioned a few examples: how the French Committee for Liberation was influenced by underground fighters driven by their sense of responsibility and solidarity in France; the seeds of civic consciousness lacked class-war spirit in Italy; the Vatican definitely veered towards the Left. Polanyi noted that "the sentiment among freedom loving people in the Russian borderlands is strong against being sacrificed on the altar of Anglo-Russian balance of power".[90] Polanyi speculated that Europeans were "picking up the threads of history where they broke in 1914"[91] by reviving popular national democratic movements in the West which are extending their influence towards the Russian and Turkish borders, where they meet the "Ariatic realms of enlightened absolutism, reproducing the modern milieu by action from the top".[92] Polanyi described the moral crisis of Europe in the following way:

> Will it emerge from it with a sufficiently strong faith in human ideals, to render its ancient civilisation once more stable, prosperous, tolerant and yet creative? Or is it weakened to the point of total indifference to public affairs; which permits a passing truce in all controversial issues?

Polanyi was hopeful that the "dusk of lethargy" will be the "dawn of tolerance",[93] and that European youth will shake off the chains of dejection and disillusionment.

Polanyi admired the vitality of the American people in handling public affairs which he considered to be having a beneficial but quite unnoticed influence on European politics. He thought that without the "rigorous individualist temper of the US the combined efforts of Intellectual Planners, Monopolists and Trade Unionists would have by this time transformed Britain into a fortress of reactionary Socialism from which all Europe would have taken colour".[94] According to Polanyi, without American influence, "Britain, though herself largely immune to these pernicious ideas, would have become the germ-carrier of their disease everywhere." Polanyi thought that British civic sense would have been a strong shield against the application of the oppressive form of these ideas on British soil even if they got adopted. But in other countries, lacking strong civic traditions, nothing would have stopped the growth of totalitarian patterns. Polanyi noted that propaganda literature was on its way in that direction from about 1941 and even named a few whom he considered to be the main carriers. In his view, "G.D.H. Cole, Kingsley Martin, Gollancz, Laski and the rest of them had 'decided' on a

Socialist Revolution under Russian egis in Europe."[95] This list offers an insight into how and in what domains socialism had started to take root in Great Britain.

G.D.H. Cole was an economist, historian and an executive member of the Fabian Society advocating guild socialism, a libertarian socialist alternative to Marxist political economy, which aimed to reach the workers' control of industry and centred around trade-related guilds. He regularly wrote to the *New Statesman*, which had been founded by Sidney and Beatrice Webb and George Bernard Shaw. He later recalled that his interest in socialism was aroused by a utopian novel, *News from Nowhere* (1890) by William Morris. But Cole was not only a socialist, but an economics tutor as well. One might recall here that he was among those who were experimenting with Polanyi's film at the W.E.A., and that he was firmly against any kind of standardization in economics teaching and was the one who reminded Polanyi that tutors might not be happy with pre-made arguments because there are still unsettled controversies in the community of economists. Cole saw socialism as a case for a "society of equals"[96] setting people free from the "twin evils of riches and poverty, mastership and subjection" and the only kind of society "consistent with human decency and fellowship".[97] Cole wrote multiple books for the Left Book Club, all published by Victor Gollancz, another person on Polanyi's list. Cole appreciated the socialist economy of the Soviet Union but emphasized that he wanted to avoid the import of dictatorial ways of exercising power if there is any other option. He noted that "Democratic Socialism offers the only means of building the new order on what is valuable and worth preserving in the civilisation of today."[98] Despite his democratic and anti-totalitarian rhetoric, in some of his writings Cole seemed shockingly and outrageously open towards totalitarian régimes. In his *Europe, Russia and the Future* (1941), Cole stated that, from an economic perspective, "it would be better to let Hitler conquer all Europe short of the Soviet Union, and therefore exploit it ruthlessly in the Nazi interest, than to go back to the pre-war order of independent Nation States"[99] with frontiers cutting through "natural units of production and exchange". He also noted that it would be much better to be "ruled by Stalin than by the destructive and monopolistic cliques which dominate Western capitalism".[100] From the latter statements, it seems safe to say that Cole wanted the 'establishment' to be destroyed in the West, even if it meant that Europe would be devoured completely by either Hitler or Stalin because, in his opinion, this would eliminate the impractical legal barriers called nation states and the corrupt power of the cliques impeding the most efficient means of economic production.

Kingsley Martin was a British journalist and academic. During his school years he joined the Fabian Society and later became a teacher at the London School of Economics under the guidance of Harold Laski (also on Polanyi's list). He worked for the *Nation*, the *Manchester Guardian* and, most importantly, the *New Statesman* (1930–60). Martin and the *New Statesman* was not so critical of Stalin's régime or the Soviet Union before the Hitler-Stalin Pact.

Even his friend, John Maynard Keynes, remarked that, when it came to the Soviet Union, Martin was a "little too full perhaps of goodwill. When a doubt arises it is swallowed down if possible."[101] Others, like George Orwell, thought that the *New Statesman* was "under direct communist influence",[102] and not only the writers but also the readers of the paper were "worshippers of Stalin".[103] Of course, Orwell's rage was not unrelated to his personal quarrel with Martin, the editor. After coming back from the Spanish Civil War, Orwell summarized his personal experience and submitted an article titled "Eyewitness in Spain" to the *New Statesman*, which was rejected by Martin because it could have undermined the Spanish Republicans. To redress the tension, Martin first offered Orwell an opportunity to write a review of Franz Borkenau's *The Spanish Cockpit*, but after receiving it, eventually also rejected the manuscript stating that it reminded him too much of Orwell's previous opinion piece and too little of what their other sources had said about Spain. Orwell's famous list of who he considered to be unsuitable for involvement in anti-communist propaganda included a few names mentioned earlier: Arthur Calder-Marshall, E.H. Carr, Patrick Blackett, J.G. Crowther and, not surprisingly, Kingsley Martin. The name of Harold Laski and George Bernard Shaw were in the notebook, but they were not included in the final list. It must be noted here that Orwell's now public list included not only the names of those whom he thought to be communist party members or agents. There were many labels, ranging from "probably symphatizer",[104] "appeaser", through "pro-Russian" to "fellow-traveller" and "C.P. member"; his classification was highly subjective and speculative. Martin was described by Orwell as "too dishonest to be outright 'crypto' or fellow traveller, but reliably pro-Russian on all major issues".[105] It sounds as though, according to Orwell, Martin was too bad to be a good communist.

Harold Laski was a professor at the London School of Economics from 1926 to 1950, an executive member of the Fabian Society (1922–36) and a co-founder of the Left Book Club with Victor Gollancz, Stafford Cripps and John Strachey. Laski was a high-achiever in economics and an outstanding lecturer. He was first a supporter of socialism and a planned economy, believing that an "international democratic system" can be established through the League of Nations, then urged for replacing even the international system of sovereign states. For Laski and many others, the Molotov–Ribbentrop pact (August 1939) was an eye-opener. The Left Book Club started an unlikely cooperation with Orwell resulting in *Betrayal of the Left* (1941), a book taking a very critical tone not only against fascism but also against Communism. It was a cooperation between Laski, Gollancz, Strachey and Orwell. Although Laski became a key figure in the Labour Party, Clement Attlee gave him no position in his cabinet in 1945. Members of the Labour Party, in general, were committed to non-violent democratic transformations. But during the 1945 general election campaign, Laski said publicly that "If Labour did not obtain what it needed by general consent, we shall have to use violence even if it means revolution."[106] No wonder this statement erased him from British politics. It was anti-constitutional and anti-democratic in a country which had strong roots in cultivating both constitutionality and democracy. Churchill and Attlee agreed on only a few things. One of them was that the irresponsible and radical escapades of Laski would threaten British society in the nebulous times following World War II. Although the spread on British soil of Laski's economic thinking was blocked by his suicidal political manoeuvre, it blossomed in a recently established country on another continent. It is hard to argue with John Kenneth Galbraith in his statements that "the center of Nehru's thinking was Laski" and "India the country most influenced by Laski's ideas". And, as was noted earlier, after the death of Gandhi, Nehru's economic views became decisive for the new nation.

Polanyi wrote a review on Laski's *Reflections on the Revolution of Our Time* (1943) for the *Manchester Guardian*. According to Polanyi, Laski considered capitalism, private enterprise, the profit motive and the neutral market mechanism to be on a highway to hell destroying our civilization. Laski urged replacing capitalism with a socialist planned economy everywhere. Polanyi noted that Laski's account was sloppy beyond measure. In his view, it did not reflect the recent statistics and also neglected the "recent progress in economic thought",[107] perhaps a reference to Keynesian economics. Moreover, Polanyi accused Laski of playing on the popular contrast between socialist planned economy and laissez-faire liberalism, pretending that there is no third way – a popular fallacy of propagandistic realms Polanyi had spent considerable time to slay publicly slain but failed to do because of the public activities of Laski and his 'fellow-travellers'. He noted that, by the time of writing his Laski review, not even Stalin and the modern socialist thinkers thought that commercial profitability could or should be completely eliminated in favour of public ownership. On the contrary, they were working on how to make use of profitability for their purposes. Polanyi asked what role did the "notoriously expansionist financial policy"[108] play in the prevention of unemployment in Soviet Russia, and what would a similar financial policy do under capitalist conditions. Polanyi also pointed out internal inconsistencies in Laski's account. First, Laski argued that "every state of welfare, necessarily determines its own appropriate values"[109] thus we cannot change our values deliberately. Then he urged people to preserve, as if they could, a certain set of values he considered to be better than others. Moreover, Laski did this without making reference to his own embeddedness in an economic niche, as if he had a 'view from nowhere', that is, without being determined by any state of welfare, a perspective he considered to be impossible. Laski did not convince Polanyi that the growth of welfare is necessarily followed by a revival of faith in values. For Polanyi, economic and moral revival are strongly linked and neither of them can make much progress without the other.

Polanyi was not the only one considering Laski a socialist anti-hero. Ayn Rand, in her *The Fountainhead*[110] (1943), portrayed the main antagonist, Ellsworth Monkton Toohey, primarily after Harold Laski. Rand depicted

Toohey as a socialist who presented himself as representing the interest of the masses but who secretly had a strong power-mongering drive. Toohey used egalitarian and altruist narratives to manipulate people, mostly by persuading them that they are not worth as much they think they are. Once someone believes that she is only an indistinguishable corpuscle in a swarm of billions, she loses her personality and will to decide her own fate. Then Toohey, like the Rat-Catcher of Hamelin, plays his magic pipe to control rats in the German legend, can play ideological tunes and do whatever he pleases with his helpless victim imprisoned in the belief of her own valuelessness. The novel's protagonist, Howard Roark, is an individualist with the virtues of independence and integrity. Rand noted that the main message of *The Fountainhead* is that there is a battle of "individualism versus collectivism, not in politics but within a man's soul".[111] Polanyi seemed to tinker with the epistemic dimension of the same battle and put his related pursuits at the very heart of his postmodern economics.

Ayn Rand's *The Fountainhead*, Isabel Paterson's *The God of the Machine* and Rose Wilder Lane's *The Discovery of Freedom* were first published in the same year (1943), earning the authors the name "the founding mothers of American libertarian movement".[112] They were all worried about the growing degree of state intervention into the economy (e.g. the New Deal) and urged the revival of old-school laissez-faire liberalism. Rand and Wilder Lane had first-hand experience with the Soviet Union before they started to write anti-communist literature. Rand was born in Russia to a bourgeois family struggling during and after the Russian Revolution of 1917. Wilder Lane met the 'enemy' during her travels with the Red Cross. While Polanyi's sympathies, similarly to these arch-libertarians, were rather with the individual than with the state, he was not developing an anti-state philosophy. For Polanyi, the state was both a threat to individual freedom and a carrier of traditions needed in order to be able to be free. It could be argued that Polanyi was against state authority and only fostered intervention when there was no other viable option on the table. But it could also be argued that he considered nationalism and nation states a positive force renewing traditions and revitalizing democracies. Libertarian accounts usually focus more on exploring the deficits of modern states and less on giving fine-grained portrayals of the alternatives to their taste. While positioning Polanyi on the liberal–libertarian axis would undoubtedly lie outside the scope of this book, and perhaps require its own volume, it can be noted here that he was more careful about balancing the pros and cons of state intervention into the economy than most early libertarians.

Victor Gollancz was a British left-wing publisher and humanitarian who became known by forecasting the Nazi extermination of six million Jews in his *Let My People Go* (1942a). He established the Left Book Club, which became a centre for collecting and disseminating socialist ideas in Britain, similar to the Fabian Society. At one time of his life, Gollancz had communist leanings, but he gave these up after the Molotov–Ribbentrop pact (1939), which shocked most of the socialist propagandists in the United Kingdom who generally interpreted the act as a betrayal of the left-wing cause. His socialist convictions, which he retained throughout his life, were slowly transforming into humanitarian activism with a decreasing attachment to party politics. In 1941, when the Nazis attacked the Soviet Union, he established the Anglo-Soviet Public Relations Association (ASPRA) to promote mutual relations between England and Russia. He was an ardent opponent of Vansittartism and wrote a pamphlet titled *Shall Our Children Live or Die?* (1942b) to fight against it. Despite being a Jew and a socialist, he established the organization Save Europe Now (SEN) in 1945 to support Germans living under terrible conditions, and in *What Buchenwald Really Means* (1945) he treated German collective guilt and argued that, despite what Vansittartists suggest, not all Germans were guilty. Orwell described Gollancz as "part of the Communism-racket"[113] in 1937 and, perhaps, in a sense, he was right. But that changed considerably through the next two decades. In 1955, Gollancz set up the National Campaign for the Prevention of Legal Cruelty (later renamed to the National Campaign for the Abolition of Capital Punishment) with John Collins and Polanyi's childhood friend, Arthur Koestler. At the beginning of the 1960s, Gollancz even campaigned against the execution of the Nazi war criminal, Adolf Eichmann in his controversial *The Case of Adolf Eichmann* (1961).

Polanyi saw a great threat not only on the left but also on the right. He thought that "the World Trade Alliance of industrialists, seconded by Trade Unionists of the Citrine[114] type, was planning to arrange a quota for all articles of international trade".[115] He was shocked that they wanted to use the 1925 figures (much had happened in the economy during 18 years, including the Great Depression and the two World Wars) as a standard for the quota, but calmed himself that "these people were rebuked in America" and as a consequence "they are not making any headway" in Britain either. Polanyi welcomed American influence perhaps in every respect, except one. He thought that American economists and businessmen were lagging behind their British colleagues in the field of finance. Polanyi noted that "British economists headed by Keynes have by this time fully absorbed and made into a basis for practical policy the modern theory of monetary circulation",[116] an achievement yet to be manifest in the United States. Polanyi also informed Toni Stolper that, thanks to a letter he wrote to the *Manchester Guardian*, he came to know "Dr. Beyen",[117] author of the Lever Project, former President of the Bank for International Settlements, whom he met at a study group of MPs.

This meeting was important for at least two reasons. First, for its influence on what Polanyi thought about the chances for introducing an expansionist budgetary policy in Britain. He recalled that the meeting "was very profitable and proved, to my mind, that there should be not much difficulty in getting an expansionist budgetary system adopted in England".[118] And second, for who this "Dr. Beyen" was or, better said, who he became in the upcoming decades. Polanyi was writing about Johan Willem Beyen, who was a financial advisor to the Dutch Government in exile (the London cabinet) during World War II; a key player in the Bretton Woods conference of 1944 establishing the World Bank, the International Bank of Reconstruction and Development (IBRD) and the International Monetary Fund (IMF); a Minister of Foreign Affairs of the Netherlands (1952–56); and, not least, one of the founding fathers of the European Union. Beyen's contribution was particularly significant in the development of the economic face of European integration. Instead of the previous sectorial type of cooperation mirrored in the European Coal and Steel Community (ECSC) established by the Paris Treaty in 1951, Beyen promoted a plan to move towards a customs union (the Beyen Plan) which affected the BeNeLux memorandum (18 May 1955), the Messina Conference (1 to 3 June 1955), and was vital for relaunching European integration by the Treaties of Rome (1957) establishing the European Economic Community (EEC). Polanyi met and talked with Johan Beyen about economic issues, mostly budgetary policy, just before the latter made his pivotal contributions to the establishment of the European and international financial system. This is not to suggest that Polanyi's economic ideas were foundational to the European Economic Community (EEC) through Beyen, but they might have had some sort of influence. The letter in the *Manchester Guardian* connecting Polanyi and Beyen was titled *Economics of Full Employment*, and was published on 13 February 1943 in the *Manchester Guardian*. In this letter, Polanyi criticized the proposal of the Lever Brothers and Unilever Ltd. to fight unemployment. According to Polanyi, in order to be able to raise business activity to its full capacity, it is not enough to drain "the high tides of circulation and filling up its ebbs by the proceeds thus gained"[119] as the Lever brothers suggested, because this would stabilize business activity at a relatively low level. Instead, the Government should raise "Government loans up to a sum equal to the deficiency of private investment and injecting the proceeds" into the economy in the form of public expenditure. Polanyi admitted that kickstarting the economy in this way was not without its risks, but considered it the best possible option in the present economic circumstances. He thought that the "main difficulty obstructing this kind of policy would have been, and still appears to be in the future, the popular dread of an indefinitely increasing National Debt", an illusion against which economists had tried to grapple with before but failed to do so. In Polanyi's view, complementing the missing private investments with public expenditures is the "most efficient" and, perhaps, the only effective policy against chronic unemployment. A task that lay ahead is to explore the "full scope of measures available to society"[120] in the upcoming post-war era, even though the dangers of expansion are much more likely to impinge in the period than of contraction. Polanyi noted that Beyen's "over-cautious expression of opinion"[121] about the Lever Project was "only due to regard for his fellow directors of Lever brothers" and that Beyen "quite agreed" with Polanyi's proposal to go beyond with deficit-spending and reach full business capacity, thus curing unemployment. While one must be careful not to read too much into this relationship, it seems safe to say that deficit-spending, fostered by Keynes, Polanyi and others, became a customary tool in the international financial system then taking shape.

After the meeting with Beyen and the MPs, Polanyi was inclined to think that an expansionist budgetary policy might be introduced in Britain, but doubted that American lawmakers would be "similarly receptive". He asked Stolper what she thought about this and added that he based his assumption on information from Hicks, who "feels rather strongly the backwardness of his colleagues in the U.S.". He closed his letter by explaining to Stolper that Hicks is a "Professor of Economics in Manchester" who is "pretty near to the top, we think, in the world list of economists".[122] It is not clear what Hicks and Polanyi meant by backwardness. They could have meant the under-developed American reception of Keynesian economics, the opposition of deficit-spending or the scarcity of American economists among the front-runners of the field. Of course, by the 1940s, American economists and lawmakers were not unfamiliar with Keynesian ideas. Keynes himself had even written an open letter to President Roosevelt a decade earlier, published in the 31 December 1933 issue of the *New York Times*, which was read by many economists and politicians. The New Deal and other government policies mirrored the American reception of Keynesian ideas and also the will and capacity to put it into practice. Stolper interpreted Polanyi's words as discerning a "lag in American economic theory as against the British"[123] and strongly agreed. While her argument that "there is no one to match Keynes or Hicks (whose high-class economic primer No. 1 we have all read with admiration)" might have been convincing at the time of writing the letter, it must not be accepted without a grain of salt. High-class American economics was already on its way with Knight, Stigler, Friedman and others, and soon a few well-known European economists (including Hayek) found intellectual shelter in the liberal atmosphere of the University of Chicago.

Stolper was among the few who seemed to understand how and in what sense the dialectic of tradition and discovery played a central role in Polanyi's postmodern economics. She pointed out that, while in the United States both "individualism in capitalistic production" in general and the "unceasing fight against monopolistic tendencies" in particular had strong traditions, the British, having free-trade for so long, did not cultivate worry about monopolists. According to Stolper, the monopolists, "left and right, found less ready vigilance when they made use of the war economy for their ulterior aims" on British soil. She saw another threat in America. Stolper thought that the "lack of tradition and instinct in matters of world affairs" about what is happening outside the United States endangered the outcome of the war and with it all that we have left of Western civilization. She explained this attitude with the widespread belief that American isolationism is the primary source of the nation's happiness. But she remained hopeful, stating that the "huge vitality of this country may find positive answers to its (and the world's) life problems".[124] Stolper admittedly found stimulating thoughts by reading Polanyi.

She wrote that "faith, versus doctrine, as the crystallizing power for liberal, versus totalitarian, thinking strikes me as a formulation with wide possibilities".[125] Stolper sent some critical remarks from her husband, Gustav Stolper, including doubts about Dick Stone's figures which Polanyi used, and an unfortunate implication of the term *full employment*. Polanyi was quite receptive to these remarks. He responded that full employment, indeed, had a somewhat "elastic nature"[126] and that it had different "regions"[127] with potential difficulties. He seemed particularly open to Gustav's insight that if full employment can be reached, it would come with at least a 10 per cent decrease in the productivity of labour for "psychological reasons".[128] Polanyi seemed to embrace the warning and reframed it in economic terms by stating that people will likely prefer "to be somewhat inefficiently over-employed rather than more efficiently under-employed"[129] and closed his letter with a witty remark: "humanity is such a funny lot, always wanting to feel important".[130]

Toni Stolper praised Polanyi's article in *Fortune* as well as his review of Hayek's book in the *Spectator* and lashed Karl Polanyi's book in her own review published in *Survey Graphic*. She wrote about Karl that she considered him "as an intellectual, not as a man with insight"[131] and she definitely did not mean that as a compliment. Stolper noted that in her mind, "the rather reckless jump from a disquisition of Speenhamland and the English poor laws straight to the destruction of Christianity and of Western individualism cum liberalism is all but scurrilous". She accused Karl's narrative of giving a "delightful playground" to pseudo-facts instead of presenting the facts' "unfathomable and awe inspiring complexities faithfully" from a less "esthetic attitude".[132] About the public perception of the European war in the United States, she wrote, months after her previous letter, that "Europe is not anything alive and meaningful to this nation, and no amount of war literature and movies is going to make it so".[133] In the US 1943 was election year which, according to Stolper, provided an even less desirable atmosphere to change public opinion. She told Polanyi about a few expectional Americans learning about world affairs, but regarded their number as far behind the critical mass needed to change the common attitude. Stolper noted that her husband, Gustav, was "doing what he can in not too narrow circles to mediate between half-open minds and strange realities" but warned that enlightening Americans about the European situation is not without its risks and that "some emigrés do this with dire results".[134]

These rival traditions claiming to explain what was happening in the economy were not created on statements by some perfect seekers of truth, but by claims of people trying to get along in life. They were scholars and members of the intelligentsia, but they were also people having interests, feelings, fears, hopes and dreams. They were very much interested in the fate of their school of thought because they knew that their personal careers as experts, and in most cases, their success in life, lay with the success of the school they practiced and developed. They were making arguments explaining the economy and trying to persuade others, and by doing so, looting the economy for authority. Robbins, who hired Hayek to counter Keynes, worked hard to purify economic science from what made Keynesian economics popular. Perhaps, this move was not so surprising from the head of the Economics Department of LSE, a department which was on a mission to establish itself by countering the hegemony of the Marshall Society and the University of Cambridge. Hogben was anything but cool-headed in describing economists and their field. He was attacking to defend political arithmetic and, with it, the professional authority of his wife and, of course, himself. The Labour trilogy of the Hammonds, on the one hand, included reviews of certain parliamentary debates with commentaries from the authors, and, on the other hand, the books themselves have also influenced British welfare reforms. Sidney and Beatrice Webb were singing the hymn of Soviet communism, which they considered to be a new civilization. Did it make no difference to them whether they were being thought of as propagandists of the socialist expansion destroying pre-existing cultural schemes or as brave, pioneering builders of a better world order? Hardly. Would this general view eventually depend on whether Soviet Communism became popular on British soil? Probably.

Practices of many of those who were looting the economy for authority became intertwined in one way or another. Polanyi's list of those deciding on a socialist revolution (Cole, Martin, Gollancz, Laski) in Europe might remind us of Orwell's list of those living in the UK and sympathizing with socialism. While there were names which were on both lists, it would be fallacious to see these people as members of a homogenous group fighting for the same purpose or to think that similar lists could not be assembled of liberal sympathizers. The names of Robbins, Hayek, Polanyi, Jaszi and Walter Lippmann would have probably been included on such list. But it would be similarly sloppy to describe them as members of a homogenous group fighting for the same purpose. This chapter has shown that Polanyi and his correspondents were wandering in many different social worlds, making accounts, having disputes with each other and, in doing so, attempting to extend their own authority, mostly versus others who were practicing and developing rival schools of thought. Internal histories of economics usually focus on the history of what later become seen as mainstream or neoclassical economics. They pay less or absolutely no attention to the rival schools which were, as this chapter has shown, pretty much out there interacting with economic science in public and personal domains.

Notes

1 Robbins 1932, 23.
2 Notwithstanding Robbins' acknowledgement that, by taking this road, difficulties might arise in cases of collective formulations of action, i.e. in the sphere of public expenditure.
3 Ibid., 24.
4 Ibid.

5 Ibid., 25.
6 Ibid.
7 Ibid., 18.
8 Ibid., 43.
9 Ibid.
10 Ibid., 44.
11 Polanyi 1939c, 1.
12 Ibid.
13 Ibid., 4–5.
14 Ibid., 5.
15 Polanyi 1939a, 1.
16 Polanyi 1939d, 1.
17 Ibid.
18 Hogben 1938, 14.
19 Hogben 1938b.
20 Polanyi 1939e, 1.
21 Ibid.
22 Polanyi 1939f, 1.
23 Ibid., 2.
24 Ibid.
25 Ibid., 4.
26 Polanyi 1939b, 1.
27 Polanyi 1939b, 1.
28 Polanyi 1941g, 1.
29 Ibid., 2.
30 Polanyi 1942i, 2.
31 Ibid.
32 Polanyi 1942n, 1.
33 Ibid.
34 Polanyi 1942d, 1.
35 Ibid.
36 Polanyi 1941c, 2.
37 Ibid., 1.
38 Ibid., 2.
39 Orwell 1940, 1.
40 Ibid.
41 Polanyi 1941d, 1.
42 Ibid.
43 Polanyi 1941e, 1.
44 Ibid.
45 Ibid., 2.
46 Polanyi 1940d, 1.
47 Ibid.
48 Polanyi 1940e, 1.
49 Polanyi 1940f, 1–2.
50 Polanyi 1940k, 1.
51 Polanyi 1940h, 1.
52 Ibid.
53 Polanyi 1941a, 1.
54 Polanyi 1941b, 1.
55 Ibid.
56 Polanyi 1942o, 1.
57 Polanyi 1944d, 1.
58 Ibid., 2.

59 Ibid.
60 The judge contributed to the New Deal administration with "Felix's Happy Hot Dogs".
61 Polanyi 1944h, 1.
62 Ibid.
63 Polanyi 1944k, 1.
64 Ibid.
65 Polanyi 1945j, 1.
66 Ibid.
67 Polanyi 1945n, 1.
68 Ibid.
69 Polanyi 1946a, 1.
70 Ibid.
71 Polanyi 1945n, 1.
72 Craig Roberts and Van Cott 1999.
73 Polanyi 1942f, 2.
74 Ibid.
75 Ibid., 3.
76 British diplomat who was the Permanent Under-Secretary of State For Foreign Affairs (1930–38).
77 Vansittart 1943, front dust cover.
78 Polanyi 1942j, 1.
79 Ibid.
80 Ibid., 2.
81 Ibid.
82 Churchill 1931.
83 Fischer 1962, 265.
84 Polanyi 1941b, 1.
85 Brock 1983, 34.
86 Gandhi established an experimental colony in South Africa (1910) which he called Tolstoy Farm, and, which provided an ideal training ground for his non-violent resistance.
87 Polanyi 1944b, 1.
88 Polanyi 1943o, 1.
89 Ibid., 1–2.
90 Ibid., 2.
91 Ibid.
92 Ibid., 3.
93 Ibid.
94 Ibid., 4.
95 Ibid.
96 Cole 1956, 5.
97 Ibid.
98 Cole 1939.
99 Cole 1941, 104.
100 Ibid.
101 Jones 1977, 25.
102 Taylor and Smith 2013.
103 Ibid.
104 Orwell 1949.
105 Ibid.
106 Laski 1945.
107 Polanyi 1943p, 1.
108 Ibid.

109 Ibid., 2.
110 It is especially topical that, during his presidential campaign in 2016, President Donald Trump (then candidate) praised the novel by stating that "it relates to business (and) beauty (and) life and inner emotions. That book relates to … everything" (Powers 2016). Trump identified himself with the protagonist, Howard Roark, an individualist lead by the virtues of independence and integrity who, despite being a nonconformist all the way, eventually built his skyscraper and reached the stars (ibid.).
111 Rand 1997, 223.
112 Powell 1996, 322.
113 Orwell 1937, 1.
114 A reference to Walter Citrine, British trade unionist, General Secretary of the Trades Union Congress (TUC) 1926–46, President of the International Federation of Trade Unions (IFTU) 1928–45.
115 Polanyi 1943o, 5.
116 Ibid.
117 Ibid., 6.
118 Ibid.
119 Polanyi 1943h, 1.
120 Ibid.
121 Polanyi 1943o, 6.
122 Ibid.
123 Polanyi 1943s, 1.
124 Ibid.
125 Ibid., 2.
126 Polanyi 1943v, 2.
127 Ibid.
128 Polanyi 1943s, 2.
129 Polanyi 1943v, 2.
130 Ibid.
131 Polanyi 1944g, 1.
132 Ibid.
133 Ibid., 2.
134 Ibid.

4 Polanyi's visual method

The previous chapter described rival traditions explaining the economy. Some promoters of these traditions decided to increase their school's popularity by making it more comprehensible for those without specialized training. The most current way of doing so was to make the economy visible in a way which mirrored their own interpretation instead of those of their rivals. Polanyi had started to think about using motion-picture technology to teach economics in 1929,[1] nine years before the first version of his film, *An Outline of the Working of Money* premiered in March 1938. This chapter seeks to explore the main influences on his visual method during these nine years of development and, in so doing, maps the surrounding landscape of economic visualizers in the 1930s and 1940s.

Oscar Jaszi, the Hungarian-born liberal politician and social scientist, in a letter of 1935, drew Polanyi's attention to multiple experiments intended to illustrate complex economic processes. He mentioned Franz Oppenheimer's plan to "illustrate the creation of the Mehrwert as an application of his geocentric theory"[2] and "a board game designed and patented by Norman Angell ... which illustrates the circulation of money and the distribution of gold stocks".[3] Jaszi did not go into details about the experiments, so one can only speculate what he meant by them. Regarding Oppenheimer's *Mehrwert* (added value) theory, Jaszi probably referred to the latter's conviction that the greatest economic bane of the capitalist system is land monopoly, which should be abolished in order to be able to have a competitive equilibrium where prices are determined by labour values. By labelling Oppenheimer's theory 'geocentric', Jaszi likely referred to its principles as mirroring *geoist* or *Georgist* economic philosophy. Although Oppenheimer was widely believed to be a Georgist, even the early interpreters acknowledged substantial differences between the economics of Henry George and Franz Oppenheimer. While George considered land rent to be the source of most economic evil and, of course, monopolies, Oppenheimer accused both land and capital with bringing forward monopolistic tendencies and their undeserved *sine qua non*, profit.[4] Both theoreticians sought a healthy symbiosis between economic progress and social justice, but took quite distinct roads. Henry George seems to have suggested a new social contract based on sharing land rent equally between all members of society. Oppenheimer did not believe in social contracts, and saw the state as a hypocritical institution providing *ex post facto* legitimation of the outcome of the social struggle by cementing the power of the winners and the powerlessness of the losers into the claimed-to-be impartial legal corpus. While no evidence has been found so far suggesting that Polanyi was familiar with Oppenheimer's economic ideas or his illustrations, there are fragments suggesting that he was familiar with Georgism. After receiving an appreciative letter to one of his later radio talks from E.J. McManus, secretary of the Henry George School of Social Science,[5] Polanyi replied that "I have respect for the writings of Henry George which I have studied with care."[6] Of course, based only on the few available fragments, it would be reckless to speculate about the Polanyian perception of the economic ideas of George and Oppenheimer or the latter's illustration of how value is being created in the economy.

Regarding the reference to Norman Angell's board game illustrating the inflows and outflows of money and the distribution of gold, apparently Jaszi referred to *The Money Game: How to Play it: A New Instrument of Economic Education*, which was first published in 1928,[7] five years before its maker won the Nobel Peace Prize. *The Money Game* was primarily concerned with teaching the fundamentals of banking and finance to those without any related formal training. The 'newness' of the instrument was its increased emphasis on the visualization of the economy by using thematic illustrated cards and its playful way of conveying an otherwise complex economic content. Angell's Nobel speech delivered in 1935 showed similarities to the Polanyian programme of economics enlightenment. The Angellian idea to educate the "ordinary man",[8] to empower the masses by making them more informed and therefore more resistant to political propaganda, seems akin to Polanyi's endeavours to teach the common "layman",[9] to raise a kind of "social consciousness",[10] and to eliminate popular fallacies in order to be able to save democracy and Western civilization. According to Angell, the most crucial educational problem was not the inadequate quantity of knowledge but our deficient ways of using the knowledge at our disposal. As he noted, what we need is "not more knowledge, but better use of the knowledge which we now have".[11] There is a similar strand in Polanyi's *Full Employment and Free Trade* which was primarily framed as surveying expert accounts of economists, mostly Keynesian ones, and making their "conversion into a matter of common sense"[12] happen. One should not go so far to suggest that Angell was working on a Polanyian programme or vice versa. But they were both very much concerned with enhancing the public understanding of a field of knowledge (Angell – social studies; Polanyi – economics) and they thought that better comprehension comes with better visualization.

Using games to teach economic ideas to the masses and to promote a certain kind of economics was not without precedent. *The Landlord's Game* (1904), another proto-Monopoly[13] game, designed by Elizabeth Magie, aimed to popularize the economic thought of Henry George and to show how land rents necessarily increase the wealth of landowners while impoverishing tenants. The game, coming from a Delawarean Georgist community, eventually found its way to publication after Magie and a few other Georgists established the Economic Game Company. After having sold her patent to Parker Brothers for $500 and no royalties, she was asked about the fairness of the deal.[14] She said she did not mind "if she never made a dime so long as the Henry George single tax idea was spread to the people of the country".[15] As Dodson pointed out, Magie was adamant about preserving the core economic ideas of the game. When the president of Parker Brothers, Robert Barton, asked her about whether she would accept certain changes to her game, she replied: "No. This is to teach the Henry George theory of single taxation, and I will not have my game changed in any way whatsoever."[16] Historians of Georgism explored how The Landlord's game has journeyed into different social worlds from the expert realms of academia to the simplest lay sphere of ordinary American living rooms. Scott Nearing, a socialist economics professor of Wharton School of Finance (1906–15) learnt the game in its birthplace, Arden, Delaware, and then used it for his economics classes to teach the students about the "antisocial nature"[17] and the "wickedness of land monopoly".[18] The game soon became popular in several American universities (e.g. Columbia, Harvard, Haverford, Pennsylvania, Princeton and Swarthmore) and got unofficial spin-offs with tailor-made game boards and pieces representing more familiar economic surroundings (ibid). Magie aimed to make a "worthwhile impression on the multitude"[19] by using an uncommon vessel, a board game, to carry economic ideas, which was not only intended to "tell them, but show them just how and why and where our claims can be proven in some actual situation".[20] Physical showing, a kind of visualization, again, promotes better comprehension.

The importance of the relation between seeing and understanding social phenomena was not a passing whim but a recurrent topos in Angell's work. In some cases, he used actual physical representations of things to foster comprehension (e.g. in *The Money Game*). In others, he played the card of metaphorical-verbal tinkering to connect visualizing and understanding. His *Europe's Optical Illusion* (1909) was not, of course, concerned with what Europeans physically see in an illusory way, but what they, according to Angell, do not adequately comprehend. The book was republished under the title *The Great Illusion: A Study of the Relation of Military Power in Nations to their Economic and Social Advantage* (1910) and became an anti-war bestseller. Angell argued that militarization and war are irrational from an economic point of view both for the victors and the defeated. The idea that a country conquering another can gain a considerable amount of economic loot from its slain body is a common fallacy which should be eliminated in the public mind. War destroys economic capacities, networks of economic agents and trust, which is the basis of healthy economic relations. A state-driven economic war machine functioning before and during a war and the war reparations paid by the defeated right after cannot provide the economic gain of a peaceful international economic order. Angell suggested deepening the economic interdependence of developed countries to make it even less likely to have a country waging war against another hoping for a fictional economic trophy. *The Great Illusion* (1910) inspired the French anti-war film *La Grande Illusion* (1937) by Jean Renoir. The script was co-written by Charles Spaak; Charles was the brother of Paul-Henri Spaak, the later Belgian prime minister (1938–39; 1946–46), and the foreign minister of the Belgian Government in London, who was, among other things, responsible for information and propaganda during the British exile (1940–44) of the Belgian Government. Paul-Henri became one of the founding fathers of the European Union (in addition to the previously mentioned Johan Willem Beyen) after the war. Unfortunately, neither the metaphorical visualization of *The Great Illusion* (1910) could prevent World War I, nor could the literary visualization of *La Grande Illusion* (1937) prevent World War II. These two efforts intended to explain the futile nature and the pointlessness of war to the masses. But did these carriers of peace fail to convince the masses or the masses fail to convince their representatives and political masters?

James D. Mooney, the president of General Motors Overseas (1922–40), was also working on experiments visualizing the economy for the masses. He designed and patented several apparatuses illustrating economic realms in the 1930s and 1940s. Polanyi was informed about Mooney's project in 1937 by Charles Sale, an official of the Rockefeller Foundation, when Mooney had started to tinker with the idea of filming his apparatus to make his visualization of the economy even more comprehensible. Sale sent an extract from Mooney's letter to Polanyi stating that "I [Mooney] feel that motion pictures of the apparatus, accompanied by synchronised spoken explanation, and reinforced if necessary by simplified charts and diagrams in 'moving cartoon' style, offer the best means of large-scale presentation."[21] No evidence has been found so far suggesting that Mooney made his motion pictures or that Polanyi contacted him directly. But this does not mean that there is no further evidence connecting their endeavours to visualize economic realms. Studying the letters Sale sent to Polanyi reveals a hidden sketch from Polanyi on the back of a page, a sketch which provides further clues. The sketch contains a circle, smaller rectangles inside and, on the circle, arrows, a few letters next to different parts of the figure, and a formula attached quite loosely on the right. One cannot be sure what Polanyi meant by each of the letters because he did not provide a legend, but a speculative explanation can be given. The circle, Polanyi's monetary ouroboros, having two parts chasing each other infinitely, most likely represents income (i) and expenditure (e). The rectangle in the middle seems to be the banking sector (B) having savings (s) and aging (a) as inflows, and profit (p) and an additional unit of capital (c) as outflows. The factory sector (F) is the receiver of expenditure (e) and the payer of income (i) on the circle and the receiver of profit (p) and the payer of aging (a) in respect to the banking sector (B) in the middle. The formula on the right seems to be suggesting that the amount of money in circulation at a given time (from 0 to time t) is the integral of (additional unit of capital (c) – aging (a) – saving (s)). Mooney did not go into the details regarding the economic content of his planned motion pictures in the letter extracted and forwarded by Sale, so what Polanyi intended to represent did not come from this source but from another. Polanyi's figure rather mirrored Keynesian ideas central to his later film *Unemployment and Money* (1940) for which it seems to provide an early static summary using arrows as place-holders of motion.[22] Perhaps the letter about Mooney's project should be considered less as a source of influence on Polanyi and more as a source of pressure urging him to speed up his own related enterprise he was working on from 1929.

Mooney framed his patents as showing novel ways to illustrate "laws of economics",[23] "economics",[24] "economic laws"[25] and "economic principles"[26] by "physical analogies".[27] Although he used various terms to denote what is to be illustrated, he did not seem to be very conscious about what is the difference between having claims about the economy and having claims about economics. All of his patents, running under these labels, claimed to illustrate certain economic mechanisms without acknowledging any kind of theory-ladenness. Moreover, they were anti-theoretical in the sense that they were to establish physical apparatuses as claimed-to-be surrogates of "abstract conceptions".[28] Mooney aimed to show "concrete, visual, physical analogies" of economic laws to help the minds of his learners to obtain a physical picture about what is happening and why, instead of confronting them with sophist-icated expert arguments made of abstract, incomprehensible concepts. His physical apparatuses portrayed the laws of supply and demand in the case of one commodity, plural commodities and the national economy in general, as well as the basics of home economics and the principles of business eco-nomics. The blueprint Mooney followed involved taking economic laws, translating them into "algebraic expressions", and then producing "physical analogies"[29] to these expressions, thereby making economic laws visible for the masses without advanced economic and mathematical training. Even though most of Mooney's devices used liquids to demonstrate what happens with certain quantities if one is changed, he warned that his apparatuses pre-senting economic laws "hydraulically"[30] are better in giving insight into "qualitative rather than strict quantitative relationships",[31] by which he meant that without having "adequate statistical data" to "calibrate"[32] the machines these are better in demonstrating economic relations and effects than in pre-dicting or calculating the magnitude of these effects. Mooney's cabinets of economic non-curiosities gave an insight into machinistic economic realms built of tanks, pipes, pistons, cylinders, shafts and communicating vessels. They portrayed economy as a set of automatic mechanisms working quite independently from the minds of those involved, whether they are constitu-tive agents of the economy to be represented or visitors with an intention to interpret Mooney's physical analogies. There was no place for strangeness and curiosities. And there was, in general, no place for soul. Similarly to economies, people visiting the exhibition were expected to be identical: seeing the same, thinking the same. Mooney did not want to teach economics in a tailor-made fashion, taking individual characteristics into consideration, but to find a common, generally applicable way of doing so. He did not want to teach anyone, but everyone.

The commitment to teach the masses connects Mooney's economics pau-perum with another visual régime, Isotype. *Neurath's International System of Typographic Picture Education* (Isotype) was well-known to Polanyi who usually referred to it as the unit symbol method of Neurath or Neurath figures. The aim of the Vienna method was to establish "one international picture lan-guage (as a helping language) into which statements may be put from all the normal languages of the earth"[33] making it, in a sense, a debabelization effort cutting through traditional language barriers. The Neurathian emphasis upon "education by the eye"[34] and "teaching by pictures"[35] seemed to have a similar, rather naive presumption like Mooney's physical analogies: seeing the same leads to thinking the same. Neurath's slogan "words divide, pictures unite" mirrors the implication that, unlike words, pictures convey the same message to everyone regardless of their previous experience, knowledge and personality. Unified visual notation brings unified meaning. Education thus becomes less dependent on teachers and more dependent on teaching mater-ials. According to Neurath, a teaching material consists of good "teaching pictures"[36] making it "possible for the least able teachers to do good work".[37] One needs to have good teachers to develop good teaching material, but, once the latter is done and ready to use, there is no need to employ the best teachers anymore. Neurath did not explain why good teachers should con-tribute to the devaluation of their expertise and the decommissioning of their authority. Neither did he warn about the dangers of standardization in educa-tion. There is nothing better for propaganda purposes than a highly standard-ized teaching method capable of reaching the uneducated masses and having no real alternatives. This is not to argue that Neurath and his fellows were intentionally building a tool for propaganda, but Isotype certainly had the potential to become one, and indeed, soon attracted the attention of big players involved in propaganda. Neurath was invited to Moscow in 1931 to help establish the All-Union Institute of Pictorial Statistics of Soviet Con-struction and Economy (IZOSTAT), which aimed to disseminate the 'great' economic and social progress of the Soviet Union, in terms of five-year plans, to its vast and quite heterogeneous masses. In the following years, Neurath, Arntz and a few others travelled to Moscow to teach their Soviet colleagues on-the-spot about how to apply and develop further the Vienna method of pictorial statistics. Although their collaboration with the Soviet government was short-lived and ended in 1934, the Izostat Institute, run by their Russian fellow-depicters, operated until 1940. After Neurath fled from the Nether-lands to England, he established the Isotype Institute in Oxford (1942) which became involved with producing propaganda materials for the British Ministry of Information. The Isotype Institute developed animated charts for films like Paul Rotha's *A Few Ounces a Day* (1941), *World of Plenty* (1943) and *Land of Promise* (1945), and contributed with Isotype charts to the book series *America and Britain*[38] and *Soviets and Ourselves*[39] (1944–47) which aimed to foster understanding between the allied powers of World War II. Isotype was also used in the *New Democracy*[40] book series (1944–48) to increase the popularity of the new British welfare state model spearheaded by the *Social Insurance and Allied Services* (1942) of William Beveridge, or as it was commonly known, the *Beveridge Report*.

Isotype was described by its makers as giving "amount pictures"[41] or "number-fact pictures" and having the greatest value in visualizing statistics and the "relation between amounts of different things".[42] In most static and animated Isotype charts, the values are not cardinal but ordinal numbers which means that one can have a particularly easy time reading the relation between different represented amounts and a particularly hard time to figure out the real-life significance of these relative amounts. Making symbols in the Isotype régime requires depicters to portray "only what is necessary"[43] and to get rid of all superfluous details unnecessary for the story to be told. Two symbols have to be the same if they are to tell the same story. One cannot use different symbols to denote the same thing. Most Isotype charts employed a set of completely identical unit symbols allocated in columns or rows of different height or width. Neurath noted that scaling the size of the consensual symbol up or down to denote the ordinal values instead of multiplying the symbol is against the principles of his visual method. Some charts combined the multiplicity of pictograms with a related map as a background to connect the values with the countries producing them. Others used supplementary "guide-pictures" with pale colours to provide additional context to the presented facts without taking considerable risk of distracting learners from the primary facts to be witnessed. After the death of Otto Neurath in 1945, his wife and long-time collaborator, Marie, became the main force behind Isotype. She shifted the emphasis from visualizing economic and social statistics towards depicting history, science and everyday life for children. Marie also fostered the democratic political transition in the Western Region of Nigeria by making booklets to help the government reach out to the masses.

Like Angell, Mooney and Neurath, Polanyi believed that one of the most pressing intellectual tasks is to find ways to forward the lay understanding of complex social and economic realms. He also joined them in embracing the underlying common principle of their fairly diverse set of projects, that is, better visualization leads to better comprehension. But Polanyi's visual method and his related agenda were different in several respects. For Polanyi, his film project was only the first step in a much grander scheme which aimed to visualize the complexity of economics for the masses. In *Unemployment and Money* (1940) he visualized the economic ideas that he considered to be the most important for common laypersons to understand, Keynesian economics. But his film should not only be seen simply as a case in point of visualizing economics but also as a first instance of using a novel visual method. The Polanyi method had characteristics not present in any of the visual régimes mentioned before, which Polanyi surely had heard about. Some of these characteristics came from the didactic face of Polanyi's sociotechnical dream about how to save liberalism, democracy and Western civilization through a film starring Keynesian economics, making it even more reasonable not to separate the didactic strand from the visual one in any related historical investigation.

The contemporary public understanding of economic ideas was, according to Polanyi, flawed for two major reasons. First, the subject matter itself was so complex that it was particularly hard to understand for those without specialized training. He drew a parallel with the teaching of geography with maps and the teaching of anatomy with dissection or an anatomic atlas and argued for a similar didactic tool capable of visualizing the complexity of the social body. By doing so, he contended he could make teaching and learning economics more effective. He argued that "a complex structure that cannot be seen cannot be understood",[44] thus the way towards better understanding of economic ideas leads through finding a way to visualize the complexity of the social body. Visualizing was seen here as cutting through complexity and fostering comprehension. Second, according to Polanyi, economists and their discipline did not show much interest in being easily comprehensible either. Polanyi pointed out that economists, like most professionals, in their efforts to make "substantial contribution"[45] to their field, "became overwhelmingly interested in one section of it rather than its general outline".[46] Making comprehensible accounts for non-economists instead of doing high-end research was, perhaps, perceived as not the most rewarding way to pursue a career as an economist. Eventually, one had to decide on how to allocate her scarce resources between these activities, and the disciplinary community values expert accounts with considerable ingenuity more than general overviews providing a popular remake or a readdress of what has been previously told before. But Polanyi also offered another possible explanation.

The cloister-like character of economics, he teased, might be not so much the result of disciplinary incentives pointing in other directions and the actions of agents who sought to realize their professional aspirations by following them, but the outcome of a strategy to make the field less comprehensible for non-experts. Polanyi recalled a conversation with an economist who did not welcome his ideas about how to establish and disseminate a better popular expression of economic ideas; he "would be rather in favour of a secret language".[47] This unnamed economist preferred taking the path of secrecy to curb the misapprehension of economics and the spread of related fallacies. This stance seemed to imply that the harder it is to understand economics, the harder it is to get it wrong. Polanyi's opinion was quite the opposite: the easier it is to understand economics, the harder it is to get it wrong. Not surprisingly, he aimed to open the "secluded community" of economists and to convince them that finding ways to reach out to the general public would not only be more desirable for the society but would also suit the community of economists better. Polanyi wittily compared economists to chess players who "learned to play chess without a chessboard", carrying the secret "board in their heads" and playing their games before a public watching "this admirable feat with puzzled inattention".[48] Polanyi was suggesting, although in a rather careful way, that economists find this admiration flattering and have no real intention of risking losing their charm in the eye of the public by letting them peek behind their well-tailored expert curtains. His own film project, without doubt, was an experiment in visualizing the chessboard of Keynesian economics for the general public. Such a move ran counter to the apparent possible motive of economists threatening the guards of the ivory tower of economics by proposing no less than disarmament.

In Polanyi's view, economists saw economic fallacies as products of a flawed lay interpretation of economic ideas. He took them as symptoms of a "craving for economic consciousness",[49] a need for an economics enlightenment. Polanyi not only provided a joint diagnosis of the economic downturn and the epistemic malfunctions of the social body but he also offered a remedy and started the treatment himself. He suggested establishing centres of economics education using his film (and future ones not yet in the making) to teach people who would become "a nucleus of educated people"[50] and would carry further what they had learnt with this new method. He hoped that, from these centres, "a calm light would spread out"[51] to the society at large, radiating much more than ideas: social consciousness. According to Polanyi, the general need for social consciousness was a "historic force"[52] becoming even more influential than the idea of nationalism and nation states. People have increasingly wanted to know how their down-to-earth motives and acts contribute to a bigger picture, how and in what sense the economy is more than a sum of their individual economic selves. Social consciousness, a kind of social sensitivity "encompassing all our activities",[53] was expected to bring new life into the lay understanding of everyday doings in the economy, and, if Polanyi got his way, should revitalize liberalism and save Western civilization.

As previously noted, some characteristics of Polanyi's visual method were closely related to his pedagogical concerns. These concerns were central to his value-laden mission to save liberalism in particular, and the Western world in general, from moral and epistemic decay. None of the other visual methods mentioned before had such large-scale programmatic reasons behind them. They had educational concerns, but they did not go into details about why a better lay understanding of economic realms would be better or why they thought this was the right time to develop better visualization for better comprehension. They seemed to imply that more knowledge or advanced knowledge was better but did not explain why and for whom. Perhaps, this 'better' simpliciter disguised social implications to avoid getting entangled in social and political debates, and by doing so, reducing the political risk of being seen as a too close friend of a political party in the eyes of its most vicious opponents. Or, perhaps, they were just too busy visualizing that they saw no time or reason to be engaged in discovering the social implications of their representational novelties. Polanyi took another road. He started to think about how to make a social change which he deemed desirable and found visualization a means to reach his rather specific end. Of these four innovators, he was the most explicit regarding the social relations of the proposed visual method. For him, it was a tool towards a postmodern liberal democracy having strong roots in living tradition and converging around recently faded Christian and Western values. He was crafting an eye for members of the *society of explorers* being always already engaged, together, in the process of knowing, having a common moral anchorage-point floating in their epistemic horizons, which they can lean on without becoming completely unable to change.

Out of the discussed visual methods, only Polanyi's had a joint unfolding of the visual régime and the content to be explained. With his film, *Unemployment and Money* (1940), Polanyi was teaching his visual method and his economics in parallel, leading his viewers step by step from simple economic examples and common symbols towards complex economic discourses and abstract visualizations. As the film goes on, the cartoonish common symbols building upon the plain visual similarity of the representation and the represented are gradually replaced by abstract ones building on what the viewer has recently learned about the relation of the representation and the represented through visual and verbal explanation. Polanyi aimed to develop a kind of visual fluency in multiple steps with his film in order to be able to introduce his lay audience into hardly understandable economic landscapes. The visualizations of Angell, Mooney and Neurath did not change their symbols through a single game, exhibit or amount picture. Once they have shown their viewers the representations of the things they want to represent they stuck to the introduced visual régime and refrained from making even the slightest modification. Their visual language was the same from beginning to end. They did not change their visualizations in the course of a single viewer experience for didactic or other purposes. Of course, this is not to suggest that they had no didactic considerations when deciding on their symbols and their invariable nature.

As previously noted, Neurath's Isotype was rather explicit about the variability of symbols by stating, in principle, that one should never use different symbols for the same symbolized. Whether this was a commitment to visual simplicity or a proclamation of didactic simplicity is uncertain, but either way, the Polanyi method ran against it. As the narrative goes from economic commonplaces towards its quite abstract conclusion, *Unemployment and Money* (1940) changes the set of visual representations to fit the narrative purpose. Coin symbols representing money are replaced with rectangles more appropriate to show the constant flow of money in the economy at large. Detailed cartoonish representations of three distinct economic sectors (mines and fields, factories and office, shops) are replaced by one rectangle called business units to become a sole visual counterpoint to homes. But this was not the only reason to think that the Polanyi method went against Neurathian invariability. In his film, Polanyi uses no less than five different symbols in the same sequence for only one symbolized element, a worker. The symbols show surprisingly detailed differences in the clothes of the represented workers. They are simply called workers without providing any additional verbal or visual clues about why and in what sense they are different. One is tempted to think that different symbols are showing workers of different occupation. But there is no further evidence suggesting this or any other interpretation. The symbols are different without telling a different story which makes the Polanyi method even less like Isotype.

There is at least, one other reason to think that Polanyi did not adapt the originally static Isotype to the motion picture to create a kind of "animated infographic"[54] as Orosz argued (2014). This reason has less to do with the number of symbols used and more to do with how symbols appear and disappear. In Polanyi's film, the replacement of symbols was not simply carried out as stopping to use one and starting to use another but as portraying the process of revisualization, a liquid-like shifting of the first symbol into the next one. Revisualization was happening on-screen, before the eyes of the viewer, and was usually accompanied by a supplementary verbal explanation. Isotype did not portray the process of introducing or terminating symbols. Visualization was framed verbally as happening not on- but off-screen in closed expert circles. The audience was expected to acknowledge only the *productum*, without having even a sneak peek into the real or perceived process defining how symbols were coming and going. The aim of Isotype was to establish a growing thesaurus of fixed symbols which can then be used for several educational projects. Making these symbols was quite an intimate act for those working on them, perhaps because this activity was mirroring their competence, or perhaps because the plethora of discarded alternative symbols, which eventually ended up hidden in the drawer, if it went public, would have hampered the spread of the 'official' ones and the whole system. Polanyi's method seemed to follow other considerations. In his visual method, transition from one symbol to another was visualized in details not disguising but emphasizing that symbols are only arbitrary visual tools being used to tell a story. While Neurath's "number-fact pictures"[55] were using fixed symbols to describe the world as it is, Polanyi's film was using shifting symbols suggesting that both reality and its interpretation is quite flexible. It would be immensely anachronistic to describe Isotype as considering its symbols to be *immutable mobiles* capable of telling the same story regardless of the context of their viewer, but it would be less anachronistic to argue that Polanyi's shifting symbolism mirrored his shaping postmodern economics.

Like Isotype, the symbols of Angell's *The Money Game* remained the same through the entire user experience. Each represented thing had one representation used on all related thematic cards. The symbols did not change. Their arbitrariness was not emphasized and was not expected to be recognized by the user. Although three distinct games could be played in *The Money Game*, each aiming to teach different economic content, none of them was delivering the message that the relation of the mind and the economy is not a one-way but a two-way process. Mooney patented several apparatuses demonstrating economic realms by using physical analogies, but none of them changed their symbolism in the course of their operation. This is not to argue that Mooney used the same symbolism for all his related apparatus. He did not. But, if the amount of money or income was represented by the level of a liquid at the beginning, it stayed being represented with it until the end of the presentation. Among the discussed innovators, Polanyi was the only one playing with the plasticity of symbolism. The others focused on establishing one symbol for each thing they wanted to symbolize, making otherwise invisible or poorly visible economic landscapes clearly visible. They paid no or little attention to provide visual clues showing the arbitrariness of their visualizing practices.

But a static symbol does not necessarily denote a static symbolized. Angell's thematic illustrated cards provided insight into highly dynamic economic realms. People are working at multiple sites, chimneys of factories are emitting smoke, trawlers are ploughing the waves vigorously. Symbols are like snapshots of an economy always on the move using resources and producing goods. Regarding economy, dynamism is of the essence: a key aspect, which would have been unnecessary to portray for these three games telling other stories, but which was, nevertheless, central for the depictions on Angell's thematic cards. Mooney's physical apparatuses also did not symbolize static economies. They visualized how a change in one factor affects others, e.g. how an increased price of a certain commodity affects the supply and demand of this and other commodities, or how an increased income tax affects residual cash. In most cases, dynamism was portrayed by a changing level of liquid running through a well-crafted system of communicating vessels manufactured for the purpose of visualizing a specific economic realm. Neurath's Isotype charts were different. They portrayed static economic or social data related to a period or date. The charts have stock and flow quantities, but these should not be mistaken with static and dynamic symbolized. A stock quantity refers to a certain quantity relating to a given date showing no dynamism but stillness in time. But a flow quantity, referring to a certain quantity cumulated through a given period does not tell anything about the dynamism of the process of cumulation in the course of this period either. Flow quantities may have piled up at an even or uneven pace, with a strong start or with an intensive finale. They are not expected to have a stillness in time but they do not show a specific dynamic either. They might be seen as always suggesting several possible dynamics and never having one actual dynamic.

Polanyi coupled dynamic symbols with dynamic symbolized. His shifting symbols represented immensely dynamic economic realms. Workers are earning wages; housekeepers are spending money to buy commodities in shops. Business units are producing parcels of goods and selling them for money. Managers are competing with each other and are being affected by the general ups and downs of money flow. Actors are observing and interpreting the economy and making decisions accordingly in Polanyi's "economic drama".[56] *Unemployment and Money* (1940) portrayed how the small deeds of economic agents affect the economic big picture, and vice versa, e.g. how changes of the "money belt", shifts in the general flow of money, make an impact on the micro-cosmos of an economic agent. The film visualizes the economy as a continuously changing landscape, a monetary perpetuum mobile never coming to a halt. Establishing the correspondence between the economic micro- and macro-cosmos through showing the minutiae of their dynamics was important for Polanyi to be able convince the masses about at least two things. First, that fundamentally invisible and hardly comprehensible economic macro-processes do affect their economic life. And second, that they can and should take certain macro-economic and social considerations into account when making economic decisions, developing a kind of economic consciousness.

Discussing how Polanyi visualized economic realms without saying anything about his visual presentations in physical chemistry would be, no doubt, an arbitrary misstep in this present historical account. In *My Time with X-rays and Crystals* (1962), an autobiographical essay, Polanyi told the story of how he was asked "to solve the mystery"[57] of a diagram, and how his successful solution boosted his scientific career. Visual representation played a pivotal role in his contributions about gases, x-rays, crystals and potential energy surfaces, the ones through which he made his name as a natural scientist. Not surprisingly, when approaching the social sciences, he followed his well-tried method of finding novel ways to illustrate his subject matter. One would say that Polanyi was a *boundary shifter*[58] using unconventional visual practices to move from one social and disciplinary world to another and, by so doing, encroaching and bending the discipline in which he was about to find a new scholarly niche. But the role of visual presentation was, by far, not the only overarching trait of Polanyi's work. His portrayal of molecules and physico-chemical reactions and his portrayal of other domains inhabited by workers, business units and flows of money show considerable resemblance.

Visualizing dynamics or transition was central both to his chemical and economic visualizations. A diagram in *Über einfache Gasreaktionen* (1931), which Polanyi co-authored with Eyring, gave a well-crafted visual insight into *transition state theory* (TST) by visualizing the potential energy surface of a reacting system. This diagram illustrates a coordinate system of a potential energy surface and all the possible outcomes with their energy (kcal) values depending on the distance of an atom x from atoms y (abscissa) and z (ordinate). Transition is emphasized by symmetrical lines and arrows showing the direction of change. In *Mechanism of Chemical Reactions* (1949), one of his last contributions to chemistry,[59] Polanyi had a figure in which "hydrogen atoms are shaded to show the penetration of the Cl particles".[60] Shading denotes the process of penetration, a transition. Polanyi could have easily used two figures, one showing the initial state before the reaction and another showing the final state after the reaction, but he visualized the process of transition instead in one figure. Similarly, his visualizations of economic realms mostly focused on processes rather than discrete states. *Unemployment and Money* (1940) provided many examples of this dynamics, from portraying the flow of money, through visualizing how decreased receipts of a business unit affects the whole economy, to illustrating the process of the aging of the equipment of business units. Money does not disappear in one place to reappear in another. It flows before the eyes of the viewer constituting a continuously moving "money belt". The decreased level of receipts may result in closing down the business unit decreasing the general flow of money and increasing unemployment, tightening the "money belt". The aging of equipment was visualized by gradually darkening the colour of a set of moving flywheels. The more obsolete the equipment becomes, the darker colour the flywheels become. Without reading too much into this commonality, it is safe to say that the tendency to make transitions visible was an overarching trait of Polanyi's work spanning decades and disciplines. Considering his film as "using a system of fluid dynamics as a model for an economy",[61] as some scholars suggest, is misleading for at least two reasons. First, because fluid metaphors cannot explain part of his visual régime (e.g. the moving flywheels with shifting colours). And second, because it does not tell anything about the relation of his economic symbolism and his other visualizing practices.

The role of visual representation has been severely downplayed by historiographers of economics compared to verbal representation. Studies have only recently started to tinker with the theory-loadedness of visualizations used in economics and other related traditions explaining the economy. The pioneering study of Giraud and Charles (2013) explored, through case studies, what role visualizing economic and social realities played in the discipline-making and remaking efforts of certain figures involved with American social sciences in the interwar period. Visual representation, they argued, might be seen as participating in the disciplinary warfare between institutional and neoclassical economics, becoming a vehicle for crafting a public eye for the economy of the Great Depression, fostering the spread of socialism on American soil and turning into an ally of the Roosevelt Administration. Giraud and Charles (2013) showed how a specific theory-loadedness of Isotype, its socialist leanings having roots in Red Vienna, was making it even more attractive to those having similar political convictions while discouraging others from using it who did not believe in this kind of socialism. And they showed something more. By pointing out how Samuelson used an Isotype-like method to visualize the production possibility frontier (PPF) of a two dimensional commodity space inhabited by gun and butter (1948), they seemed to argue that visual representations are not only theory-loaded but that they can be theory-reloaded as well by finding new attachment and place in another disciplinary niche.[62] Taking root again in this way can be driven by experts and their down-to-earth reasons for expanding the authority of their expertise in the eyes of the general public. Visual rhetoric, similarly to its verbal counterpart, can be used to reach out to the masses gathering influence and fabricating power for a specific theory or discipline and the people behind it. Histories of economics that pay no attention to the role of visuals in the evolution of the discipline are making an immanent aspect of economics invisible.

Many accounts have argued that visual representation played no, or only a peripheral, role in the history of twentieth-century economics. Most of these accounts seemingly overlook that what counts as economics and core economics is an outcome of quite flexible interpretation. Those writing internal histories of the discipline too often took certain boundaries of economics for granted in making accounts about the 'key figures' of 'mainstream' economics. Driven by the delusion of the 'survival of the fittest' economic ideas, internal historiographers have learned to ignore that they base their histories on a circular reasoning: the fittest ideas survive (1); those ideas that survive are the fittest (2). Focusing on the victors of the struggle of ideas and the *heroes* bringing them to life, they praise the big and successful ideas and usually tell little about the small and unfit. The more one opens up the hard shell of internalist winner narratives, the more one sees how and in what sense the boundaries of economics are blurred, and not least, that how those making histories are not witnessing but making some ideas fit and others unfit. The study of Giraud and Charles (2013) showed how a visible element of economic disciplines, visual rhetoric, was so far pushed into oblivion by the verbal bias of claimed-to-be mainstreamers and their overtly loyal historians. By leaving the disciplinary safe space of orthodox economics, one could excavate immensely rich yet untold stories of the discipline which have never made it into the final cut of its internal historiographers. This book, in a sense, offers a similar lesson. Polanyi's uncommon ways or strange practices of conveying the message of his economics to the audience through a film were not very successful in making others see him as an economist, orthodox or otherwise. This perhaps explains why, despite being the first to make a film about economics, and despite having meaningful correspondence with celebrated economists like John Maynard Keynes, Friedrich August von Hayek, Lionel Robbins, Richard Hicks and Joan Robinson in the 1940s, he was, until recently, an unknown figure in the history of economics. Both accounts might be seen as cases in point suggesting that making visual representations regardless of their theory-loadedness was not being valued so much in the community of economists in the interwar period.

Five years after the premiere of his film, *Unemployment and Money* (1940), Polanyi published *Full Employment and Free Trade* (1945), a book intended to popularize a Keynesian understanding of the economy. In April 1945, just a few months before the first edition of the book came out, Polanyi wrote to Harold Shearman that he "made some use of the film symbolism in the illustrations to this book".[63] And indeed, two figures of his *Full Employment and Free Trade* (1945) were very much like the visual method of *Unemployment and Money* (1940). The first figure portrays the money cycle, the never-ending chase of spending and earning. For two out of the four economic sectors Polanyi did not use the same term but renamed them in his book: "fields and mines" changed to "primary production", and "factories and offices" to "manufacture". The name "shops" and "homes" remained the same. The second figure depicts three different money belts: one being too narrow causing depression, one being optimal for full employment, and one being too broad causing inflation. Symbols of the first figure went through considerable polishing by – as the R.J. monogram at the bottom of the figures suggests – Reginald Jeffryes, who was the original artist collaborating with Polanyi on his film. The second figure was simpler, perhaps in order not to distract the eye from what is the most important, the different width of the three money belts in respect to economic capacities. Both figures portray dynamic symbolized, each having multiple arrows showing the direction of change. Polanyi hoped that his book, if it became popular, might "reopen the issue of a wider use of the film for economics teaching",[64] fostering the spread of both his visual method and his vision. *Full Employment and Free Trade* (1945) was, in this sense, another attempt to kickstart his film project to save Western civilization through economics enlightenment.

Notes

1 Scott and Moleski 2005, 163.
2 Polanyi 1935b, 1.
3 Ibid.
4 Heimann 1944.
5 Polanyi 1946h.
6 Polanyi 1946k, 1.
7 Although *The Money Game* was first published by J.M. Dent & Sons (London) in the United Kingdom in 1928, Jaszi probably heard about the American edition which was published one year later by E.P. Dutton (New York).
8 Angell 1935.
9 Polanyi 1937b, 12.
10 Polanyi 1936a, 5.
11 Angell 1935.
12 Polanyi 1948a, v.
13 Some claimed that *The Landlord's Game* (1904) and *Monopoly* are not distinct games but different versions of the same game designed by Elizabeth Magie. Others emphasized that although Magie had earlier patents, Charles Darrow had his own for *Monopoly* which he sold to Parker Brothers in 1936, and by doing so, eventually made the latter company immensely prosperous, and himself the first person in history to become a millionaire from game design.
14 Dodson 2011.
15 28 January 1936, *The Evening Star*, Washington D.C., quoted in Dodson, 2011.
16 Wolfe 1976, quoted in Dodson 2011.
17 Ketcham 2012.
18 Ibid.
19 Magie 1940, quoted in Dodson 2011.

20 Ibid.
21 Polanyi 1937a, 1–2.
22 While it would be tempting to consider this illustration the very first visual draft of the interrelated ideas later becoming the plot of *Unemployment and Money* (1940), Beira has pointed out that there is an even earlier circular diagram predating Polanyi's film, which was, even according to Polanyi, an early carrier of the main message of his film: the money cycle. However, this diagram, while containing much of the film's plot, lacks elements, e.g. bank, aging and renewals, which are being addressed in the somewhat later figure I have recently found in the archives on the back of a page of Sale's letter.
23 Mooney 1934.
24 Mooney 1949.
25 Mooney 1947.
26 Mooney 1941.
27 Mooney 1934, 1947, 1948, 1949.
28 Mooney 1934.
29 Ibid.
30 Mooney 1941.
31 Mooney 1934.
32 Ibid.
33 Neurath 1936, 17.
34 Ibid., 22.
35 Ibid., 26.
36 Ibid., 27.
37 Ibid., 26.
38 The series includes *Only an Ocean Between* (1943) and *Our Private Lives* (1944) by Lella Secor Florence, and *Our Two Democracies at Work* (1944) by Kingsley Bryce Smellie.
39 The series includes *Landsmen and Seafarers* (1945) by Maurice Lovell, *Two Commonwealths* (1945) by K.E. Holme, and *How Do You Do, Tovarish?* (1947) by Ralph Parker.
40 The series includes *Battle for Health, a Primer for Social Medicine* (1944) by Stephen Taylor, *Women and Work* (1945) by Gertrude Williams, *There's Work for All* (1945) by Michael Dunlop Young and Theodor Prager, *Human Problems in Industry* (1946) by Norah M. Davis, *Women and a New Society* (1946) by Charlotte Luetkens, *Education – The New Horizon* (1947) by Harold Charles Shearman and *Full Enjoyment* (1948) by Norman Crosby.
41 Neurath 1936, 30.
42 Ibid.
43 Ibid., 28.
44 Polanyi 1936a, 1.
45 Polanyi 1937b, 13.
46 Ibid.
47 Polanyi 1936a, 2.
48 Ibid.
49 Polanyi 1937b, 11.
50 Ibid., 13.
51 Polanyi 1936a, 4.
52 Polanyi 1937c, 32.
53 Polanyi 1936a, 5.
54 Orosz 2014.
55 Neurath 1936, 30.
56 Polanyi 1937d, 15.
57 Polanyi 1962, 1.

58 Pinch and Trocco 2002, 313.
59 Berces 2003, 60.
60 Polanyi 1949, 8.
61 Moodey 2014, 28.
62 Giraud and Charles 2013.
63 Polanyi 1945k, 1.
64 Ibid.

5 Correspondence on the spirituality of science and economics

As a confident to Polanyi, Toni Stolper witnessed the inception of her friend's ideas and how they evolved. After returning from his period of forced silence (due to a throat problem), which he spent in North Wales, Polanyi wrote a lengthy letter to Stolper informing her about how he progressed during these calm rainy days and where he was headed next. In this letter, Polanyi noted that he was aware that his conceptions regarding metaphysics and ethics still needed refining but currently he was working on a book with a working title *Full Employment in Theory and Practice*. He also noted that he had started to write on the subject of economic policy first, but the manuscript grew "too vast",[1] about 80,000 words. Following the advice of John Jewkes, he decided to narrow the topic and make a selection accordingly from what had been written with an aim of 55,000 words. He also informed Stolper about writing an introduction to a couple of his recent essays which would be published in Karl Mannheim's sociological series. This seems relevant for this discussion mainly because Polanyi framed his introductory essay as dealing with "the history of the movement which Hayek has called scienticism [scientism], or rather with the history of science to the first expression of the claim, by Saint-Simon and Comte, that science should rule society".[2] Apparently, Polanyi was drawing a parallel between his and Hayek's anti-scientism and saw them joining ranks against social physics, a theoretical tradition which was more concerned to see society through the lenses of science than to see science through the lenses of society.

According to Polanyi, the scientific or materialist view of science and the long-lasting reign of the critical method "led to the subjection of science to behaviourist and utilitarian exigencies".[3] Does it sound like proudly marching under the banner of behaviourism, as Mirowski proposed?[4] Polanyi argued that science is "ultimately based on faith and on traditional devotion to certain ideals". The task that lies ahead then is to kickstart a "renaissance of ideals"[5] to restore the cognitive basis of science which was destroyed by its own hubris. Polanyi welcomed the abatement of the planning movement in Britain, which he explained by the fact that most supporters hoped for more active social policies but they "never conceived very seriously"[6] the more extreme policies, such as trade planning. This ideological 'tie-in sale' had lost its charm as other plausible options (e.g. Keynesian economic policy) emerged offering the desired welfare services without having unwanted collateral effects. Polanyi emphasized that trade planning "received a decisive shock by coming up against American views",[7] suggesting yet another positive influence of the American spirit on the European public arena of economic discourses.

Stolper noted, in the first paragraph of her response, that she and her husband considered Polanyi among the few "real spiritual brothers".[8] Of course spiritual brotherhood, in this case, can mean at least two different things: having strong ties based not on blood but on faith, or being allies in a common endeavour to have science be seen as spiritual, an antithesis of material. Their correspondence suggests that they were both. In this case, common faith rested on the spiritual nature of science and on certain convictions about how and why it would be desirable to convince the masses about its spirituality. Stolper informed Polanyi about the "snapshot view of the sentiment" in the US after the liberation of Manila and worried because she saw that a "vaguely optimistic blank" has been started to give space to a "greater puzzlement"[9] in foreign affairs. Stolper shared with Polanyi what she thought about the US presidential election of 1944. In this context, it seems rather interesting to take a look at how she characterized the candidate she did not vote for than the one for whom she cast a vote. Stolper described Thomas E. Dewey, the Republican candidate, the governor of New York, as "cold, unimaginative, extreme outsider in foreign matters",[10] a description which perfectly fit what she had previously characterized as an undesirable attitude towards the European situation. Stolper thought that a sentiment was yet to develop in the American public in order to be able to better understand world affairs. Dewey, for her, seemed unable to cultivate such a feeling. And so did the other candidate, Franklin D. Roosevelt, whose "too impulsive and playful" acts after winning the election held not so much promise to ease the puzzlement of his compatriots and to lead them towards what Stolper considered to be a more mature public sentiment. Hope, according to Stolper, lies in the "immense vital weight" of the people of the United States which is quite unrelated to what their representatives do, and the endurance of the British to keep "tiredness" and "exhaustion" at bay which have already started to "prey [even] on the most valient and able minds of men and women"[11] on British soil.

For Polanyi and Stolper, such tiredness was not so much physical as moral, a shrivelling of the soul which, according to Polanyi, started to poison Western civilization long before the Great Depression and World War I. With the Cartesian blade of radical scepticism, fostered by liberalism, we have slain the world of dogma but, to a certain degree, sacrificed our souls by doing so. Liberalism was a maker of its own destruction. It hatched and nurtured radical naturalism which does not accept any autonomy of "rational, moral or religious principles",[12] not even the ones carefully parenting it through centuries. Burke had stated in a similar vein that "the age of chivalry is gone; that of sophisters, economists, and calculators has succeeded, and the glory of Europe is extinguished forever".[13] But, unlike Burke, Polanyi thought that the faded glory could be re-established, the spirit of freedom could be revitalized and "kept alive".[14] Most of what Polanyi was working on can be interpreted as planning and implementing such a rescue mission by redefining and reinvigorating liberalism. He did not consider liberalism as such, but the most widespread kind of liberalism, the problem. In his view, society needs to place "positive faith in certain principles"[15] in order to be able to be free. At this point, after shaking off medieval fetters, we need freedom not so much *from* something than *for* something. Scepticism is not helping us make progress towards a better society any more, but is pushing us away from it. A new moral anchor has to be forged for liberal society which will lead hopeful wanderers towards a good society.

Polanyi aimed to establish a quarterly journal, *Our Times*, to make space for efforts made in this direction. The proposal for the journal, which he sent to Toni Stolper, summarized his general philosophical outlook and the programme which he would be working on in the upcoming decades. Polanyi noted that the primal role of society is to provide moral and intellectual order, to "foster charity, justice and truth among men",[16] which is strongly embedded and therefore necessarily interpreted in its historical context. According to Polanyi, the "static society"[17] of the Middle Ages was replaced by a dynamic one due to three major influences: Protestantism, Scientific Enlightenment and Capitalism. The liberal principles were first challenged by the Russian Revolution which proved that such principles lack the necessary resistance because they were forged by mistaking emptiness with neutrality. This moral and metaphysical void is what Polanyi addressed and wished to refill. But a dynamic society needs a dynamic moral anchor, otherwise its basis becomes a sequence of disillusioned moral dogmas. This led Polanyi to the concept of the society of explorers,[18] which is not included per se in the proposal. Polanyi suggested following the guidance of traditions and customs when making decisions in society; this can help us to avoid both "anarchist"[19] and "absolute pacifist"[20] extremes, which put all their trust in individual conscience but downplay law and social conventions and deeply religious heuristics relying more on the word of God or on the opinion of a religious community and consigning less sphere to individual aspects in decisionmaking.

Polanyi argued that the common narrative of interpreting "history as a process of continued liberation from the yoke of tradition"[21] is fallacious, and, in fact, harmful for those seeking a way towards a better society. He noted that it was the French Encyclopaedists and positivists who were leading the way to nowhere in a barely noticeable way, not enhancing but "fatally" imperilling freedom by destroying "established beliefs" in the name of making progress. Polanyi argued for a new idea of progress which is not anti-traditional but pro-traditional, in the sense that it embraces a "permanent framework of beliefs and customs" with a never-ending cycle of evaluating and reinterpreting these. This explains why nations and international order (rather than a supranational one) are desirable and foundational to Polanyi's liberalism. Nations are old-established embodied traditions growing and shifting, and being symbiotic with their societies. Nations tend to decay if their related beliefs remain in abstract and dogmatic realms, and they can only survive by becoming "incorporated into national ways of life". According to Polanyi, the "cultivation of charity and justice and the respect for truth must be made a national concern and become national virtues, embodied in national traditions". Nations are not dogmatic and outworn mementos of the politico-legal nature of past generations but the living and changing foundations of continuously renewing dynamic societies.

Polanyi pointed out that, in countries like Russia and Germany, the lack of strong traditions in civic liberties let "the march of modern scepticism" destroy the "beliefs on which liberty rests". Polanyi drafted three points of action: drawing together the nations retaining the tradition of liberty; showing that traditions per se are not contradictory to liberalism; and carrying liberalism to regions which were drifting towards totalitarianism or were already under totalitarian influence. Polanyi argued that perhaps the "excessive 'realism'"[22] of Western countries overlooked that other nations have their own internal habits of truth and justice which are not necessarily similar to or compatible with their Western concepts. And concepts and morals are "closely related".[23] In Polanyi's view, one cannot have a concept of man considering "his actions as completely determined by data which do not include his moral obligations" and cultivating a faith in the reality of moral obligations. It also makes it impossible for a society to plausibly think about itself as serving a moral purpose or as functioning as a free society ruled by a moral order. Machine-like, amoral, impersonal data-processors cannot dream about a moral utopia. Whosoever dreams about it is nothing like machines.

Liberalism, like any other system, requires that its principles and practices of validity be "harmonised into an organic whole". Without such harmonization the clash of rival claims, having roots in different spheres of thought, cannot be settled in a comforting way. Clashes of spheres often surface as clashes of principles. According to Polanyi, economic hardship is not a sufficient cause for social disintegration. By carefully studying economic and political problems one finds, in general, moral problems. But, as Polanyi pointed out, such careful examination is scarce. Common hardship is not likely to be the cause of disintegration. It is "far more plausible that the attribution of such events to economic causes is itself a symptom of the moral crisis in which their true origin lies". The reason why we primarily search economic realms for answers instead of others tells us something about the nature of our modern crisis. The lack of morality in these discourses reflects the "denial of the distinction between good and evil",[24] a demarcation which Polanyi considered to be necessary if our true intention is to solve the crisis and not to sweep it under the carpet of shallow symptomatic treatment. This is not to argue that there is a line between good and evil of universal validity or that such a line could or should be drawn. It is to argue that communities cannot avoid developing and cultivating their own concepts and moral ideals because moral convictions are always already present in the very fabric of every society.

Marxist socialism, in a sense, reversed the scheme of liberalism by framing the extension of the role of the state to economic realms as a *sine qua non* of an overall benevolent transformation of society driven by moral considerations. Economic productivity and efficiency were not generally considered to be of primal concern. Discourses about the economy, if they emerged at all, were deeply pervaded by political ideology and propaganda, and were more concerned with conveying moral messages than portraying the bare economy. Socialists have failed to see that a "society cannot be fashioned from outside but only developed from inside".[25] The idea of imagining, planning and rebuilding a society from scratch, disregarding the traditions of the nation, is like tossing a seed to the ground without seriously considering the ecosystem and the environment it is entering. Such unconscious and reckless moves were, in Polanyi's view, not limited to socialism. Liberal economic policy also was left without an adequate theoretical basis and mainly relied on inconsistent fragments from nineteenth-century expositions when it was more important to frame "liberalism as a going concern" and less important to produce fine-grained accounts to counter rival claims of another ideological flavour. The situation has changed. Liberalism had to adapt to the new circumstances and answer to socialist objections and concerns. Otherwise its own historical and social insensitivity is likely to spell its end. Polanyi drew awareness to the task ahead: to lay down the foundations of a new system of liberal economic policies with a broad social backing, a task which can be only accomplished with a "new[,] radically sharpened theory of democracy and civic liberties".[26] His programme was to make liberal economic and political theory "intelligible"[27] again and to channel the public sentiment and the power of the masses from having "vain destructive aspirations" to making prudent gradual progress of a conservative nature and solving "real issues"[28] instead of battling with windmills. For Polanyi, liberalism and conservativism were not foes but allies. Although he was one of the most dauntless fighters against dictatorial régimes his intellectual crusade did not make him blind to the flaws in Western democracies. He warned that "unprincipled democracy is lawless and its dominion tyrannical".[29] And it was precisely with this necessary principalization which Polanyi imagined to reconcile the conquering forces of heated liberal progress and cool-headed conservative faith in traditions.

These two forces, if finding a way to balance each other, can make a democracy function properly, not so much pulling or pushing society but growing in accordance with society. But, if they fail to find their consonance they can instead threaten the disintegration of society, giving space either to revolutionary forces neglecting or acting against constitutional order; or to dictatorship ruling in the name of a claimed-to-be democratic constitution and pretending to be deaf to active, living, organic voices of the people; or to both of these polarizing democratic deviances. The two forces being more or less in harmony are always present in every society, providing its dynamics. Stolper, in her response to Polanyi, seemed to embrace this dialectic and used it to make a topography of liberalism. Her diagnosis defined three categories: in countries becoming a prey to totalitarianism liberalism was forced to go underground or to become radical if it was to survive; in the UK liberalism was challenged by and defeated totalitarianism in a "deliberate battle body to body";[30] in America liberalism won without the "mortal anxiety of the strife" and without experiencing the real threat of being defeated. Stolper thought that the programmatic nature of Polanyi's *Our Times* would, out of these three categories, have the hardest time in the American atmosphere. According to Stolper, Americans feel themselves in the light-hearted "state of the man who 'couldn't define an elephant, but who knows one when he sees it'".[31] As if "they won't let the elephant be shorn of his tusks or trunk – their traditional freedoms of telling their President to go to hell, of smashing all monopolies except their own pet one",[32] or "of having their press report to them about all and everyone as long as it is 'news', of taking the side of 'the common man' against lords and kings without looking too closely at the ones or the others".[33] Americans have heuristics, practices and instincts leading them in anti-totalitarian directions but they are generally unable to grasp "the philosophical fundamentals of political and personal liberty" which "have not yet become sufficiently problematical to them". For them, accounts about the cruelties of the dictatorial régimes of Hitler and Stalin are "mere words or thrilling scenes out of Hollywood" and not first-hand personal experience soaked in tragedy and brutality. According to Stolper, Americans had a kind of "soul-deafness" to these personal multiverses and Polanyi's proposal would have found them in a "psychologically most unfortunate moment to make them begin to think in clean terms of spiritual verities"[34] because they were too busy hating Nazi Germany and loving anti-liberal Russia. Stolper suggested to Polanyi that his journal would probably reach a wider readership by having a more comprehensible subject of American world politics than of sophisticated philosophical accounts about liberalism. She also warned Polanyi that "a discussion of Western Liberalism today will be too narrow in its scope if it does not include in its spiritual field that very much alive, but very little durchdacht [studied] elephant of American Liberalism".[35]

Stolper pointed out that the defeated countries have economic hardships which make it even harder to export liberalism to these desperate lands.

> How can we manoeuvre those who will be in need of a soup kitchen society, endorsed with some glamour more beloved than being to make the soup palatable, into looking at the Liberalism of the West as something indecently, tauntingly, unspiritually rich?

she noted. "Can we show them Liberty without Mockery?"[36] This is a train of thought which might provide insight into why it was so hard for liberalism to spread into previously unknown landscapes. For people who are living desperate lives due to bad economic conditions and are surrounded round the clock by non-liberal patterns of how to live a good life, what the liberal eye most likely sees as driven by a kind of perverse morality, decisions are more about how to survive with their family than about how to live a life fitting to abstract ideals. Stolper seemed to be suggesting that disseminators of liberalism have mistakenly implied that all people perceive liberalism similarly regardless of their background, personality and life experience, and that it is beyond dispute that liberalism is the best for everyone everywhere. Perhaps these implications explain why it was particularly hard for classical liberalism both to adapt to the changes in the disenchanting West, and to expand its influence to the rather bred-in-the-bone East.

From a letter to Stolper, we know that Polanyi became acquainted with, moreover, "became very attached to"[37] the writer, Storm Jameson, who mostly made her name by writing fictional novels, including a few fascist and Nazi dystopias. One of her novels, *In the Second Year*[38] (1936), explores life in a fascist Britain five years after the year of its publication. The novel is a highly readable and buoyant account introducing the common reader into the bitter microcosmos of feeling, thinking and dreaming in a fascist régime. Rather than portraying a macroscopical general outline of a possible grim future, the book took a perspective focusing on the personal minutiae of what is happening which resembles, among many other things, Polanyi's personal economics. However, too much should not be read into this similarity. The novel as a genre comes with a focus on personal minutiae. This is a generic aspect more than a special spice sprinkled from the author's shaker of creativity. In the second place, focusing on the personal details in making a specific fictional account, and making a consistent and general philosophical account about how and why all knowing is personal, is not the same. And third, based on the archival materials, we cannot be sure about whether, and in what sense, Polanyi and Jameson found similarities themselves in their literary realms or their attachment was based on other common points.[39] Jameson's *Then We Shall Hear Singing: A Fantasy in C Major* (1942), another book about a fascist dystopia, provides better insight into the similarities of how these two understood totalitarian régimes. The story of the book revolves around a Nazi scientist, Hesse, who brainwashed the people of a conquered village by lobotomizing them. Hesse was on a mission to destroy the personality of his victims not only in the present but also in the past (memories) and the future (dreams). He was making spiritless depersonalized machines out of people, biorobots, waiting for commands from their master. If Hesse was portrayed as a typical Nazi anti-hero, and there is evidence suggesting that he was, then Jameson perhaps thought that seeing and treating certain human beings as machines without soul was a typical and characteristic trait of the Nazi ideology. Polanyi, like Jameson, saw machine-like concepts of man working in the heart of totalitarian régimes. Machinistic concepts, which have soaked into the very fabric of their lapdog economic craftsmanships, treating people more as bearers than makers of their economy.

Stolper appreciated Polanyi's work in economics and assured him, more than once, that they were on the same page. However, Stolper was critical of Keynesian economics, one of the most essential sources of the Polanyian understanding of the economy. She affirmed how much she enjoyed his chapter on the Russian economy, but voiced her concerns, in a humble tone, about Keynesian economics. She contended that she has "not progressed deep enough to the core of Keynesianism yet to lose that uneasy feeling about making a quantitative science out of the art of economics".[40] It is not clear, based on her brief remark, whether Stolper was more worried about transforming economics from art to science or transforming qualitative to quantitative. The two transformations were strictly interwoven in her account. Polanyi was, of course, working on a new concept of science embracing both natural and social sciences. Therefore, it would have been either pointless or burdening for him to analyse whether and why some explaining traditions fit to this widely loved 'old' view of science (if such an oversimplified and unrefined explanandum might be considered worldly enough to talk about at all) while others do not. There is no point in renovating a building if you are to demolish it altogether and replace it with a new one. Why would Polanyi have used a benchmark he thought to be outdated and wrong? He was more interested in, and also much better, throughout his whole life, giving pioneering new insights than in criticizing rival ideas in a systematic way. This might explain why he did not go into details in his response to Stolper. Polanyi's postmodern economics was not limited to understanding the economy, an aspect of knowing which, for him, mostly mirrored Keynesian ideas. According to Polanyi, knowing the economy always comes with two other aspects of knowing: believing and belonging – matters which Keynesian economics ignored, and matters having a rather qualitative and more artistic nature. Of course, without a longer description, one can only speculate what Stolper meant under the succinct terms she used.

Polanyi was particularly pleased to have his brother Karl's approval of *Full Employment and Free Trade*. The two brothers had a famously strained relationship, mostly because their differing political views. Michael was a liberal and Karl a socialist. Michael gave a glimpse into his relationship with his brother to Toni Stolper by stating that Karl "used to disagree strongly with me before I had the opportunity of explaining my point of view".[41] This time, Michael had a written explanation in the form of his new book avoiding such a discursive barrier and, indeed, he earned the rare approval of his older brother. Michael and Karl were both working on making the connection visible between the economic and the social. However, they claimed to find this connection in a sharply different form. Karl, in *The Great Transformation* (1944), differentiated between the formal and the substantive meaning of economics. The former is in line with Robbinsian economic science and refers to an abstract explanatory tradition about making rational choices with scarce resources having possible alternative uses. The latter meaning referred to how society and its members de facto struggle to meet their material needs.

Karl's perspective was, unlike his brother's, macroscopic. He studied societies as evolving historical entities and portrayed them as either part of the industrialized Western world having capitalist market-based economies, or as part of the less developed bloc relying more on *reciprocity* and *redistribution* and less on *market exchange* in making economic transactions. According to Karl, the two meanings of economics coincide in the West but took diverging roads elsewhere. He thought that economic agents in the West make rational choices between alternatives to maximize utility and reach the best outcome possible, while economic agents in other nations had an essentially different compass showing them what to do. In Karl's view, the latter can only be discerned from a substantivist perspective. Interestingly, in Karl's account, people of the West are living their lives in a Robbinsian utopia where the formalist and substantivist perspective perfectly fit. In this heaven of economic science untainted by irrational influences the best way to satisfy material needs is to make rational choices and the best way to make rational choices is to satisfy material needs. Of course, Robbins never claimed such a land to exist. Moreover, he emphasized that his economic science was not addressing everything economic and neither should it be considered as doing so. Another deviation of Karl Polanyi's formalist approach from the Robbinsian portrayal of economic science is, perhaps, even more crucial. Robbins first and foremost wanted to speak to his fellow economists and other rival experts in a normative voice to strengthen and promote the disciplinary tradition he called economic science. Karl Polanyi took certain pieces of this disciplinary tradition including its modelling axioms and transformed it into what he considered to be a real-life description of Western economies. Robbins and his fellow economic scientists had made a model to be able to grasp an admittedly thin piece of the economic cosmos. Karl Polanyi mistook this model for a general claim about economic reality and, on the top of that, promoted this to the public as being true; by doing so, relied on a sloppy and fallacious understanding of Robbins' well-tailored and finely polished deductive logical argument.

If the West is the heaven of economic science, there should also be a hell. Realms of non-capitalist, less industrialized landscapes are inhabited by outlaws of economic science building a system of economic comradeship and a state having great economic power without being constrained by such Robbinsian disciplinarity. For Karl, the way an economy works is determined by the society in which it is embedded. Economic agents are not makers but vessels of economic meaning. They cannot change the rules of the game they play. For Michael, the way an economy works is an ever-shifting accumulation of how economic agents know the economy through their practices of understanding, believing and belonging. Economic agents have freedom to understand the economy in any way they please, to believe certain assumptions underlying their understanding and to belong to a community sharing the belief in these assumptions. Personal knowing of the many is what constitutes an economy. And, when the levee breaks, changes alter even the most tenacious patterns of economic life. Karl starts by describing overarching broad social tendencies and makes his way towards interpreting the micro-cosmos of economic agents. Michael starts with the mind of a single eco-nomic agent and progresses towards understanding large-scale social change. Although the two brothers were taking very different roads and reached highly dissimilar conclusions, this does not mean that their interpretations did not meet at all. Michael's letter to Stolper did not go into details about what precisely did earn him his elder brother's approval but one is tempted to spec-ulate that it was the portrayal of the role of tradition in economic settings. For Karl, tradition was essential to understand the economic life of non-Western countries, realms which he thought to lay outside the power field of economic science. For him, tradition was mostly needed to be able to provide an external explanation for the strange economies which cannot be grasped by the 'normal' internal explanation of economic rationality. For Michael, tradition was essential to be able to portray how knowing the economy develops, and also to explain why a reimagined, less extreme and more con-scious liberalism is the only way out of the contemporary moral, economic and political crisis.

Karl Mannheim, Polanyi's childhood friend, was particularly worried about the social sciences which he perceived to follow a new "fashion to make dis-connected investigations without a philosophical outlook behind"[42] them. Mannheim even asked Polanyi to point out, in his new book, "the tragi-comedy that the Social Sciences try to enhance their dignity by becoming exclusively mathematical just when the scientists themselves feel the need to go back to a meaningful analysis of Reality". One would, of course, go too far by suggesting, based on these brief remarks, that Mannheim indicated a general tendency in the social sciences to move towards coherence theories of truth while the natural sciences are shifting towards correspondence theories of truth. However, it seems reasonable to think that Mannheim viewed the mathematization of social sciences as a pragmatic strategy to build scientific authority. Labelling this Mannheimian claim as describing an instance of *boundary-work* would be anachronistic, and perhaps, mistaken because unknown elements, like the social scientists' true reasons behind the feats of mathematization or the audience for which these were performed, would matter for the classification. Mannheim did not even claim to know the reasons behind the scientists return to the "meaningful analysis of Reality". He only claimed that they "feel the need", but he did not say anything about why. Mannheim might have seen it driven by similarly pragmatic reasons or by a recent progress in the internal logic of natural sciences, or both. It is highly unlikely, based on his sociological accounts, that Mannheim thought natural sciences to be free from every kind of earthly mundaneness, but it would be also unfounded to attribute to him the kind of social and historical sensitivity we are using today in our inquiries about science. In any event, he was convinced that Polanyi thought the same way, and he would join ranks with him against the excessive mathematization of the social sciences.

Hicks pointed to a similar tendency regarding a specific social science, economics. But, unlike Mannheim, he did not consider the increasing mathematization of economics undesirable but a novelty he need to catch up with. He asked Polanyi for private coaching about how to solve integral equations because he did not want to take this kind of mathematics on trust. "It gets beyond my maths, but since the Economists also are beginning to use that kind of thing, I want to understand it",[43] he noted. Unfortunately, as far as we know, these afterschool sessions on advanced mathematics with Hicks never happened. Polanyi asked Hicks to write an introduction to his upcoming economics book which the famous economist did not want to do. His argument about why he does not want to do it marks the beginning of a fascinating exchange of letters between the two regarding the role of public understanding of economic ideas. But this is another story to be told.

Some of Polanyi's correspondents blamed economics for unnecessarily and wrongfully seducing science into non-spiritual lands. Hugh O'Neill, one of Polanyi's friends in Manchester, warned that a "Christian student of natural science needs no utilitarian motive for pursuing his researches"[44] because he has every motive he needs: hope for a better understanding of God's creation. O'Neill regarded utilitarianism as a threat, a possible surrogate motive diverting scientists from spiritual, Christian ways of life. He reminded Polanyi that "men of science supported Malthus and led us to neo-Malthusianism by calculating that by now the world would be chronically short of food"[45] and used this unholy alliance in his rhetoric to show that scientists are not necessarily better in explaining the world than philosophers and theologians and nor they are necessarily superior in furthering human welfare than non-scientific philanthropists. Polanyi, similar to O'Neill, thought that scientists have left the spiritual road which they should follow. However, the desired spirituality of science and scientists was quite different for the two thinkers. O'Neill argued for the necessary (re)establishment of the power of Christian dogmas over science, while Polanyi meant the cultivation of an anti-dogmatic social sentiment having roots both in Christian and democratic traditions but being essentially the backbone of a *Sturm und Drang* for the upcoming post-modern era.

Polanyi warned that one of the greatest threats to science and also to society is the social insensitivity of scientists. They are so busy making technical inquiries into their specific narrow topics that they do not realize what is going on and what is at stake in public discourses about science in general. According to Polanyi, this tendency might explain why, although most scientists oppose the planning movement, they did not bother too much to express their dislike in public arenas. In Polanyi's view, the reason is that scientists considered the movement mainly as just one "empty intellectual fashion"[46] of the many coming and going relatively unaffected by what scientists think and do. But, for Polanyi, the planning of science movement was an instance of a wider wave opposing "scientific thought to traditional religion and all other spiritual realities". A wave, launched by the claimed-to-be utopian social physics of August Comte, who "envisaged a new society released from religion and metaphysical obscurities, a society which, guided by the rule of a council of scientists, would achieve complete satisfaction of all its material wants". This mechanical view of science has fostered an understanding that scientific and spiritual, knowing and believing should be seen as dichotomies. For Polanyi, these aspects are instead allies being always already tied together. Science has a kind of inherent but long-forgotten spirituality. There is no knowing without believing.

According to Polanyi, Marx continued where Comte left off by suggesting that if the overall aim is to satisfy the material needs of the society then these needs should be made as our guiding principles, not science. This claim was later used by the modern Marxists to argue for a "socially controlled" science which is constantly being adjusted to social needs, towards "results that are directly profitable to the community". Polanyi pointed out that this "branch of social materialism" is similar to another branch cultivated by the modern fascist states. They both call for a science subservient to public good, the latter being defined by the uncontested opinion of the ruling Government. He seems to realize that once such a monopoly of defining public good is being established by the Government, there is no way of turning back. The right to distinguish good science from bad and science from non-science is, as well, given to the Government by a public which knows little about science. The rug of authority has been successfully pulled from under the scientific community. The Government has established arbitrary power over science.

For Western democracies flirting with seeds of dictatorial régimes without even knowing it, such a description was a menacing dystopian future. For the Soviet Union, Nazi Germany and fascist Italy, it was already more of the bitter present. Thus, Polanyi urged scientists to leave behind their indifferent stance, and to "counteract this doctrine" by showing to the public that science was and still is most beneficial for society if not controlled from outside. To show that many scientific discoveries which were too "remote" and "intricate" for the public mind and had "no utilitarian value to speak of", such as the discoveries of Newton and Darwin, actually "remodelled and enlightened every particle of the popular mind".[47] Polanyi is suggesting here that discoveries having the most utilitarian value do not necessarily have the most social value. Far from being a well-crafted axiological account, Polanyi's brief remark might be seen as suggesting here that utilitarian value theory either implied that only foreseeable costs and benefits matter (and, perhaps, even that there are by definition no unforeseeable costs and benefits) or that there is such a thing as a view from nowhere[48] from which utilitarian judgements are being made using good and bad simpliciters. Of course, based on such a fragment, this explanation is highly speculative. Nevertheless, it offers an important addition to strands to be discussed later, e.g. the Polanyian relation of morality and order. Polanyi reminded scientists about their social responsibility by calling them to rhetorical arms by suggesting scientists share in the conviction that all the ideals of man must stand or fall together in their conflict with the materialist conception of society, and that it is the duty of science to defend the whole spiritual realm of which it forms an integral part.[49]

Polanyi portrayed science as essentially spiritual and scientists as guardians of the spiritual realm reaching well beyond scientific spheres.

The letters of Polanyi and his interlocutors reflect that the spirituality of science was, indeed, in grave danger, and in dire need of guardians. Sir Geoffrey Jefferson,[50] a professor of neuro-surgery, pointed out to Polanyi that

> the general public are going to demand from science plastics rather than ideas, and will be very cross if they do not get them, or if we show a reluctance to give them what they want. They will throw us to the lions.[51]

Adolf Polanyi, the eldest of the famous Polanyi siblings, seemed to think that public thinking was overloaded with terms of economics which made us leave the desirable spiritual road:

> We must begin to learn and see that the world has to live not in terms of export and import balances, of exchange and interest rates, of prosperity or crisis, of production of useless goods that bring, when used to blood and disaster, but first and above all in terms of the sanctity of human life and the rule of law and freedom of the human soul.[52]

Although Adolf did not accuse economics or its practitioners directly of causing the despiritualization of public thinking, he did accuse the invasion of terms which were originally inhabitants of the expert realms of economists. Adolf suggested a precise kind of conscience as a remedy, the conscience of Napoleonic France. By the latter, he meant that a nation only enjoys the "intercourse and protection of civilized nations" if it shares certain beliefs with these nations about the rights and freedoms of individuals as compatible with that of the others'. Adolf envisioned a world driven by "moral courage". A world in which no one, not even a "nation or government have the right or shall have the possibility of covering up by the fiction of Sovereignty the criminal lunacy of any single or banded gangster or gangsters". This is a conscience which reminds us of the engagement of American foreign policy of Wilsonian origin to promote democracy far beyond US borders. Adolf suggested such a conscience be the guiding light for the people in their pursuits to tell good from bad in social issues. He criticized other rival consciences by stating that "I don't want the freedom of all and every nation to decide its form of living and I don't want the freedom of trade or of other nonsense".[53] He did not want a tiny spot of 'anything goes' on the surface of the globe and considered such a thing as morally unacceptable. He also described freedom of trade as nonsense and a surrogate for his Napoleonic conscience impeding the homecoming of people to the spiritual realm which they should have never abandoned. Adolf's view and his choice of words mirrored strong Christian convictions which he transformed into a political standpoint. By stating that "Western Democracy can still claim the privilege of repentance at the 11th hour and cherish a hope of redemption due to the repentant sinner",[54] he seems tinkering with the idea that Western Democracy has a soul itself.

Adolf was not the only one from the interlocutors of his brother, Michael Polanyi, to think that Christianity is inherent in the soul of modern democracies. Another correspondent, Charles Singer, a physician and historian of science, technology and medicine, exchanged fascinating letters with Polanyi about the nature of the crisis and the untold entanglements of social, political and religious spheres. According to Singer, the "Christian impulse"[55] was a "prodigious façade" but had weakened and was "failing and fading on all sides". He considered the weakening of this impulse a threat to the "formal and historic basis of our civilisation".[56] Singer argued that people writing on the "theory of living"[57] such as himself and Polanyi often overlook that "there is, in fact, no such thing as a 'true religion', a 'cast-iron philosophy', a 'fully satisfying material order'". He noted that it might be claimed that these things exist, but they "likely remain unattainable by human effort".[58] In Singer's view, what we really have in common is our human feelings, which lie, through different interpretations, at the heart of most contemporary social, ideological and political battles. Singer developed his own theoretical scheme around 'religion'. By religion he, by definition, meant a "body of beliefs that is sufficiently emotionalised to evoke consistent major actions of individuals and of groups".[59] Singer perceived four effective religions affecting the spiritual life of Europe: nationalism; Christianity; 'Religion of Humanity'; and 'Prophetic Religion'. Interestingly, seeing these arenas of living finding each other in spiritual realms did not lead Singer to frame science as particularly spiritual or organic to this overall scheme. He suggested a demarcation between the method of scientific discovery, a "very personal and individual thing", and the method of scientific demonstration which he described as "fairly rigid" and "definite". Singer's idea that "there is almost no human power or faculty that has not, at some time or other, been involved in the process of discovery"[60] mirrored similarities with Polanyian ideas.

Polanyi recognized the commonalities in their understanding but also found differences. He disagreed with Singer about whether "modern social aspirations"[61] are forms of the 'Religion of Humanity'. Polanyi considered these aspirations to be rather "centred on material welfare", and noted that what Singer calls the 'Religion of Humanity' was, in fact, a "philosophically unsatisfactory position of an idealism" feeding on the "scraps of faith left intact" after the centuries of ideological battles. Polanyi aimed to explore this battlefield of ideas for useable scraps to smith new, more durable weapons and armour of faith for whatever the future holds. He told Singer that he "seek[s] safe anchorage ground for positive ideals in the tradition of science and in the whole structure of society which is associated with functions similar to the progress of science".[62] Polanyi's pursuit in the philosophy of science was not an isolated enterprise but part of his social philosophy focusing on revitalizing three things: liberalism, democracy and Western civilization.

Bringing positive, active, productive ideals to the fore was not an easy task. Adolf, again, proved himself to be a worthy correspondent as the two brothers delved into the depths of the question: what makes certain ideals grow while others diminish? According to Adolf,

> no human ideal can grow to active and operative significance and no civ-ilisation can grow the natural growth of things alive that does not place the respect of the individual life at the bottom and foundation of its laws and tenets.[63]

Of course, this does not mean that there are no other kinds of ideals and civilizations. These are preying on the death of individuals to be able to get, through this soul sacrifice, their "lifeless idea[s]"[64] going and their collective imaginary creating their own vital and historical realities.[65] Realities which could be "an inconceivable horror to all brains and souls that connect life with living and not with being the negligible shadow expression of a Military Power hallucination"[66] of a lunatic who considers himself the only legitimate weaver of such nightmarish realms and the only true leader of his people. But Adolf warned that "no civilisation based on the mass contempt for life and less that based on the contempt of the life of the mass can resist and strife". He noted that society, like any other structure, falls apart without the friction of its parts. Cohesion comes from friction, therefore dreams of immovable worlds, of "Nickelsteel inflexibility" and "Euclidian ruthlessness"[67] tend to evaporate. And no calculations, however precise they may be, can hold together structures of social, material or mental nature. The world cannot be plausibly described once and for all – particularly not by using such an immutable tool as mathematics.

According to Michael Polanyi, the main difference between his scheme and that of Singer was that, unlike his British correspondent, he attributed a "fundamental significance to the disparity of English and Continental ways".[68] Polanyi referred to the English way as "secular Protestantism" and to the Continental way as "materialist fanaticism". While he considered the latter as being "Satanic, essentially irreligious, idolatrous", this anti-Continentalism must not be read as anti-nationalism. On the contrary. Polanyi was pretty much in the pro-nationalism camp. He wrote to Singer that "from my point of view Nationalism is a positive moral force (or rather a moral framework) incorporating 'secular protestantism' in England and America, while it is abused for a manifestation of 'materialist fanaticism' in Germany". He did not attribute the devilish deeds of Nazism to nationalism but the latter's exploitation by a kind of "materialist fanaticism". Polanyi thought that he and Singer had an "essentially similar outlook" which would enable them to bridge any gap between them, but did not think that there was a desperate need for doing so. He called Singer's idea of a 'Prophetic Religion' a "very important one" which he could "well imagine" pointing "to the future solution", therefore he "will think about it".[69]

Polanyi convinced Singer that the strong tradition of civic liberties in England "had its roots in religious liberty" which also contributed to the relatively advanced state of science in the country. But not everybody was happy with Polanyi's bridging practices attempting to connect science and religion. After reading Polanyi's *The Autonomy of Science* (1943), Clifford Copland Paterson, an electrical engineer at General Electric Company, wrote a critical letter to Polanyi about his depiction of science and the Bible which he considered to be a "sad blemish"[70] in an otherwise "brilliant exposition". Paterson particularly disapproved of Polanyi's sentence that "the choice open to the public is only that believing in Science or else in some rival explanation of nature such as ... the Bible".[71] He criticized Polanyi for basing his argument on an outdated view, stating that "I should have thought you the last man to 'detect' rivalry between science and the Bible".[72] Paterson made it clear what he thought about science and religion: "Surely the Bible deals with moral issues (spiritual ones if you like) whilst Science deals with material ones. To me and very many others the two are complementary."[73] Regarding his own view, Paterson noted that he saw the two "converging into one entity".[74] Like many others, he misunderstood Polanyi. Polanyi was talking about the historical trend of how the public learned to see science and religion as being the mutually exclusive rivals of each other. He did not argue that there is, or should be, a choice between science and the Bible. He argued that many people claim to see and consider themselves making such a choice, and that this aspect of the public understanding of spiritual realms fits into a historical process. To calm Paterson, Polanyi noted that they agree more than he thinks and even added that he first presented *The Autonomy of Science* (1943) at the local Theological Society because his friends there believed that his "views are conducive to a new solidarity between science and religion".[75] No written response has been found so far. Perhaps there was none because Paterson thought that there was no point in continuing the correspondence. But, of course, this is highly speculative. Despite misinterpreting Polanyi, he had, after all, a very different view about the relation of science and religion. Paterson claimed that science and religion are essentially different but converging enterprises, Polanyi claimed that there are unnoticed common elements in their very fabric and that we have too hastily learnt to see these enterprises as incompatible and mutually exclusive explanations of the world without making deep philosophical inquiries to understand their 'true' nature.

A letter of Polanyi to Ludwig Lachmann, a German economist of the Austrian school, a student and later colleague of Hayek at LSE, might shed some further light on Polanyi's views. Polanyi returned a manuscript to

Lachmann and made a remark stating that Huxley's "materialism is not, I believe, the generally accepted view of evolution".[76] By going into details, he emphasized that "scientists may like to believe that they do not pre-suppose purpose in evolution, but philosophers do not all agree with this".[77] This remark is, of course, more about whether these groups like or do not like to admit that they presuppose purpose in evolution, and less about whether they are actually presupposing it. Polanyi recommended a book to Lachmann which he described as written from a non-Huxleyan perspective embracing a purposeful evolution: *Science, Religion, and the Future* (1943) by Charles E. Raven. This book reflects remarkable similarities with Polanyi's outlook, e.g. the three tasks to save modern society (an intellectual task to achieve integrity, a moral task to achieve sympathy and a religious task to achieve community) might remind us of Polanyi's three aspects of *knowing* (understanding, believing, belonging), but it goes much further. While Polanyi was reimagining knowing and, by doing so, crafting a heart for a postmodern economics and science, Raven was reimagining all the different faculties of human belief by attempting to provide a unified perspective embracing the religious belief in God and the scientific belief in what is the best method of inquiring about nature.

What can we know about the religious faith of Polanyi, and how this presumably unscientific topic might fit into our grand narrative? In a letter to Karl Mannheim, Polanyi made an unexpectedly intimate confession about what he believed in certain periods of his life. He told Mannheim that at a very young age he was "a materialist and an eager discipline of H.G. Wells",[78] that his "religious interests were awakened by reading the *Brothers Karamazov* in 1913", and that, for the five years between 1915 and 1920, he was "a completely converted Christian on the lines of Tolstoy's confession of faith". By describing the development of his religious faith, Polanyi referred to worlds of literary fiction and authors most known about their fictional realms. He could have referred to the Bible, to other religious texts or to gatherings of a religious nature to portray how his religious faith changed through the years, but he did not, at all. By being a materialist and an "eager discipline"[79] of Wells, Polanyi probably meant that, at this early period of his life, he believed that material progress fostered by the advancement of natural sciences could, in itself, lead humanity towards a brighter tomorrow. In *The Brothers Karamazov*, religious faith was contrasted to doubt, a kind of logical scepticism making a verdict against everything apparently metaphysical: God, religion, morality and, basically, all that is humane. Dostoevsky argued for the side of faith by showing that positive, active belief and engagement lead to a happier and better life than the systematic bitter dehumanization of our phys-ical and metaphysical surroundings. Based on the letter to Mannheim, it seems that Dostoevsky's argument either convinced Polanyi or, at least, pushed his faith and understanding towards previously neglected spiritual realms. The third reference stating that Polanyi, for a few years, was a Christian of Tolstoyan kind[80] most likely refers to the newly discovered appraisement of personal faith, the element which later became central both to his postmodern economics and his philosophy of science. Polanyi described the development of his own religious faith by referring to writers and writings of fiction. Why should we not consider then the fictional realms Polanyi and his correspondents referred to in our pursuits to understand their economic thought? What makes us think that we are entitled to make such an arbitrary demarcation to make their references to fiction invisible in our historical accounts? This book argues that we are not entitled at all, and that the exploration of these invisible realms might provide a better understanding of 'serious', 'non-fictional', 'scholarly' topics such as economics, long-believed to be separable from the world of fiction.

Perhaps to avoid the misunderstanding of his early materialist convictions, Polanyi made it clear to Mannheim that he was critical of the measures of the Communist régime in Hungary (the Hungarian Soviet Republic), as well as that he was "the only male member of the University who refused to 'volunteer' for the Red Army and was threatened in various ways in consequence".[81] Polanyi also emphasized that his first writing about politics in 1917 was a critique of the "materialist conception of history", which also suggests that his Wellsian materialism was unlike the mainstream materialism of the era. Believing that scientific progress brings material progress which best serves society is not equal to believing that only material matters or that the most plausible account of human history is the one seeing every human enterprise as a continuous struggle over scarce material resources. Of course, the analysis of the shades of materialism would require its own volume. In this case, we are only attempting to show that Polanyi's early materialism was not the same as the radical Marxist philosophy sweeping through Continental Europe. Polanyi noted that regarding civic liberty, he "needed no conversion to this ideal but merely instruction in it, on grounds prepared for its reception" – a training about the "true nature of civic liberty"[82] which Polanyi claimed to receive after coming to England, the land where, according to Polanyi, tradition and progress found, in a sense, a healthy way of coexistence providing practical experience for those working on social reforms.

Polanyi realized that he needed to clarify to Mannheim that, despite the great emphasis of the social in his accounts, he was not creating socialist narratives. Polanyi noted that he rejects "all social analysis of history which makes social conditions anything more than opportunities for a development of thought"[83] and expressed strong disagreement about what he considered to be Mannheim's view, which is, "thought is not merely conditioned, but determined by a social or technical situation" (ibid). Interestingly, Mannheim's magnum opus, *Ideology and Utopia* (1929) also pointed to the importance of utopias, and argued that societies are striving to reach certain utopias through the development of related ideologies. These utopias, however, were not generally seen as inhabitants of fictional realms. On the contrary, they get their power from the people who believed their claimed-to-be non-fictional status and their practical feasibility. Mannheim's relationism suggested that there are social determinants of knowledge-claims, and that knowledge-claims are only true in a specific time and social space. While Polanyi was against attributing determinative power to social or any other factors in knowledge-making, he was definitely not against narrowing the scope of evaluating the truthness and falseness of knowledge-claims to a specific time and social space. Unfortunately, they were too busy emphasizing their differences to find their commonalities such as the pioneering insight of the local-boundedness of truth values.

It must not be forgotten that, in the 1930s and 1940s, internalist perspectives of science and history were on the rise. Alfred Ernest Teale, a lecturer of philosophy at the University of Manchester, portrayed science and scientists as almost empyrean entities in one of his letters to Polanyi. Teale wrote that "the scientist is not pleasing himself, as he pleases himself whether he will play bridge or billiards or politics".[84] He has free choice but his "choice is not arbitrary nor a mere personal preference, a question of likes and dislikes – but one which is in a very real sense determined by the growing insight into the field of inquiry opened up by previous advances". For Teale, scientists are faceless agents of an infallible metahuman enterprise which "indicates certain lines of profitable investigation and prevents the waste of time and energy in blind alleys". Teale's portrayal of science and scientists sounds a bit naive, even for this early date. Perhaps, this might be explained by Teale's motives. He thought that if his view "could be demonstrated it would put an end to the demand for planning in the interests of social usefulness".[85] While Teale and Polanyi were both making rhetorical manoeuvres against their common enemies, the planners, they chose different strategies. Teale wanted to show that science is less social than the 'planners' claimed, Polanyi attempted to show that it is far more social, and that it is social but in another sense.

Mannheim's remark that Polanyi made "emotional decisions, where still a further confrontation of evidence and argument is feasible"[86] suggests that he considered the sphere of emotion and the sphere of facts, evidence and argument to be separate. For Mannheim, emotion begins where science ends. For Polanyi, emotion and moral are inseparable from science. In his *au contraire* to Mannheim, Polanyi argued that the paramount task of a research director is "to keep up his collaborator's morale",[87] to encourage them to carry on despite all the failures which greatly outnumber successes in the natural course of scientific inquiry. Having and keeping motivation for doing research, caring about certain emotions of those being involved in scientific activity, was, for Polanyi, not some auxiliary activity of scientists but an essential part of science. He had a similarly externalist view regarding morals. According to Polanyi, "as Christians and Westerners, we are dedicated to seek and uphold human interpretations more especially in the terms of our own moral tradition. That is what we are here for, as I understand our purpose in life". Scientists are not emotionless amoral machines producing scientific knowledge from data. They are passionate creatures following a moral compass in their pursuits to understand the world they live in. Accounts like Gibbon's portrayal of history seeing the past as "little more than the register of crimes[,] follies[,] and misfortunes of mankind" or Marx's view of history as "the manifestation of economic necessities conditioned by technical progress" were, for Polanyi, defective because they paid no attention to the morals of their makers – a constructive force, which these authors apparently did not consider to be important in making science, and which they rendered invisible. Polanyi claimed that "those who have become accustomed to regard material forces as the ultimate reality in human affairs will not find it easy to entrust their minds ever again to a more intangible aspect of these affairs".[88] He thus warned that once scientists embrace the materialist view and it becomes "their second nature",[89] it is particularly hard to enlist their support for a spiritual perspective.

Polanyi argued that evidence "can neither kill nor create fundamental beliefs. What we accept or reject in these matters is life itself". To an extent, we are born to our "forms of existence", to another extent, we choose and reject them. According to Polanyi,

> even in the midst of such enormous tides of rising and falling convictions there remains fixed a deeper secret pivot of faith round which we keep revolving; we follow throughout a code of duty of which we are so unconscious that we could not formulate one single syllable of it.

This pivot of faith is always already present in all of us whether we acknowledge its existence or not. It affects our knowing and being, and, if we are scientists, the science we are making. In Polanyi's view, there is no life without convictions. "There is no way out",[90] he noted. Scientific accounts framed as being universal, portraying ultimate realities, as if they were being written from "a view from nowhere"[91] are always hiding their moral origins which would reveal their partiality. We have to choose from various convictions "in such a fashion that what we instinctively love in life, what we spontaneously admire, what we irresistibly aspire to, should make sense in the light of our convictions".[92] In Polanyi's view, when we started to see a prospect to reach out to these, we went through a "conversion". If faith meets apparently contradictory evidence, we are more inclined to convince ourselves about the fallaciousness of the evidence than to change our faith in light of the new evidence. We are much better in finding "ever renewed confirmation for our fundamental beliefs"[93] than in admitting that we should change what we believe. The latter suggests that Polanyi was not in favour of Popperian falsifiability as a criterion for the demarcation of science from non-science. If evidence is less likely to trump a priori faith than vice versa, how can a new observation, taking the form of an existential statement, falsify a universal one believed to be true?

Leonard Hyman, a bookseller who specialized in music literature, wrote a letter to Polanyi after hearing one of his speeches on the radio, offering a brief comparison of Hayek's *The Road to Serfdom* (1944) and Polanyi's *Science and the Decline of Freedom* (1944). Hyman regarded Polanyi's "approach to this problem of the Machine Age"[94] illuminating and considered it a "pity that Hayek sees no connection between the decline of freedom and the rise of technocracy". According to Hyman, the relation between these two tendencies is "too obvious any longer to be overlooked",[95] and there are people, similarly to Polanyi, who realized this connection. Well, there were, at least, two of them. Enid Bradford, an industrial chemist, complained to Polanyi about the excessive control and organization of the daily work of industrial scientists. Bradford described in detail how a specific company, her employer, J. Lyons and Co.,[96] treated employees like soulless machines. The uncontestable supremacy of bureaucracy, the prohibition of communication with outsiders, the techniques playing on the fear of people who need to make a living for their family and themselves, the representation of the firm as if it were "father, mother and God rolled into one",[97] and the indirect socialization pushing employees to give up their "will and free thinking" and to become a corporate zealot are symptoms of techno-fetishist business practices of the Machine Age. Bradford warned that "human creative intelligence is a rare gift and cannot be organised and controlled by the time clock and recorded on a time sheet". Carrying organization too far "kills all interest in and enthusiasm for any work".[98] Bradford seemed to perceive an increasing gap between industrial science and academic science. Her not-so-flattering description of the mechanic milieu at J. Lyons and Co. might be understood as an insider's account of the ruthlessness of doing cutting edge chemical research in the private sector during World War II. However, Bradford's normative statement that the "industrial chemist should be of the highest character because he stands between the consuming public and the avariciousness of the industrialist"[99] suggests something more. According to Bradford, industrial scientists were the moral guardians of doing business at their companies. They should not simply take orders from their superiors and run like hungry mice in the bureaucratic labyrinth mirroring corporate power structures. They should realize that truth, honour and integrity are not limited to the academic world and they can and should have their own moral compasses regardless of what is coming downstream on the corporate ladder.

Bradford's intransigence was converging around robust moral convictions. She reminded Polanyi that industrial scientists have responsibilities not only towards their employer but also towards the society they are living in. The general public and the employers, in her view, should also change their attitude towards scientists. "With the shifting values of the world today the only real capital is brain power",[100] she noted. For this reason, the "trained brain should be [treated as] a gilt-edged security". Bradford claimed to find a relation between the evolution of a firm and the common treatment of scientists. As the firm grows, the capitalist is not satisfied any more with the ad hoc help of a "consultant" scientist and decides to have her own "paid employee" and laboratory. As the private laboratory grows it becomes "a vast brontosaurus like I.C.I. with an ungainly body scarcely under the control of the limited brain power". According to Bradford, the overall experience is that the chemist is usually "regarded as a superior sort of artisan", but only as an artisan. She found this tendency undesirable and wanted the chemist to be generally seen as equal to the financier due to her "real knowledge". But does this "real knowledge" make chemists valuable for the company because it provides better understanding of the world or because it yields more money? Should companies reassess the value of their scientists because of their 'pure knowledge' or their 'useful knowledge'? Bradford seemed to argue for both. She portrayed scientists as unrivalled knowers dealing with the world, from chemical compounds to international affairs, with their "beautiful clear-cut mind".[101] But she also drew examples of the unfair financial contribution of scientific ideas, although she admitted that assessing the "cash value for an idea"[102] is anything but easy.

Bradford wrote to Polanyi that she was on a mission to convince industrialists that science is not a "commodity" but a "directive force" which they cannot neglect nor completely put under control. Her bitter remark that we confuse money, the index of power, with knowledge, the real power, as if money were the "primary thing", transformed her narrative into a social critique. Polanyi seemed to feel sorry for his fellow scientists living this 'machinistic life', or, as he rephrased, "wheels within wheels governing the employees' faith in an irrational manner".[103] Bradford's philosophy that "the joy of living is bound up with the sense of adventure and enterprise"[104] was probably sympathetic to him, particularly because Bradford contrasted it with the "sheltered, planned and theoretically perfect life". They seemed to agree that all good life is driven by a personal spiritual attachment to the world, and that there are people who, intentionally or not, work against the faith in this spiritual realm. However, Bradford and Polanyi attributed different weights to the reasons behind these despiritualizing practices. Bradford was only concerned about how the growing inhumanity of cutting-edge research and the divinization of the profit motive might affect the minds of scientists and the general public. While Polanyi was also concerned about this inhuman and anti-spiritual tendency of modern economies, both present in realms of laissez-faire liberalism and socialist planning, he portrayed a more direct relationship between these machinistic traits of modern economies and the common layperson (e.g. his Dickensian depiction of corporations and the poor) than Bradford, who treated scientists as a kind of moral in-betweeners. Polanyi, unlike Bradford, perceived another source of despiritualization coming from the sphere of politics and ideology. This was not driven by the greed of capitalists or the control-mongering of corporate managers but the desire for political power. Contemporary politicians were, indeed, cultivating streams embracing machine-like implications of man and society. Knowledge claims about how the world is and what to do in life were generally framed as having universal validity, being infallible and providing a similarly good future for everyone having an ear to hear or eye to see political propaganda. Society was, for politicians, like a mechanical device which, if it broke down, could be opened up to search for and to replace bad components. Voters, believers, followers of political movements were mostly treated as machines. Politicians acted to find out what makes these machines tick to earn their support. Perhaps, because they did not see these hidden inhuman implications themselves or because they did no see any other choice. Or, perhaps, because they realized that one is less likely to make political capital out of a philosophy spearheading the primacy of personal spiritual attachment to the world.

Spiritual and personal were, perhaps, widespread topoi of common talk but somewhat unexpected in scholarly debates. When Polanyi, talking about tolerance on "The Brains Trust" BBC radio programme on 9 January 1945, described John Milton as "a pioneer of tolerance"[105] he seemed to touch on a sensitive scholarly issue. While he received letters of acknowledgement from listeners appraising his speech for going deeper than "verbal fireworks",[106] Bertrand Russel and John Edward Bowle immediately let Polanyi know that they were missing "a paragraph or two on the significance of Locke in the context".[107] In his response to Bowle, Polanyi agreed that he should have put a greater emphasis on Locke, but admitted that he is "intellectually dissatisfied with Locke's position",[108] mostly because, unlike Locke or his followers, he does "not believe that tolerance can be logically established so easily". Based on Polanyi's early postmodern philosophical inquiries, one is tempted to think that Polanyi did not think that tolerance (or anything else) could be well-established, at all, on purely logical grounds, easily or otherwise. Why, then, did he add "so easily" to his confession if he thought that tolerance cannot be "logically established" at all? Did he simply not want to fight the big fight at this point, or did he generally consider it rather pointless to wrestle with old-school positions coming from a cloister of an unfriendly scholarly niche? In any event, Polanyi wrote to Bowle that "Milton's more emotional and political approach seems to be more appropriate to me as a profession of faith in tolerance".[109] However, a disclaimer must be made here regarding Milton's tolerance. Milton's concept of tolerance, seen in his *Areopagitica* (1644), was widely discussed and criticized as being partial and as only fighting for the freedom of speech and expression of a highly circumscribed group, Puritan revolutionaries, instead of fostering these rights for people of all kinds and faiths.[110] But even if we are inclined to accept these critical remarks, it does not necessarily affect how we understand Polanyi's interpretation of Milton's tolerance. Polanyi did not claim Milton's approach to be better than Locke's because he considered it impartial or as making a better argument for a general claim on tolerance. He claimed it to be better precisely because it was admittedly emotional and political. It was a view of tolerance which was not making attempts to disguise its moral and political origins but prides itself on making them visible. Regardless of what one thinks of its moral and political currents, Milton's concept of tolerance seemed, indeed, "more appropriate"[111] from the perspective of Polanyi's early postmodern philosophy as the latter was suggesting that every statement, including scientific ones, bear moral, social and personal imprints.

A correspondent of Polanyi, Andrew Bongiorno, whom he came to know through Oscar Jaszi, seemed to agree with Polanyi that one cannot tackle partiality in making scholarly accounts. According to Bongiorno, partiality, or "prejudice"[112] as he called it, is not only desirable for science but also for society. "Thus far we have been saved from moral and political disaster by moral and political prejudice", he noted. In his view, "prejudice is all in favor of freedom" in America, even though the "majority, of those champion it most loudly are [indeed] busy undermining its metaphysical and religious foundations". For Bongiorno, similar to Polanyi, moral, social and political engagements constituting prejudice were not harmful to science but immanent to its fabric. Bongiorno and Polanyi did not believe in the Mertonian crusade to purge out every kind of social, moral and political taintedness out of science for the betterment of science and society. For them, the construction of such a naive, oversimplified picture of science was either a bona fide fantasy of the zealots of CUDOStan or a well-timed rhetorical hit to earn prestige and authority in the turmoil of World War II. In their view, it may be claimed that modern science, if well-cultivated, is a crystally realm of universal purity, but it is obviously not. While Merton and his comrades were worrying about how emerging and already present prejudice affects science, Bongiorno was afraid about how the fading of prejudice might affect science. For the Mertonians, only a dead prejudice is a good prejudice, regardless of its content. For Bongiorno, prejudice gets weaker as it moves away from philosophy and religion, leaving greater scope to nihilism which has already been "distressingly prevalent in academic circles".[113] Both Merton and Bongiorno sought what is better for science and society but saw immensely different, quite contradictory paths. Polanyi agreed with Bongiorno in considering nihilism and cynicism a greater threat to science and society than moral and political ladenness.

Interestingly, for many, postmodernism was not an enemy but an ally to nihilism. For Toynbee, the postmodern era was a chaotic epoch of epistemic *bellum omnium contra omnes* following the progressive modernism of Enlightenment origin. Lyotard described postmodernism as what comes after the age of grand narratives. For him, we are living in the ever-shifting, ungraspable clouds of language elements playing language games with rules in the making. Although there are noticeably cognate elements in the philosophy of Lyotard and Polanyi, e.g. the similarity between the Lyotardian putting "forward the unpresentable in the presentation"[114] and the Polanyian *tacit knowing*, their differences are not less significant. Lyotard's local determinism of the language bricoleur would have been unacceptable for Polanyi who rejected all kinds of determinism root and branch (see his correspondence with Karl Mannheim). Also, Polanyi rather considered the human mind to be itself the constructive force rather than the place of elusive constructions of mixed up and messed up agency. Baudrillard argued that melancholia and nihilism have devoured reality and pushed us towards living in a postmodern *hyperreality*, a realm where dreamers have no *real* strings attached in their practices weaving the world our minds inhabit.[115] For Polanyi and Bongiorno, pluralism and the denial of objective, universal standards did not come with nihilism but with the realization that we are always already embedded in a moral, social and political niche affecting our scholarly inquiries. According to their view, we cannot and should not attempt to escape from this influence, which is not deterministic but neither completely eliminable from our knowing and being practices.

Similar to his postmodern ideas, Polanyi's view of positivism had a strange flavour. In a letter to Franz Gabriel Alexander, another Hungarian medical doctor, a founder of the Chicago Institute for Psychoanalysis, Polanyi remembered their walks and talks alongside the Danube during their Budapest years before they both left for Germany and then respectively for England (Polanyi) and the United States (Alexander). Polanyi recalled one particular question from their riverside talks: the question "whether history ought to be taught at all, or else[,] replaced by education in sociological laws".[116] Polanyi presumed that, in America, "one may still find positivists of the old type" who would vote for social studies over history. But he also perceived "the opposite pole of positivism"[117] to be present in America, more precisely, to be converging around the University of Chicago due to Robert Maynard Hutchins and Mortimer Jerome Adler. Polanyi did not go into details regarding this new, extreme type of positivism, but it seems safe to suppose that he meant by it the school suggesting a move from empirical social sciences towards Aristotelian and Thomist philosophical inquiries. Hutchins, as president of the university, even proposed a significant change to the curriculum along these lines which never became implemented due to the resistance of the university. Although Polanyi did not say anything in this letter about either of these positivist extremes, we know from many other sources that he was not in favour of any kind of positivism, whether it was extreme or not.

While some warned about the dangers of seeing socialism as the sole vessel of progress, others warned about the dangers of seeing religion as the sole vessel of faith and spirituality. According to L. Victor Block, who wrote a letter to Polanyi after one of Polanyi's radio talks, "orthodox churches and dogmatic religions have quite failed"[118] to cultivate "better spiritual relations between individuals and nations". By the time of writing the letter, Block had been establishing a society to foster these spiritual relations and asked for Polanyi's criticism as well as his patronage. Block noted that "the word spiritual has become so suspect and corrupt"[119] that he does not use it in the entire folder about his society. Polanyi would have probably agreed with Block about the rather negative social connotation of the word "spiritual". Although he grounded both his postmodern economics and philosophy on personal attachment to the world, which seems to resonate with spirituality, Polanyi did not use the word either. While Block aimed to improve the spiritual relations between individuals and nations, Polanyi aimed to bring forward a philosophy suggesting that the world as we know it always has a personal dimension. Block argued for a spiritual reworking of social relations and politics; Polanyi was on a mission for a better understanding of what was, so far, perhaps too conveniently, seen as the relation of the knowing subject and the object of knowing. One might say that this view sounds like having a psychological flavour. And she would not be the only one claiming so.

After reading about one of Polanyi's broadcasts, a psychologist, J. Guilfoyle Williams, expressed agreement with some of Polanyi's ideas and suggested Polanyi read his related upcoming book, *The Psychology of Childhood to Maturity* (1948). Williams particularly agreed with Polanyi "regard the fallacy of reductive analysis and the need for emphasis on the social instincts and spiritual aspects of mankind",[120] the latter which he claimed to discuss in the "maturity"[121] part of his book manuscript which he offered to send to Polanyi before publication. Polanyi thanked Williams and succinctly remarked that "the problem of connecting rightly the foundations of psychology with the metaphysical foundations of morality"[122] was amongst the most important problems of their age. Polanyi did not claim explicitly in his response that he, Williams or anyone else was doing this. However, the unlikely flirtation of Polanyi's postmodern philosophy with Williams' developmental psychology suggests that both scholars thought that they were working on different facets of the same problem.

The idea of respiritualizing science and social thinking earned Polanyi the admiration of Olwen Ward Campbell, author of *Shelley and the Unromantics* (1924) and *The Lighted Window* (1940). In a 1946 letter to Polanyi, Campbell noted that she has just finished a book on the problem of unhappiness in which she investigated the question of "finding a moral basis for modern society and restoring faith in moral institutions".[123] According to Campbell, the main enemy is the "scientific attitude"[124] or "scientific materialism"[125] which had a ruinous influence on "men's confidence in their own spiritual nature and even moral responsibility". In her view, the task which lies ahead is to establish generally acceptable, "civilised principles", a moral common ground. Campbell noted that she and Polanyi were not alone in their point of view, and referred to Edward Hallett Carr's argument about the lack of moral basis for the reconstruction in his *Conditions of Peace* (1942), and quoted a fragment from a pastoral of Richard Downey, the Roman Catholic Bishop of Liverpool, saying that "a complete system of social[,] economic and moral doctrine, humanly speaking, … is the only remedy for the world's disease". Campbell favoured assembling a committee to "discuss the possibility of framing such [moral] code"[126] and asked Polanyi whether he has received several letters after his broadcast which would indicate large public concern. Polanyi replied that, actually, there were many welcoming his radio talk, and that this point of view he shared with Campbell is apparently getting increasingly popular. However, he noted that his "share in the further work should be concerned with the more rigorous philosophical foundations, without which the movement may peter out at any moment as a pure matter of sentiment".[127] This is an understandable, quite pragmatic statement from Polanyi, but perhaps not the most fortunate wording for Campbell, a litterateur of romanticism and a soon-to-be active political feminist who one year later became the organizer of the Conference on the Feminine Point of View (1947–51) following in the footsteps of her suffragette mother.[128]

Others saw Polanyi as building a "new humanism".[129] N.S. Hubbard, an employee of I.C.I. Metals Ltd., thought that there are two kinds of contemporary humanisms. Theistic humanism, which tends to annihilate the material aspect of human nature, and material humanism, which tends to annihilate its spiritual aspect. In Hubbard's view, none of these humanisms is "truly human" and both lead to inhumane fanaticism. What he thought could make a humanism "truly human" is treating human nature as "compounded as it is of material body and intellectual soul". And this was what he found in Polanyi's new humanism. According to Hubbard, although naturalism is seen as the ascending new humanism from the eighteenth century, it has been degenerating into materialism. Quite surprisingly, Hubbard seemed to tinker with theoretical questions later becoming central for the not-yet nascent discipline, philosophy of science. He suggested that even if there is no royal road, views must be "formulated" and theories "must be propounded" to get science going. Theories are only "instruments for the investigation of reality" which, of course, is never completely "compassed by the theory".[130] Still, theories too often become mistaken for reality. Hubbard deemed the main obstacle to the spread of this view to be the prejudice of physicists against Aristotelean metaphysics and the "notion of potentiality".[131] Interestingly, potentiality was also central to some of Polanyi's pioneering early contributions to chemistry, particularly to his insights about potential energy surfaces. Hubbard claimed to know why physicists are so reluctant to accept spiritual reality. Physicists claimed that their discipline is concerned with all reality. If there is such a thing as spiritual reality, a realm admittedly unknown to modern physics, then their claim is much less plausible, moreover, just getting falsified. Physicists are not the sole masters of the cosmos and everything knowable anymore, thus they should either extend the scope of their discipline to investigate spiritual reality or make alliances with practitioners of other disciplines. Conserving the status quo by denying the existence of spiritual reality apparently is easier. Hubbard suggested to "reverse this attitude"[132] by making intelligible aspects of reality to be seen more important than its sensible aspects. By the latter, he hoped to get a more meaningful analysis of reality considering a person as a compound of body and soul, and to find a new balance between the more sensible truths of lower order and the rather intelligible truths of higher order which might also contribute to a novel interpretation of Christian life. No doubt, this is a Herculean task, but one that, in Hubbard's view, he and Polanyi have already started to carry out by developing their respective philosophies.

Notes

1 Polanyi 1944l, 2.
2 Ibid., 2–3.
3 Ibid., 3.
4 Mirowski 2002, 7.
5 Ibid.

6 Ibid., 6.
7 Ibid.
8 Polanyi 1945d, 1.
9 Ibid.
10 Ibid., 2.
11 Ibid.
12 Polanyi 1945e, 2.
13 Burke 1793, 1.
14 Ibid.
15 Polanyi 1945e, 2.
16 Ibid., 1.
17 Ibid.
18 Mullins 2010.
19 Polanyi 1945e, 3.
20 Ibid.
21 Ibid., 4.
22 Ibid.
23 Ibid., 5.
24 Ibid.
25 Ibid., 6.
26 Ibid.
27 Ibid., 7.
28 Ibid.
29 Ibid., 1.
30 Polanyi 1945m, 1.
31 Ibid.
32 Ibid., 1–2.
33 Ibid., 2.
34 Ibid.
35 Ibid., 3.
36 Ibid.
37 Polanyi 1945o, 6.
38 Perhaps the title playfully referred to *In the Fourth Year: Anticipations of a World Peace* (1918) by H.G. Wells. In this book Wells explored the League of Nations as a counterpoint against the idea of imperialism and made a political-ideological deep dive into the battle of ideas behind World War I and what was expected to come right after.
39 In the second volume of her autobiography, *Journey from the North* (1970), Storm Jameson mentioned Polanyi only once. She first called Polanyi and Arthur Koestler more intelligent people from whom she could learn (Jameson 1970, 130). Then, in the immediately following paragraph, she described Polanyi as leading the way before her along an unused slate railway by jumping the consecutive wooden sleepers of the railway and setting the mood by repeating "verse after verse of Verlaine, in an enchantingly gentle voice" (ibid.). An unknown correspondent sent Polanyi a cutting of the related paragraph and put it right after: "it is a charming recollection, but why mention your superior intelligence on the previous page if that's all she remembers of your endless talks?" (Fragment to Michael Polanyi). Polanyi was probably thinking the same. But Jameson not seeing similarities between them, or at least not including these in her autobiography, does not mean that there were none.
40 Polanyi 1945q, 1.
41 Polanyi 1945s, 3.
42 Polanyi 1944m, 1.
43 Polanyi 1943t, 1.

44 Polanyi 1942b, 3.
45 Ibid.
46 Polanyi 1942k, 1.
47 Ibid.
48 Nagel 1986.
49 Polanyi 1942k, 1.
50 He wrote a couple of letters to Polanyi in December 1942 from Ruthin Castle (North Wales), which was functioning as a private sanatorium for the wealthy between 1923 and 1950. John Maynard Keynes was among the notable patients of Ruthin Castle spending three months there from 19 June until 23 September 1937. However, the treatment Keynes received at Ruthin shortly proved to be ineffective, which led him to a friend of Polanyi, another Hungarian-born physician who had fled to England, Janos Plesch.
51 Polanyi 1942m, 3–4.
52 Polanyi 1942l, 3.
53 Ibid.
54 Ibid., 5.
55 Polanyi 1943a, 1.
56 Ibid.
57 Polanyi 1943c, 1.
58 Ibid.
59 Ibid., 2.
60 Ibid.
61 Polanyi 1943b, 1.
62 Ibid.
63 Polanyi 1943e, 3.
64 Ibid.
65 Polanyi 1943e.
66 Polanyi 1943e, 3.
67 Ibid.
68 Polanyi 1943j, 1.
69 Ibid.
70 Polanyi 1943n, 1.
71 Ibid.
72 Ibid., 1–2.
73 Ibid., 2.
74 Ibid.
75 Polanyi 1943r, 1.
76 Polanyi 1943q, 1.
77 Ibid.
78 Polanyi 1944b, 1.
79 Ibid.
80 A disclaimer must be made here. Although Polanyi wrote that he was a "Christian on the lines of Tolstoy's confession of faith", his confession must not be mistaken for claiming to be a member of the Tolstoyan movement. The latter movement was criticized even by Tolstoy himself, who realized that the systematic propagation of any doctrine is incompatible with his view focusing on personal conscience.
81 Polanyi 1944b, 1.
82 Ibid.
83 Ibid., 2.
84 Polanyi 1944e, 1.
85 Ibid.
86 Polanyi 1944c, 2.

87 Polanyi 1944f, 1.
88 Ibid.
89 Ibid., 2.
90 Ibid.
91 Nagel 1986.
92 Polanyi 1944f, 2.
93 Ibid.
94 Polanyi 1944j, 1.
95 Ibid.
96 Interestingly, the later British Prime Minister, Margaret Thatcher, worked for the same company as a research chemist between 1949 and 1951. Thatcher was developing ice cream emulsifiers during these years at J. Lyons and Co. which earned her the nickname "ice cream maiden" (*New Scientist*, 7 July 1983), a soft and sweet foil to her most known sobriquet, "iron lady".
97 Polanyi 1944n, 2.
98 Ibid.
99 Ibid., 3.
100 Polanyi 1944o, 1.
101 Ibid.
102 Ibid., 2.
103 Ibid.
104 Ibid., 1.
105 Polanyi 1945c, 1.
106 Polanyi 1945b, 1.
107 Polanyi 1945a, 1.
108 Polanyi 1945c, 1.
109 Ibid.
110 Illo 1965.
111 Polanyi 1945c, 1.
112 Polanyi 1945j, 1.
113 Ibid.
114 Lyotard 1984, 81.
115 Baudrillard 1994.
116 Polanyi 1945l, 1.
117 Ibid.
118 Polanyi 1946d, 1.
119 Ibid.
120 Polanyi 1946e, 1.
121 Ibid.
122 Polanyi 1946i, 1.
123 Polanyi 1946j, 1.
124 Ibid.
125 Ibid., 2.
126 Ibid.
127 Polanyi 1946l, 1.
128 Her mother, Mary Ward, also an active political feminist, played a pivotal role in the Cambridge Association for Women's Suffrage.
129 Polanyi 1946o, 1.
130 Ibid.
131 Ibid., 2.
132 Ibid.

6   Economic evil and machineness

Polanyi and his contemporaries were on a mission to hunt down the evil behind the economic and moral crisis of their time. Some of them claimed to find it in the all-can-be-left-behind policy of laissez-faire liberalism or the boundless greed of capitalist investors. Others considered such evil to be coming from the state: its nature, size, maladministration and relation to the economy. Some saw it coming from the deepest and darkest depths of human nature. However, most accounts identifying the economic evil were better in fanning the flames of sentiment than in calming the troubled intellect. While there were many who claimed to know what was going on and what should be done, only Polanyi and a handful of others dared to study the economic evil long enough to find out that it resides both in systems of laissez-faire liberalism and of social-ist planning. Most scholars have taken one blurry side or the other. In *The Great Transformation* (1944), Karl Polanyi argued that laissez-faire liberalism was estab-lished and propagated to realize an imaginative vision which was a "stark utopia".[1] In his view, the best way out of this inhumane "satanic mill"[2] of market society is to give space to the spontaneous protective mechanisms of society and to let people reclaim their primal social "habitation".[3] Instead of having an artificial subordination of society to the laws of the market, the latter should be subordinated to the natural laws of living in a human society. Jaszi and his fellow-minded authors of *The City of Man* (1940) dreamed about an Atlantic utopia without nation states and national governments relying on a world government, a "Universal State"[4] or "State of States"[5] guarding over world democracy and world humanism. For them, the evil was not coming from the market but from the nation states which, by their mere existence, fostered isolationist sentiments and impeded the emergence of other novel sen-timents, including the idea of global democracy and responsibility. To tackle the "evil titanism"[6] of nation states, they proposed establishing a supranational entity cutting through national boundaries and embracing a philosophy prioritizing morals over economics and not economics over morals.

Similarly to Michael Polanyi, authors of *The City of Man* (1940) thought that Western civilization was threatened by its totalitarian rivals, the Nazi, the fascist and the Soviet régimes. They pointed out that considering technolo-gical superiority the sole harbinger of victory is fallacious because no "mechanical equipment could redress by itself the wrongs of a mechanical destiny".[7] The bane of democracy is the "decay of the soul",[8] the loss of faith and hope, people living the routine of "liberties and comforts"[9] without having personal spiritual attachment to it. "Mass-man"[10] and "rootless man"[11] cannot build true democracy and neither can machines. Democracy "cannot be run by robots and automatons, by serfs and slaves. Its vigor rests upon the cultivation and discipline of the person, as a self-acting and self-controlling agent."[12] The view considering democracy as "dispersive atomism"[13] should be replaced by a new vision seeing it as a "purposive organism"[14] following a plan. Machines and machine-like attributes were portrayed as being wrong and inhumane. Mass production was framed as "intrinsically vicious"[15] and "subduing the diligence of the human person serving the machine to the automatic beat of the machine itself".[16] Technology was depicted as socially constructed but not being completely under social control: "If the machine, man's creature, seems to have developed a brutal power of its own, there abides in the human mind a presentiment that it can and must be domesticated somehow."[17] How to tame your technology (or golem) is, of course, the central theme of a masterpiece of philosophy of technology, *The Golem at Large* (1998) by Harry Collins and Trevor Pinch. Without attempting to find predecessors and forerunners in a hopelessly anachronistic enterprise, it should rather be noted here that the technophobia of the authors of *The City of Man* (1940) succinctly summarized by them as the "immaturity and the overgrowth of the machine age"[18] was not only concerned with the economic hardship of individuals due to the industrial mechanization of the sector in which they were employed, but also with the spiritless and mindless nature of machines and its consequences for the social order, the system at large. They argued that machines have, quite imperceptibly, brought not only quantitative but also qualitative change to economy and society.

The authors claimed that industrial mechanization is not neutral to values, social philosophies and politics but fosters certain ways of exercising power while downplaying others.

> Every large machine-industry – which is the material productive source and the basis of Socialism – requires an absolute and strict unity of the will. … But how can we secure a strict unity of the will? By subjecting the will of thousands to the will of one.[19]

– as they quoted Lenin in anything but agreement. In their account, Marx, similarly to Lenin, viewed the economy and the "labor-state",[20] as "one colossal factory".[21] This factory was also seen as providing a "blueprint"[22] for fascism for how to make a "world-wide regimentation" of "self-contained despotism".[23] The machineness of the economic microcosmos of doing factory work was depicted here going hand in hand with the machineness of the economic macro-cosmos of technocratic industries and dictatorial economies. The authors drew a parallel between how an employee is being treated in a modern factory and how an individual is being treated under dictatorship. And the common point was the mechanistic conduct of affairs paying only little or no attention to what is individual, personal and humane.

Connecting evil and machineness in economic realms was, likewise, a pivotal element in Karl Polanyi's *The Great Transformation* (1944). However, unlike the relevant narrative of *The City of Man* (1940), *The Great Transformation* anchored evil and machineness in the idea of the self-regulating market system and claimed to find its origins in the historical alliance of commercial society and the large-scale machinization of production. Mass production based on machines does not only create output but transforms "the natural and human substance of society into commodities".[24] Machinization, for Karl, was not only a technical add-on improving an already existing self-regulating economic system, but its maker. Machine, an "artificial phenomenon",[25] was giving "highly artificial stimulants"[26] to the society, and by doing so, transforming it significantly. Rage against the machine was, according to him, understandable and rightful. The economic world stabilized by Speenhamland should have been destroyed either by destroying the machines themselves in a Luddite rage or by establishing a regular labour market. The "machine civilization"[27] has been struck by economic calamities of a national scale (e.g. Speenhamland, Poor Law Reform of 1834). Machines caused "social dislocation"[28] which needs to be addressed. "If a human society is a self-acting machine for maintaining the standards on which it is built, Speenhamland was an automaton for demolishing the standards on which any kind of society could be based",[29] he noted. Karl pointed out that Jeremy Bentham suggested using the manpower of many convicts instead of a steam engine to get machinery going which was designed by his brother, Samuel Bentham. Karl drew a parallel between the business of the Bentham brothers and the grand-scale social machinery of the era having the poor as surrogates of Benthamian convicts, both struggling under the application of Bentham's idea of an all-seeing Panopticon. Karl even accused Bentham, although not in a very explicit way, by building ideological scaffolding for the "mechanical revolution"[30] with utilitarianism, his new science of morals and legislation. Science, understood as a "practical art based on empirical knowledge"[31] in the eighteenth century, was asked to provide guidance about how to approach the new mechanical realm. Bentham aimed to develop a universal method to quantify humane aspects of the world with his utilitarianism which would have, if successful, made the next step towards having a common denominator of human and machinistic realms and thus ending the incommensurability threatening society with disintegration. Karl quoted Leslie Stephen about the panoptic nature of the market system which, being the product of the commercial masters of machines, mirrored the construction of a "mill to grind rogues honest, and idle men industrious".[32]

While machinization of production was an evil in its own right in Karl Polanyi's *The Great Transformation* (1944), it was not portrayed as necessarily evil in *Soviet Communism: A New Civilisation?* (1935), the colossal socialist narrative of Sidney and Beatrice Webb. In the latter, the machine "is not a thing of evil, but a blessing to mankind".[33] The machine was to bring shorter working days, ease the burden of workers and, eventually, to become a "ubi-quitous slave of mankind".[34] The Webb's quoted an interesting fragment from Barbara Wootton's *Plan or No Plan* (1934), suggesting that the world itself should not be seen as mechanical because that would be incompatible with dialectical materialism. According to Wootton, the acts of people should fit to "conscious necessity",[35] to "fall in with" "the nature of things" "instead of trying to kick against the pricks". In her view, the universe is not "a mechanistic affair, a mere structure of atoms blindly controlled by a balance of forces". It should be understood in terms of "growth" rather than "equi-librium" and visualized as an "organism" rather than as a "machine".[36] Inter-estingly, Wootton found the implicit idea of a possible balance or equilibrium in the mechanical worldview, a perspective which she ipso facto considered to be incompatible with dialectical materialism. Thus, following such strange and quite flawed logic, the incontestable nature of dialectical materialism gave birth to the socialist worldview which was framed as anti-mechanical and essentially organic. Although the Webbs declined to see the world as one big machine, they did not consider machines to be inherently evil or to increase the social hardship of man. On the contrary, the evil was not seen coming from the material apparatus but from "the utilisation of these machines without regard to human needs".[37] In their view, it was not the machines but their bad management under a capitalist system which has "led us into our present ghastly predicament".[38]

The Hammonds' Labour trilogy offered a more sophisticated account of the social role of machines. The couple pointed out that only part of the workers' mechanophobia can be explained by their rightful fear of losing their job due to the increasing mechanization of the new age. The other part came from "a feeling of hatred and terror that no magician among economists could have dispelled by the most convincing demonstration that machinery could not hurt the poor".[39] This spirit of resistance comes from the inhuman and impersonal nature of the new system which deprived workers of their "instincts and sensibilities",[40] destroying their customs, traditions, freedom and previously held social ties. Macaulay's proud statement that "nowhere does man exercise such dominion over matter"[41] was melted and recoined by the Hammonds to become a no less spirited slogan: "nowhere does matter exercise such dominion over man".[42] The detailed regulations about do's and don'ts are like the musical score defining the "brutal rhythm of the factory".[43] The Hammonds argued that "no economist of the day, in estimating the gains and the losses of factory employment, ever allowed for the strains and violence that a man suffered in his feelings"[44] when he lost a considerable amount of his personal freedom and found himself locked up without "even the right to whistle". People are compelled to watch and work with the tire-less machinery that "knows no suffering and no weariness", causing overwork for the gain of the company and "nervous strain"[45] for the loss of its workers.

In the mechanized capitalist system, the poor were "in the grasp of a great machine that threatened to destroy all sense of the dignity of human life".[46] Not only do the rich get richer and the poor get poorer, but the latter were being increasingly dehumanized in the machine age. It must also be noted here that the Hammonds examined cases which seemed to contradict such an oversimplified portrayal of the social effects of the increasing machinization of industry. They gave an example of Mr. Smart's sweeping machine (1803) which was aimed to be employed instead of boys to sweep chimneys in order to reduce the health hazards of climbing boys of a young age, but which shortly met obstacles in its wider take-up. In the capitalist system, human life was treated "as one among several forces which drove the wheels of rapid wealth, and as nothing more".[47] The extensive application of a new invention with the capacity to lighten the burden of the poor, like Smart's sweeping machine, could be easily impeded by the rich and powerful if the status quo seemed to be more rewarding for those at the top. Although they flashed a few examples about machines siding with humans, the Hammonds argued that mechanization generally comes with dehumanization in the economy.

The Hammonds pointed out that economics was, among other things, a tool for the powerful to reach their goals. "In the House of Lords there was King who used Political Economy to threaten the rich, and Lauderdale who used it to punish the poor",[48] they noted. Their accounts are not so much concerned about how economists were using their political attachments to enhance their scholarly authority but with how politicians were using economics in their rhetorics to further their political aims. Of course, some economic theories were more usable for these purposes than others. The Hammonds pointed out how the Smithian view of trade reflected in the concept of the *invisible hand* discouraged the public from seeing trade as consciously "snatching advantages from each other"[49] and fostered seeing it instead as "unconsciously helping and developing each other" while following their self-interests. This idea could be used by the upper classes to explain why the state should not intervene in the economy to protect workers from monopolists and inhuman working conditions. It appeared as if there was an implicit principle suggesting 'the state can do no good' in the economy. But the idea could also be used to explain why deregulation, the abolishment of economic privileges and "mercantilist superstition"[50] is necessary. According to the authors of the labour trilogy, "Ricardo's brilliant and rather labyrinthine deductive reasoning has led later students to the most diverse conclusions."[51] The so-called *Ricardian vice* was portrayed here as fostering various diverse interpretations making a foundation which "Socialism and Individualism alike have built on". In the Hammonds' view, Ricardo's instant message to the general public was that the "unfailing principle of self-interest" might eliminate other human motives from economic realms, that the power of supply and demand is omnipotent and that "the laws governing profits and wages were mechanical and fixed".[52] They did not argue that these are Ricardian teachings but they did argue that these are the most influential common interpretations of Ricardo's contributions to economics.

Born, who defined himself as an anti-capitalist and anti-liberal who was not a socialist, thought that "personal profit is a very unsatisfactory regulating principle and that the so called 'laws of the market' are a deception".[53] For him, the evil was coming from the idea of the market developed to provide rhetorical pseudo-legitimation to the almost limitless power of the rich over the poor in capitalist countries. In Born's view, regulation of economic life is necessary and desirable. His poster country for having economic regulation and being efficient at the same time was Russia. Not surprisingly, he did not draw examples from everyday Russian economic life but instead only referred to the country's successful military resistance against the Nazi threat, which he traced back to economic efficiency without trying to provide any further evidence. His rejection of what he considered to be the "economic laws"[54] of "'liberal' economists",[55] his support for economic planning, his proposal to reform education for service and collective spirit and, particularly, his idealistic portrayal of Russia makes his coming out about being non-socialist less plausible. But not everyone saw the appraisal of socialism, the Russian experiment and the efficiency of a state-driven economy so closely connected. Arthur Koestler, Polanyi's childhood friend, the author of *Darkness at Noon* (1940) and *Scum of the Earth*[56] (1941), declined to see the Russian Experiment as a "valid test for State-Socialism".[57] In Koestler's view, the state "can be an employer as liberal and more generous than the Nuffield Trust or the K.W.I.".[58] Thus he did not see the evil of the Russian Experiment coming from the state-drivenness of the economy or its socialist character but from other unspecified sources.

According to Jaszi, state-drivenness does necessarily "lead to semi-fascist systems".[59] Hence the evil does not or not only come from the bad management and the ideology of these systems but it is also immanent to their centralized power structure and their ways of exercising power. There is no such thing as a good and extensively "planned system of economics".[60] One simply cannot have both. Not surprisingly, *The City of Man* (1940), co-authored by Jaszi, reflected strong anti-state sentiment. Others, such as the Shakespeare-expert and literary critic Lionel Charles Knights, argued that it was not the state-planning but the "sillier side of doctrinaire Marxism"[61] and the one-party system which caused the social evil most commonly attributed to the so-called socialist planning. In Knights' view, a "moderately enlightened State" can be better in allocating resources without limiting scientists' freedom on purely scientific matters. Knights asked Polanyi "if spurious theories are endorsed by the State and made the basis of vast practical schemes (like those described in Russia) won't their spuriousness be shown after some time by the fact that they don't after all, <u>work</u>?" It must be noted, in Knights' defence, that he emphasized that he was a "non-scientist"[62] and a "non-specialist"[63] approaching an unknown landscape. However, his question, perhaps even indicating a mildly condescending tone, was anything but clever. There is no fair test, no *experimentum crucis*, no clearcut line of demarcation deciding what does and does not work in either good or bad systems. What does matter instead is the right and opportunity to form and spread free opinion about what is going on. State-centred systems can use, and in fact, tend to use their political legitimation and legal power to curb this right and opportunity. Some with indirect methods, others with more direct ones. State planning systems often aim to collectivize not just the economy but the minds of their citizens by monopolizing what they think about the economy. After reaching the point of no return, there is no one inside the bubble who is really the master of her own understanding anymore. Information in- and outflows are under strict state control and the panoptic dystopia becomes a harsh reality. Neither those at the top nor those in the mud think anymore that the executive power has de facto responsibility and accountability. How can a fair test of 'anything' exist in such a hellish realm? How can the "spuriousness"[64] of a state-driven theory be discovered when the state is the sole interpreter of both theories and reality and, like all centres of power, is anything but humble?

T.S. Eliot, the British-American essayist, poet, literary critic and playwright, a regular attendant of The Moot, seemed to recognize the threat which an expansive Government could pose to individual freedom. In a letter to Polanyi, he drew a parallel between "the nature of scientific enquiry and its relation to Government"[65] and "the nature of art (especially of course literature) and its relation to Government". Although Eliot did not go into details – he just stated that Polanyi's book "confirms the sort of conclusions"[66] he progressed towards in his meta-literary inquiries – it seems safer to think that, by the latter, he meant he saw a possible threat to the autonomy of art and science from the Government. Polanyi realized that the extension of Government control does not only threaten individual freedom, but, in certain fields (e.g. Patent reform) and particular circumstances, it can also promote its advancement. In Polanyi's view, reforms of increased state control can only achieve "partial solutions",[67] there always remains a "field of unmanageable relations"[68] beyond the grasp of top-down policies.

The way Laura Polanyi-Striker, Michael's sister, a historian and active feminist, portrayed economic freedom might be less useful for the pursuit of economic evil and more useful for inquiring its more popular counterpart, economic good. According to Polanyi-Striker, in the United States, "everybody could – even can – make a living without giving up any of his habits, ideologies, ideals, ways – he came away with from the old countries: very often because these had become obsolete there".[69] There is no trade-off between private freedom and economic well-being, at least not within certain bounds. There is a minimum of both which is not up to bargain. Following this logic, the contrast of economic good, economic evil, would come from systems demanding their economic agents to sacrifice everything, their morals, personalities and uniqueness, on the altar of chasing economic well-being. Of course, once such one-dimensional materialism has been spread in a society, and piling up wealth becomes an end in itself and the only end people can dream of, economic power defeats its less mechanical rivals in the race to define what makes a good life.

A letter which Polanyi received from Gilbert Murray, a Professor of Greek[70] at the University of Oxford, provided an unexpected summary of pro-state socialist intellectuals on British soil. According to Murray, he was too lazy to write a letter of acknowledgement to Polanyi about his broadcast on *The Challenge of Our Time*, but, as he phrased matters:

> the blasphemies of Jack Haldane stimulate me. He was so able and so wrong. But I fear people will not begin to see things sanely until we are free from the after-effects of the War. Bernal was the worst. Koestler brilliant and attractive but open to attack.[71]

Others warned that Bernal, Haldane and a few other socialists are seen as "prophets"[72] and their "enthusiasm"[73] makes them dangerously attractive, particularly for the youth. E.J. McManus, secretary of the Henry George School of Social Science, thought that Haldane fallaciously defined "social evil as 'economic', i.e. as springing from the laws of Political Economy – the laws governing the production and distribution of wealth".[74] He argued that just because the "effect of collective wrongdoing manifest itself"[75] in the sphere of economy, we should not identify social evil as being economic, just as we do not blame physiology for having diseases and injuries. Hill drew Polanyi's attention to Crowther's review of *The Royal Society, 1660–1940* (1944) by Henry George Lyons. In his review, Crowther voiced his fear that if the Royal Society refused to participate in the central planning of science, scientific authority and administrative responsibility would break up, eventually resulting in the dominance of administration over science. "Huge administrative machines will grow without ideas and possibilities of their own, repulsive to men of intelligence, and finally without brain and soul."[76] Hill characterized Crowther's review as being

> his usual comic stunt of saying that Russia should be our model in everything: in this case the Royal Society should model itself on the Soviet Academy and throw all its high principles of the last hundred years to the winds.[77]

Hill was convinced that the editor (Kingsley Martin, 1931–60) of *The New Statesman and Nation* in which the review was published would not allow them to publish a counter-strike in the same journal because he was, similarly to the author, committed to the point of view it represents.

Is it possible to fight against both these economic evils at the same time? If yes, how can one avoid unconditional surrender to either the market or the state in her pursuits in economic life? How to escape both aimless drifting and uncontestable order? These are questions which seemed to influence

Polanyi's endeavours to lay down foundations for a postmodern economics. Polanyi's middle road was anything but conventional. He hoped to "establish an anchorage for the reasonable government of society".[78] A floating anchorage-point consists of certain morals and beliefs of a group of fellow-minded people providing them both stability and dynamics in their inquiries into what is 'out there' in the economic wilderness and how to survive. I cannot agree with Mullins (2010) more that Polanyi's early vision of a liberal society, his later vision of the society of explorers, and his *tacit knowing* concept were all connected. To use the most unfortunate Whig term possible: 'the missing piece' is Polanyi's even earlier concept of *knowing* which, so far, has remained quite unnoticed in the depths of his archival materials.

The Polanyian concept of *knowing* as an ensemble of three aspects: understanding, believing and belonging offers new opportunities for the interpretation of economics. The first, understanding the economy in a specific yet unfixed way, was not without precedent. As Toni Stolper pointed out, even "Keynes himself, after having made his illuminating contributions … has had to move on from there to the various thin edges or brittle walls of his edifice where unruly life showed signs of gnawing and tearing at it".[79] Of course, the portrayal of Keynes as a "dynamist"[80] by someone else does not tell us anything about what Keynes himself thought about the evolution of his own ideas. However, a fragment he sent to Polanyi might. Keynes wrote to Polanyi that

> I am rather doubtful how far I shall feel moved to go back and pick up what I was saying and thinking ten years ago. So it may be that I shall leave the Keynesians a free run unimpeded by me and will be myself writing something else.[81]

Thinking about the development of economic theories as consecutive runs suggests that neither Keynes himself thought about his enterprise as laying down additional perfectly crafted bricks of positive economic knowledge. On the contrary, he envisioned an infinite process of polishing and fine-tuning of what has been, so far, falsely believed to be true. But it also suggests something else. Keynes was conscious about the fact that what happens after the roll out of his economics is not completely under his control. Once a theory is 'out there' it is getting, intentionally or not, shifted and bended by both Keynesians and non-Keynesians. Understanding a theory may come to a halt but it is never finished.

Polanyi usually framed his economics as Keynesian. Indeed, much of the content of his 'economics' was Keynesian. He fostered deficit-spending, state intervention in the economy (when it was necessary), depicted a macro-economic model of Keynesian flavour and raised attention to the importance of money flow and monetary policy. But all this falls into only one aspect of Polanyian knowing, understanding. Much of what makes Polanyi's economics postmodern lies with the other two aspects. Believing certain assumptions and belonging to a group sharing those assumptions were not something generally considered to be part of knowing the economy in one way or another. Of course, axioms have been part of economic theory-building for a long time, but having assumptions and believing in assumptions is not the same. While the first is a technical statement about what the author(s) thought about the limitations of the theory and its possible applications, the latter implies a personal attachment to the theory. Or, in other words, the personal attachment of the subject of knowing to the object of knowing. Robots might have assumptions in the form of pre-given rules to follow, but they cannot believe or disbelieve in these assumptions. Their makers might believe in these assumptions, but this aspect of believing is immanent to the knowing of robot-makers not the robots themselves. Belonging to a group of fellow-believers is also a prerequisite of Polanyian knowing, suggesting that there is no such thing as a 'lone wolf' knower. One might be enough to understand or believe, but it takes more than one to form a group. Knowing, for Polanyi, is not an individual enterprise but a personal journey we always share with kindred others. Since a group of fellow-understanders and believers is being formed providing the third aspect of knowing, belonging, those involved in it ipso facto become subjects of a specific kind of knowing. Machines might simulate understanding, but they cannot be believers and belongers, therefore they cannot be subjects of Polanyian knowing. Polanyian knowing is, at least in this early period, inherently humane.

The concept of economic man (*homo oeconomicus*) treating humans as 'purely' rational decision-makers driven by self interest, individuals capable of mapping the world, of evaluating the alternatives and of deciding themselves accordingly, was immanent in most contemporary theories labelled as economics. But this was not the case in Polanyi's postmodern economics. Knowing the economy was, for Polanyi, not an individual feat but a group exercise. Deciding that something is good or bad, rational or irrational, true or false, eventually relied on what a certain group thinks. However, this does not sanction the subordination of the individual opinion to that of the community. Far from it. Every individual, through her attachment to the group, constantly shapes what the group thinks. And, if the two do not find a mutually satisfactory outcome, the individual can at any time join another group into which she better fits. This is not intended to be a portrayal of a disintegrating society but one which admits that there are epistemic differences in every society which should not be swept under the carpet but which should instead be taken into consideration as a natural trait of continuously evolving human societies. Having diverse individuals and multiple groups does not necessarily mean disintegration. Perhaps these individuals and groups eventually converge precisely because they can be different and have the freedom to follow their own ways. Regardless of whether they eventually converge or not, they are, from a Polanyian approach, essential for knowing the economy.

Knowing is a personal journey taken with fellow-minded associates. It is not a sequence of individual epistemic states. Polanyi's *homo oeconomicus explorans* is an individual who understands the economy the way her peers do, believes in the same assumptions about how to understand the economy as they do, and belongs to a group sharing those assumptions. She is on an ongoing mission with her peers towards better knowing. This concept of man pertaining to Polanyi's postmodern economics is nothing like the *homo oeconomicus* who is incapable of change or of having personal attachments to others and what they think, believe or do. One should not avoid making a list-like comparison here to please those who fancy succinct logic instead of lively descriptions. In a hopelessly small and rough nutshell: *homo oeconomicus* implies that a person making an economic decision has all the knowledge she needs and does not have any knowledge she does not need (1), that she does not and cannot believe in anything (2), and that she does not and cannot belong to any community, she is an isolated individual (3). Polanyi's concept of *homo oeconomicus explorans* is strikingly different. His concept implies that a person making an economic decision does not and cannot have all the knowledge she needs (i), that she does believe and has to believe in something (ii), and that she belongs and has to belong to a community, she is never an isolated individual (iii). Knowing is a personal, group-laden and not completely explicable process. Unlike what the *homo oeconomicus* concept suggests, economic decision-making is not an asocial, purely individual or entirely explicable act. The explorativeness of knowing the economy, the assumption that one cannot anchor her economic knowledge to any objective point of reference and therefore the best thing to do is to join a group of fellow-minded explorers in their 'always already' flawed, never-ending pursuit, made Polanyi's economics postmodern.

Polanyi's *homo oeconomicus explorans* was a concept describing those who do not follow a 'state-dictated' understanding of the economy mindlessly; nor do they accept that they cannot grasp anything beyond their individual economic self-interest. This was a *sine qua non* for both a kind of postmodern economics and a new theory of democracy. Bright wanderers, fellow associates of economic knowing, were both constituents of specific dynamically changing economic and political realities. Such realities affirming the involvement of the state was not necessarily evil but not necessarily good either. People have the twin freedom of knowing and not knowing. They can be part of a bigger scheme without giving up their individuality. Polanyi developed his postmodern economics to save Western democracy which he saw as threatened by two main enemies. The internal enemy of extreme scepticism devoured faith, confidence and hope in traditions of Western civilization. And the external enemy of dictatorial régimes eager to transmit their destructive patterns of exercising power. The concept of *homo oeconomicus explorans* offered a fiduciary alternative to scepticism by asking people not to believe in dogmas but to join others with similar beliefs in their personal inquiries of economic knowing. And it also offered an epistemic alternative to the omniscient state of the Nazi and Soviet ideologies and the quasi nescient economic man of laissez-faire liberalism blind to anything other than her economic self-interest.

From the Polanyian perspective, people are not so much knowers or non-knowers but rather vessels of knowing which is an immanently personal, always already flawed, never-ending process one always goes through with her fellow explorers. The fiduciary and the epistemic aspects of Polanyi's concept strengthened each other. Without epistemic considerations, the fiduciary aspect would have easily ended up being seen as a religion. And without faith and trust, the epistemic aspect would not lead towards what those involved in knowing considered to be better knowing but towards any knowing they find others to believe in with.

Polanyi was fighting the same battle on two fronts. With his novel concept about how to see man in the economy, he was twisting the Soviet Leviathan's tail and shook a fundamental axiom of liberal economics. He was doing this in a period when war alliances usually outshone even principal differences, and when dichotomies of good and evil were on the rise. It was a time when Polanyi was being told not to be so critical of Russia, because the country was one of the most important allies against Nazi Germany. For many, an enemy of our enemy was our friend. But where are the boundaries of this friendship? For some, it included ignoring whether our friend severely curtailed the autonomy of science and human rights. For others, including Polanyi, it was not. He was developing a theory running against both socialist economic planning and laissez-faire liberalism exposing their unspoken commonality: seeing men in the economy as identical and essentially mechanical entities. Socialist planning treated people as faceless implementers of multi-annual plans only having the traits which are necessary to realize top-down schemes. Laissez-faire liberalism treated people as conformers to economic models, as only having the traits which are necessary for them to fit into pre-made schemes. One can rightly argue that liberal economic theories were never assumed to explain everything economic, just an admittedly narrow slice of the world. Chapter 3 showed a famous instance of this attitude in the efforts of Lionel Robbins to demarcate economic science from everything else. Robbins claimed that economic science is the discipline which studies human behaviour in a specific way, as "a relationship between ends and scarce means"[82] implying that such means "have alternative uses"[83] and by so doing, narrowing the scope of the discipline. The Robbinsian perspective on economic science does not explain or care about much of what is happening in economic realms and is only concerned with studying human behaviour as rational decision-making between alternatives stirred up by very few outside the circles of math-loving economists. Economics was pushed further on the road of coherence theories of truth by Robbins, drifting away from the conviction that the primary source of plausibility should be seen as coming from the correspondence of reality and theory. Economists have become increasingly interested in developing coherent theories and less interested in making theories which explain what is 'out there' in the economy. As a consequence, economics has increasingly started to treat people as if they were obedient, dreamless polygons in an ever expanding *Flatland*. People are regarded as if they cannot think, feel or do what they please. People do only what is explicitly permitted for them by the theories. From this perspective, people are not makers, shapers or benders of theories, just passive conformers or invisible bystanders waiting for their mechanical fate.

Polanyi's *homo oeconomicus explorans* does not limit what people can and should do in relation to economic theories. His focus on personal knowing implies understanding a theory, believing in certain assumptions underlying it and belonging to a community sharing those assumptions. But how to understand, what to believe and where to belong is quite flexible. An individual can develop a new understanding, change the set of assumptions she believes in, and join or even form a new community of believers anytime she wants. Nothing is set in stone. Lay and expert realms of economic knowing are not completely separated. But this does not lead to epistemic anarchism. Knowing connects people through the way in which they develop personal attachments to the world. People establish knowing communities, societies of explorers for their common journey towards better comprehension of the economy. These social spaces act as moral and epistemic compasses showing how to keep an eye on traditions and yet able to make new discoveries. They play a similar role to the House of Lords in the British constitutional system. The role of the House of Lords is basically to cool down the heat of politics and activism, to warn that thinking again might provide better insight into the possible consequences of a decision. The role of Polanyi's society of explorers is to maintain a moral and epistemic anchorage-point which slows down the rooting of hasty new sprouts of knowing by reminding explorers what their society is made of. They reflect traditions without chaining people to traditions. Showing the common grounds without arguing that there can be no other common ground. Emphasizing commonality without restricting individuality. They are providing a prudent way towards better knowing, a way which intended to lean on "sober and considerate agreement"[84] in the very personal practices of knowing.

Polanyi's postmodern ideas cut through the conventional dichotomous thinking focusing on traditionalism or liberalism, nationalism or liberalism or conservativism or liberalism. Polanyi suggests that leaning on tradition is not necessarily dogmatic and having freedom to do something does not mean that there are no strands which people incline to follow instead of others. Polanyi's *homo oeconomicus explorans* is the economic man of strange realities. She does think, feel, believe, act and change in both known and unknown ways. Unlike *homo oeconomicus*, she is not and cannot be completely explicated and comprehended. She relies upon and continuously renews herself from the tacit dimension. Being an open-ended model emphasizing her own limits, she gives more space to be affected by and become a vessel of what is happening 'out there'. She is a creature of an economics leaving behind mechanicality and claimed-to-be universal patterns of explanation and groping towards organicity and the personal minutiae of economic realities. Polanyi outlines an economics which seeks the correspondence of theory and reality, even if that means grabbing little and taking little due to the intangible nature of personal realities; an economics, which cares more about what can plausibly be told about the economy and less about what has already being told in previous accounts; an economics, which cares more about the small than the big, talks to the laypeople instead of experts, and which does not hide but proudly undertakes its moral and social origins.

Mechanicality was, as this chapter explored, usually considered to be the source of evil in economic realms by Polanyi's correspondents. Some saw this evil machineness coming from the state rule of the economy; others saw it residing in the ruthless efficiency of the unchastened market. Polanyi saw the evil in both places but he was not satisfied with the mappings of others and traced it further himself to the economic theories of socialists and liberals. At a time when pointing out commonalities of socialist planning and laissez-faire liberalism was a rare and dangerous feat, Polanyi claimed to find the evil in the heart of both these theories: in how they treat the person in the economy. For laissez-faire liberalism, an individual was a rational decision-making automaton who is always true to herself, never does anything stupid and only cares about making the best choices possible. For socialist planning, an individual was not a decision-maker but a mechanical implementer fulfilling her economic destiny drafted in three- or five-year plans made by omnipotent programmers of the party. None of them addressed an individual as having the freedom to see, know or do what does not fit into pre-made schemes. Polanyi's postmodern economics works from the other side. It presupposes that most things are not known and cannot entirely be known, and advised that the best thing one can do is to grope along the three interrelated aspects of knowing in her inquiries into the economy. From this perspective, our own moral currents and social conventions make a platform on which we inevitably rely through our never-ending explorative epistemic practices, whether we are conscious about it or not. One might ask that if such a moral and social platform affects us anyway, what is the point in making it conscious? Essentially that, by making this inevitable kind of partiality conscious, one is less likely to see her own personal knowing as having knowledge of universal validity. And being more humble about what we know, if it goes viral, would lead towards a more enlightened society and a more conscious democracy.

Notes

1 Karl Polanyi [1944] 2001, xxv.
2 Ibid., 35.
3 Ibid., 41.
4 Agar *et al.* [1940] 1941, 24.
5 Ibid.
6 Editorial note in *The Listener* 1 June 1944.
7 Agar *et al.* [1940] 1941, 15.
8 Ibid., 16.
9 Ibid., 17.
10 Ibid., 18.
11 Ibid.
12 Ibid., 30.

13 Ibid., 33.
14 Ibid.
15 Ibid., 90.
16 Ibid., 90–1.
17 Ibid., 91.
18 Ibid., 90.
19 Ibid., 53–4.
20 Ibid., 53.
21 Ibid.
22 Ibid., 57.
23 Ibid.
24 Karl Polanyi [1944] 2001, 44.
25 Ibid., 60.
26 Ibid.
27 Ibid., 105.
28 Ibid., 103.
29 Ibid., 103–4.
30 Ibid., 125.
31 Ibid.
32 Ibid., 126.
33 Webb and Webb 1935, 1139.
34 Ibid., 1020.
35 Ibid., 952.
36 Ibid.
37 Ibid., 1139; Flamm 1935, 347.
38 Webb and Webb 1935, 1139.
39 Hammond and Hammond [1911] 1917, 17.
40 Ibid., 18.
41 Ibid., 17.
42 Ibid., 18.
43 Ibid., 20.
44 Ibid., 21.
45 Ibid.
46 Ibid., 36.
47 Ibid., 251.
48 Ibid., 195.
49 Ibid., 196.
50 Ibid.
51 Ibid., 203.
52 Ibid.
53 Polanyi 1942e, 1.
54 Polanyi 1942n, 1.
55 Ibid.
56 Koestler was so close to Polanyi that he even informed him about getting news from Leo Valiani, who was the flesh and blood person behind one of Koestler's literary characters, Mario. As Koestler noted, he

> received a letter from the "Mario" of "Scum of the Earth" – he has safely reached Mexico after a year in hell in French-Marocco. I booked him as a loss long ago, this is the most cheerful news that reached me for a long time.
> (Polanyi 1942g, 1)

Later Valiani returned to Italy and became one of the leaders of the anti-fascist resistance and literally signed the death sentence of Benito Mussolini in April 1945.
57 Polanyi 1943l, 1.

58 Ibid., 1–2.
59 Polanyi 1942o, 1.
60 Ibid.
61 Polanyi 1943m, 1.
62 Ibid.
63 Ibid., 2.
64 Ibid., 1.
65 Polanyi 1945f, 1.
66 Ibid.
67 Polanyi 1945g, 1.
68 Ibid.
69 Polanyi 1945p, 12.
70 Murray was one of the most influential scholars of Ancient Greece in British universities from the end of the nineteenth century until the mid-1930s. He was a Professor of Greek at the University of Glasgow (1889–99), and then Regius Professor of Greek at the University of Oxford (1908–36). No wonder he provided the basis for Adolphus Cusins, the scholar of Greek literature in George Bernard Shaw's play, *Major Barbara*. Murray was also the inspiration for another fictional character, the ghost of Gilbert Murray in Tony Harrison's *Fram* (2008) which portrayed the two main characters' ideological transformation, one from socialism to social Darwinism, the other from social Darwinism to socialism.
71 Polanyi 1946f, 1.
72 Polanyi 1946g, 1.
73 Ibid.
74 Polanyi 1946h, 2.
75 Ibid.
76 Crowther 1944, 375.
77 Polanyi 1944p, 1.
78 Polanyi 1943i, 1.
79 Polanyi 1946n, 2.
80 Ibid.
81 Polanyi 1946b, 1.
82 Robbins 1932, 15.
83 Ibid.
84 Polanyi 1941d, 1.

7 Epilogue

Towards a Polanyian personal economics

There is an old Hungarian saying: he who grabs a lot takes little. Polanyi seemed to consider this true of the mainstream liberal economics of his time which aimed to explain much through abstract theoretization and, by so doing, lost touch with realities of many living outside expert circles. And he was not alone. Ernst Friedrich Schumacher, in his *Small is Beautiful: A Study of Economics as if People Mattered* (1973) offered similar insights. In Schumacher's view, the economics of all is the economics of none. What economics needed is a revision focusing on the small-scale and humane aspects of economic life, empowering people by finding "intermediate" or "appropriate technologies" based on their needs as humans and not on their obligations as conformers to economic theories. Schumacher entered the scene of British economic government in the early 1940s, when Keynes, after reading Schumacher's "Multilateral Clearing" (1943), rescued him from internment and helped him to establish himself as a government economist. "Multilateral Clearing" (1943) was published in *Economica*, the journal which played a pivotal role in the Keynes–Hayek debate, as well as in Polanyi's endeavours to be seen as having economic expertise. Interestingly, no correspondence has been found so far between Schumacher and Polanyi, although the archival materials of the Schumacher Center Library suggests that Schumacher was a committed reader of Polanyi's work.[1] Schumacher's early work mostly included pieces of mainstream economics. He only started to develop heterodox ideas after travelling to Burma in 1955. His turnaround from orthodox to heterodox economics and his late commitment to human-scale, sustainable local economies might be briefly grasped here by recalling his 1973 Gandhi Memorial Lecture in which Schumacher described Gandhi as the "greatest People's economist"[2] having an economic thought "compatible with spirituality as opposed to materialism".[3]

Another influence on Schumacher was Leopold Kohr, one of his teachers, a friend of George Orwell, and a fellow intellectual who intended to smash the 'bigness and hardness' bias in economics and replace it with a conscious emphasis on 'smallness and softness'. In *The Breakdown of Nations* (1957), Kohr argued for small states instead of nation states and bigger political-legal conglomerates. In his view, such homecoming of the small and local would diminish many political and social problems by decentralizing power and by bringing politics back to the close quarters of people. One cannot help seeing the contrast with *The City of Man* (1940) of Jaszi and his co-authors. Both books argued for changing the international system of nation states to solve wide-scale social problems, but while *The Breakdown of Nations* (1957) suggested going smaller, minimizing the aggregation of power, *The City of Man* (1940) suggested going even bigger, maximizing the aggregation of power and replacing developed nation states with one supranational legal-political entity. According to Kohr, the main problem of Europe "is one of division, not of union"[4] and the division should be remade in a way having parts approximately equal in size and taking "traditional tribal frontiers"[5] into consideration. Ivan Illich, an admirer of Kohr, described his work as not making an alternative economics but as developing an "alternative to economics".[6] In Illich's view, Kohr took the biological morphology of D'Arcy Thompson and J.B.S. Haldane and transformed it into a social morphology. By the latter he meant that Kohr was not interested in the "timeless and weightless critters fabricated by social scientists" lacking any kind of natural proportion of form and size, not being real-life inhabitants but imaginary monsters of social worlds. Kohr refused the fancies of both planning and progress and instead suggested finding the form that best fits the size by inquiring into the nearby social, cultural and environmental micro-cosmos. Kohr argued that one is better off focusing on "a certain appropriateness", on what is a good way of doing something for certain people in a certain place and time. As Illich has pointed out, this Kohrian perspective, in a sense, reversed the conventional way economics treats problems. While economics goes from having scarce means with alternative uses to reach the best outcome possible, Kohr's social morphology goes from what is the best for a specific person in a certain environment to find the best means possible for this specific outcome. In Illich's understanding, "where scarcity rules, ethics is reduced to numbers and utility", and "the person engaged in the manipulation of mathematical formulas loses his or her ear for ethical nuance; one becomes morally deaf".[7] One might recall here the pertinent term of Toni Stolper, "soul-deafness"[8] which was a symptom of having no or only little sentiment towards the personal 'otherness' of others. Stolper described American public opinion in World War II with this symptom; however, she claimed to find the cause of this deafness in the historical and political roots of American isolationism and not in the social effects of economics. Illich argued that not only the language of mathematics, e.g. thinking about values instead of an "immanent, concrete proportion",[9] but its dominant modes of thinking "could norm the realm of human relationships". Making it even more explicit, he pointed out that "algorithms 'purified' value by filtering out appropriateness, thereby taking the good out of ethics".[10] Similar ideas are found in Polanyi's quotation of the two Dickensian characters, Gradgrind who knows everything about value and economics but nothing about morals and how to live a good life, and Bounderby, who posed as one of the fittest survivors of the capitalist struggle but was instead a forger of his own history.

Illich was, of course, not only a remarkable interpreter of Kohr and a stalwart opposer of economics but a prolific scholar himself. His ideas about the relation of education and society offer exciting parallels with the Polanyian project of saving liberalism, democracy and Western civilization through education. In *Deschooling Society* (1971) Illich argued that institutional education is fundamentally flawed, and it works to institutionalize society under the false premise that everyone can and should be schooled in the same way without taking their individual differences into account.[11] What is needed, according to Illich, are "educational webs"[12] or "learning webs"[13] helping each individual "to transform each moment of his living into one of learning, sharing, and caring".[14] Illich suggested using computer technology for establishing "peer-matching"[15] networks to find those looking for the same kind of activity. He dreamed about a sharing-based virtual computopia of everyone in the earliest days of ARPANET, almost two decades before Timothy Berners-Lee introduced the World Wide Web to the general public (1989), and more than three decades before Web 2.0 hit the digital road. In *Tools for Conviviality* (1973), Illich countered "modernized poverty",[16] dependency of the average person on the technocratic élite and the institutionalized expert knowledge of their taste. He posited new instruments which would be developed and maintained by the community of users and, by doing so, empower average citizens. Illich's vision influenced many, including Lee Felsenstein, a pioneer of personal computer design, mediator of the Homebrew Computer Club in Silicon Valley. Felsenstein's design philosophy admittedly mirrors Illichian ideas, e.g. "to change the rules, change the tools". But is a personal computer personal in the same sense Illich dreamt about his convivial tools to be?

Illich's *convivial tools* are, in a sense, counterpoints to machines. A convivial tool has its origins in the "autonomous and creative"[17] intercourse of persons and their environment. Its applications are being explored through personal use. Machines have a predetermined single purpose. Humans can run them, use them, but cannot find new uses for them. There is no personal intercourse, no social symbiosis. For Illich, conviviality is "individual freedom realized in personal interdependence and, as such, an intrinsic ethical value".[18] Tools may be compatible with conviviality, but not machines. One is tempted to think that the personal computer did not mean the same for the pioneering brains of the Homebrew Computer Club like Felsenstein and for the common user. But would such a difference have meant that, from an Illichian perspective, personal computers are convivial tools for their designers and mere machines for their average user? Early thinkers and designers were hobbyists exchanging and building computer parts and sharing ideas for self-actualization and for having fun. They were mostly interested in computers in the making. Computers, for them, were both artefacts of self-expression, showing their skills and their personal attachment to the world, and allies in reimagining and remaking the world. Necessarily having personal intercourse with their environment, designers were makers of their individual freedom through their interdependence with computers. Computer designers became computer designers by designing and making computers. And there is no computer without someone fabricating it. This relationship was, of course, nothing like the ways in which the common user was being engaged in computer-related activities. But this does not mean that the latter users were not having a symbiotic relationship with their computers. Using them for technical purposes such as calculating or exchanging messages, and for practical purposes such as constructing an identity of a competent computer-user, they were building and maintaining a different kind of symbiosis with personal computers. Being unable or unwilling to develop or significantly improve the computer themselves, they established personal interdependence through using the device. Their related individual freedom was not coming from tailor-making computers of their taste, but from making an ally in the finished computer to reach their personal aims. Personal computers might be seen as convivial tools for designers and common users alike, yet for quite different reasons. An anachronistic but immensely relevant question might be raised here: could Polanyi's centres of economics education be seen as an instance of "educational webs"[19] or "learning webs"[20] and his economics film as a "convivial tool"?[21]

Polanyi and Illich both criticized conventional practices of knowing. Polanyi argued that economists do not try hard enough to make their discipline comprehensible for the masses. He also claimed to find another cause of the unsatisfactory public understanding of economic ideas: the complexity and invisibility of the social body. As a solution, he crafted a heart for a postmodern economics, treating knowing as an ensemble of three interrelated aspects. He proposed a novel programme based on centres of economics education using visual notation for presenting economic matters to teach those without advanced mathematical skills. Polanyi hoped that, from these centres, a "calm light",[22] a kind of economics enlightenment "would spread out"[23] to change knowing the economy, and, to save Western democracy with a "social consciousness"[24] compatible with liberalism. Illich did not criticize education of a specific discipline but the entire educational system. His philosophy mirrored his rage against the establishment and the conviction that mass education is a tool for the technical élite to push and keep the common person in mental and epistemic slavery in order to be able to preserve the status quo. For him, institutionalizing education was a means for institutionalizing society. He wanted society to be deschooled and then reschooled based on the common people's way. Illich imagined "learning webs"[25] or "educational webs"[26] through which people can establish learning networks without any significant control from state authorities or acknowledged experts. He was not a fan of technocracy, and his anarchist adventure implying that there is no need for experts in education at all because they are necessarily, whether they are aware of it or not, mercenaries of the big and powerful, was extremely radical and made his epistemology more like that of Feyerabend's[27] than of Polanyi's.

Illich's anti-scientific and anti-expert attitude is a stark contrast with Polanyi's attitude. Illich promoted the concept of the "Epimethean man",[28] as opposed to the Promethean man. While the first posits an organic view of man converging around nature and individuals, the latter embraced a mechanical view converging around institutions. According to Illich, the Promethean man or "homo faber"[29] forgot that technological progress was not the ultimate purpose in life. He was eagerly waiting for the "rebirth of Epimethean man",[30] a man of hope and trust and not a man of expectations. The "Epimethean man"[31] does not seek his end by chasing goals set by others (e.g. an increasing quantity of unneeded commodities), but by following her own spiritual and personal way in life.[32] Unlike Illich, Polanyi saw the way out from the contemporary moral crisis by improving and spreading expertise, and not by decommissioning it. He held that better and more economics is desirable both for the individual and for the society. Polanyi was a traditionalist, in the sense that he imagined prudent gradual change based on living traditions of communities, and, unlike Illich, he did not foster an edgy push of the reset button to send the whole educational system and social establishment to the hellish realms of fire and brimstone. Illich was more of a destroyer than a builder. He gave what he thought to be a well-deserved beating to the contemporary social system, but he did not offer a fine-grained alternative. Emphasizing the role of hope and trust, nature and the individual might be considered good when addressing how to live a desirable individual life, but not good enough when one needs an explanation of social life. Illich said little about how he thought individuals would interact with each other, and about what would be the social outcome if he had his quite anarchistic way. Polanyi's centres of economics education were intended to provide a "nucleus of educated people",[33] a living and knowing community with members sharing traditions of the past, and perhaps, visions of the future. Polanyi imagined these knowing communities as growing, and eventually, after reaching the tipping point, affecting the whole society. Emphasizing hope, trust and faith was central to both thinkers, but while Illich sought to foster these aspects of knowing by working against science, Polanyi sought to facilitate their reception by reforming and revitalizing science. Illich's heated epistemological radicalism therefore might be seen as a counterpoint to Polanyi's coldheaded epistemological temperance.

Could Polanyi's economics film, *Unemployment and Money* (1940) be seen as a "convivial tool"[34] in the Illichian sense? It aimed to foster "individual freedom"[35] by empowering people with better and more knowing, and by lessening the influence of common fallacies. It intended to foster such freedom through "personal interdependence".[36] Polanyian knowing was not an individual feat but an epistemic journey always to be taken with fellow-minded others. Although these two attributes were making it very much akin to Illich's "convivial tools",[37] there was at least one important attribute pointing to the other direction. Applications of "convivial tools"[38] are being explored and re-explored through personal use. Their users gave them purpose through an "autonomous and creative"[39] intercourse of man and device. Polanyi's economics film was different. It had a pre-made purpose coined by Polanyi, which was not expected to be revised or replaced by simple users. In his original concept, Polanyi did not address the possibility that users can find new purposes for his film. He did not seem to be worried so much about the fact that, after the rollout, he could not really control anymore what would happen with his film. The feedback received after the release of his film suggests that he should have. Some economics tutors used it as a surrogate for teaching, some others as a new way to visualize economic matters. Few grasped the original purpose, and even fewer conveyed this pivotal message to their audience. Regardless of what eventually happened with his film, Polanyi's related concept was not being made to embrace the "anything goes"[40] attitude of Illich. On the contrary, the purpose was considered to remain fixed in order to be able to reach the desired social outcome. Polanyi's film was a flexible means towards a specific end. Illich's "convivial tools"[41] were flexible means towards a necessarily unspecified end. This is a difference, suggesting that Polanyi's economics film cannot be plausibly labelled as a "convivial tool"[42] in the Illichian sense.

By exploring Polanyi's endeavours to craft a heart for postmodern economics, this book intended to shed new light both on the history of economics in the 1930s and 1940s, and, on the later historiography of this period. By not directly focusing on the celebrated heroes of economics but rather those living and working on the fringe of the discipline, I have shown that one might construct a more layered, more ambiguous and less anachronistic picture of interwar economics. Mirowski's portrayal of economics as evolving from economic protoenergetics to cyborg economics, from one kind of machineness to another, seemed to be an overstatement if one includes small and misfit theories, devices and sentiments in her inquiries. Admirers and visionaries of mechanical and mathematical realms were, no doubt, in the majority among those who later became praised members of the pantheon of economics. But in the considered period there were many intellectuals, including Michael Polanyi, who were cultivating anti-machinistic and anti-mechanical visions and promoting a more humane approach for disciplinary inquiries into the economy. For figures like Polanyi, mechanicality meant quite different yet not so flattering qualities: inhumanness, despirituality, amorality, emptiness, unsophisticatedness, unwordliness, in and outside of economic realms. There was no consensus about the desirability of mechanicality in social sciences, and many who were seeking answers focused rather on the mind than on behaviour. Internal historiographers of economics have taken the easy way for decades by stigmatizing everything which did not fit into their contemporary concepts as non-economics and therefore irrelevant for their expert accounts. And, until recently, they got away with it quite well. But they should not anymore. Why? And why should non-experts, who usually consider themselves unaffected by the disputes of economists and their historians, care?

Because in the past, we trust. Or rather, in what is most commonly believed to be the past. Giving wrongly-knitted accounts about what has happened affects what lessons we draw from the past and therefore what heuristics we follow to find our way towards a better tomorrow. Makers of our past are, indirectly, also makers of our future. And a small flaw in a historical account can become a giant fallacy for mankind. Something similar is happening when the struggle of liberalism and conservativism or liberalism and socialism is being portrayed as the never-ending battle of two homogenous blocks – stories of good guys versus bad guys – and not stories of people having interests, tastes, motives, hopes, beliefs and practices, all a bit different and all being subject to quite flexible interpretations. What a shame that most people still buy cheap dichotomies by uncritically joining either side and becoming blind to the weaknesses of their chosen ideological home. Of course, politicians like oversimplifications. They come handy in their rhetorical practices of uniting and dividing people. But scholars should not like them so much. Dichotomies might make it easier to give coherent accounts, but there is a trade-off: accounts being painted with a broad brush are losing touch with the reality or realities of what they claim to represent. One could say that there is no objective demarcation line dividing too simple from not too simple accounts. And she would be undoubtedly right. But this does not mean that there are no scholars paying insufficient attention to details or that we should not help them fine-tuning their accounts whether they want it or not. Certain economic concepts are becoming attached to certain sociopolitical systems, suggesting that what seemed to be an internal problem of expert communities at first glance is also a social problem reaching far beyond expert realms. Exploring the attachments of past economic concepts and sociopolitical systems might help us to understand attachments of their contemporary successors.

We are living in a world of computers, virtual realities and digital economies in the second decade of the twenty-first century. Information networks enmesh the entire globe, containing a plethora of information about virtual citizens and connecting more people than before. Algorithms are tracing our interests, tastes and thinking through search patterns, providing us tailor-made content adjusted to our preferences, and by doing so, growing a bubble of our increasingly consistent past selves. One can craft immense economic and political power just by being able to peek behind the veil of this vast global information system, not to mention those who can even use it for their own purposes. Few would deny that this grand-scale technological advancement transforms our society, but people do not agree about how. Some frame this transformation as a realization of a virtual utopia having traits such as those Illich envisioned. For them, virtual worlds are realms of freedom fostering free speech, personality and self-fulfilment regardless of who we are in the non-virtual world. Others rather see it as digital Panopticon tricking people into putting themselves under the control of those maintaining the surveillance of virtual roads and having the monopoly to lay down new roads and to close down others to drive the epistemic traffic in the desired direction, e.g. to increase the sales of a corporation or to spread the influence of a political party. At the time of writing this book, Mark Zuckerberg, founder and CEO of the social media giant, Facebook, was put under pressure by various political platforms both in the US and Europe in the wake of the Cambridge Analytica fiasco. By following the statements made in the consecutive stops of Zuckerberg's tour of justification,[43] the careful observer can identify the clash of these widely varying visions. What shocked many representatives and citizens on the two side of the Atlantic was not the data breach but that, according to the charges, third parties could have used the leaked data to influence the operation of two flagship democracies. Perhaps the ancient fear has come to the surface here, that technology can defy us and can be used against one of the most celebrated achievements of humanity: democracy. Voices claimed that the Cambridge Analytica case threw doubts on the democratic nature of certain elections and the legitimation of certain governments. But were these claims rather fuelled by the bitterness of rivals losing political battles or by the sober insight of intellectuals having a keen eye to the newest digital entanglements of technology and society? And if this technology could have influenced even the working of our political machinery without noticing it in time, how could we know that it has not already affected our economics as well?

The age of social networks and global databases brings the rise of *big data*, a shaping discipline focusing on collecting, manipulating, analysing and visualizing very large data sets and using tools and methods designed especially for this purpose. Big data is being used to track the behaviour of the masses and to help decision-makers both to adapt to this behaviour and to change it in the desired direction. Mapping what is 'out there' and sending targeted marketing messages using big data to increase the sales of specific commodities or the popularity of certain politicians became part of our business practices and political cultures after the millennium. Relying on big data for describing the economy and in figuring out what to do is becoming increasingly popular in business circles, while in parallel, theoretical economics seems to be losing its once held charm. Economists apparently do not worry so much about big data, which they consider as a distinct data science or as an unwanted and ill-mannered stepchild of statistics and cybernetics rather than as a young offspring of economics expanding to their disciplinary territories by devouring their authority and devaluing their expertise without meeting considerable resistance.

At a first glance, big data, like political arithmetic, does not seem to foster any theoretical stance. But examining it more closely reveals that, like most economic expertise discussed in this book, it embraces a mechanical view of man. For big data, people are numbers in equations having no real human qualities. One could argue that tracking the digital footsteps of people in virtual realms might provide insights not only into their behaviour but also into their sentiments, beliefs and understandings. But being concerned about

whether someone has clicked on the 'like' button of a page and being concerned about what she thinks and feels about its content is quite different.
Likes should not be mistaken to be revealed preferences about the content.
Liking a page might be less about revealing preferences about the content and
more about revealing preferences about which content we want to be publicly associated with. And this is more than a shout-out to virtual hypocrisy.
Comparatively few people like pages of trash cans, mats, toothpastes, socks
and lighters compared to high-budget Hollywood movies or trending singers
of popular music. Does this lack of likes mean that we do not have preferences about trash cans, mats and lighters at all or that we are less likely to
publicly perform certain preferences than others? If the latter, what does this
tell us about the methods and explanations of big data? That it cannot really
grasp internal mental states but only publicly performed and quite asymmetri-
cal clues for these. Big data does not necessarily tell anything about our personal attachment to the world, but it does necessarily tell many things about
how we want others to see our personal attachment to the world. It is, no
doubt, a remarkable feat to handle such an insane number of carefully constructed virtual selves, but this is an exercise which is not necessarily about
telling, analysing and explaining anything immanently personal.

People in the economy are only subjects of big data and are expected to
have no power over the discipline. Although big data relies heavily on computers, it treats neither any hardware nor any software as "convivial tools"[44]
in the Illichian sense. People in the economy have no freedom to find new
uses of these tools, and cannot have "autonomous and creative"[45] intercourse
with the physical or the virtual pillars of big data. Similar to extreme economic liberalism and socialist planning, big data handles people as fitters of
pre-made schemes. People cannot do anything unexpected, e.g. like a content
they do not really like or browse specific pages for the sole purpose of mis-
guiding algorithms mapping their online activity whether they want it or not.
These concerns, sentiments and practices are invisible for big data. And so are
the personal aspects of knowing the economy. Big data does not really care
about how people understand the economy, what beliefs they have or what
group of believers they are part of. People are only tastes in a vat. But if not
the common economic agent, then who is the master of this nascent discipline? Those who have the greatest global networks and databases at their disposal to make the best big data inquiries possible. But those having an inside
view of how this expertise works are far more scarce than those having an
inside view of the working of traditional economics. And it is almost impossible to check whether this powerful few are running big data inquiries on us
or whether they are doing it right – not to mention the attempts of economic
and political power players to use big data to change our behaviour without
anyone even noticing it. Without considerable checks and balances, how can
we know that big data is not being used to build a sociopolitical order which
might be the best implementation so far of the Benthamite Panopticon and
the Orwellian *Big Brother*, which necessarily and quite swiftly bring forward

an unprecedented decay of both individual freedom and public liberty? Big data does not address how personal aspects could affect its disciplinary fabric nor how personal understanding, believing and belonging might influence its own perception. Because of such detachment from personal, humane, moral and spiritual realms, how can we know whether we are witnessing the emergence of a new economics tailor-made for a digital democracy or the rise of a lapdog discipline ready to serve whoever is on top?

An economics not based on the personal aspects of knowing might or might not be an ally to dictatorial political régimes. But an economics based on the personal elements of knowing ipso facto cannot be an ally to non-democratical political systems. Polanyi's personal economics was seriously concerned about democratic social order, liberalism and Western civilization. It was being crafted with the specific purpose to foster these by being compatible with postmodern democracy and being incompatible with dictatorship. Polanyi has considered economics to be necessarily ladened with values whether one admits it or not, and he was on a mission to develop an economics which embraces the values which he thought to be the most desirable. Polanyi reckoned that the mechanical view of man in the economy was a common feature in the contemporary theories of extreme liberalism and socialist planning. Personal, humane, spiritual and moral aspects of man in the economy were severely downplayed by most economists, who usually framed these realms as lying outside the scope of their discipline. Polanyi, however, based his postmodern economics on the three interrelated aspects of personal knowing providing a floating moral and social anchorage ground which a person could draw on when making economic decisions without being constrained. His solution avoided both the aimless drifting of laissez-faire liberalism and the state-dictated, centrally planned economic rationality of socialist planning, and suggested that one can embrace both tradition and discovery, as well as community and individuality in her personal inquiries into the economy. Unfortunately, until now only a few have understood Polanyi's lesson about why we should take economics personally.

Notes

1 Schumacher's personal library contained a copy of Polanyi's *Full Employment and Free Trade* (1945) and *Science, Faith and Society* (1964).
2 Schumacher 1973.
3 Ibid.
4 Kohr 1957, 232.
5 Ibid.
6 Illich 1994.
7 Ibid.
8 Polanyi 1945m, 2.
9 Illich 1994.
10 Ibid.
11 Mirroring a similar message in Pink Floyd's *Another Brick in the Wall* (1979), released eight years after the publication of *Deschooling Society* (1971).

12 Illich 1971, 2.
13 Ibid., 32.
14 Ibid., 2.
15 Ibid., 34.
16 Illich 1973, 84.
17 Ibid., 24.
18 Ibid.
19 Illich 1971, 2.
20 Ibid., 32.
21 Illich 1973.
22 Polanyi 1936a, 4.
23 Ibid.
24 Polanyi 1937c, 32.
25 Illich 1971, 32.
26 Ibid., 2.
27 When arguing against scientific medicine and the expert knowledge of doctors, Feyerabend quoted a passage from Illich in his *Three Dialogues on Knowledge* (1991), stating that a military officer would be relieved from duty if he had the same death-rates among his soldiers as an average hospital.
28 Illich 1971, 44.
29 Ibid., 48.
30 Ibid.
31 Ibid., 44.
32 This is a message quite similar to a contemporary hit, *Make Your Own Kind of Music* (1969) by Mama Cass Elliot.
33 Polanyi 1937b, 12.
34 Illich 1973.
35 Illich 1973, 24.
36 Ibid.
37 Illich 1973.
38 Ibid.
39 Illich 1973, 24.
40 A reference to Paul Feyerabend's epistemological anarchism mirrored in *Against Method: Outline of an Anarchist Theory of Knowledge* (1975).
41 Illich 1973.
42 Ibid.
43 Joint hearing of the Senate Commerce and Judiciary Committees (10 April 2018); hearing of the House Energy and Commerce Committee (11 April 2018); hearing of the European Parliament (22 May 2018).
44 Illich 1973.
45 Ibid., 24.

Bibliography

"A Monetary Movie". *Glasgow Herald*. 27 April 1940.

Abbott, Edwin. 1884. *Flatland: A Romance of Many Dimensions*. London: Seeley & Co.

Agar, Herbert; Aydelotte, Frank; Borgese, G.A.; Broch, Hermann; Brooks, Van Wyck; Comstock, Ada L.; Elliott, William Yandell; Fisher, Dorothy Canfield; Gauss, Christian; Jászi, Oscar; Johnson, Alvin; Kohn, Hans; Mann, Thomas; Mumford, Lewis; Neilson, William Allan; Niebuhr, Reinhold; Salvemini, Gaetano. 1940. *The City of Man: A Declaration on World Democracy*. New York: The Viking Press.

Alexander, William. 1981. *Film on the Left: American Documentary Film from 1931 to 1942*. Princeton: Princeton University Press.

Angell, Norman. 1909. *Europe's Optical Illusion*. London: Simpkin, Marshall, Hamilton, Kent & Co.

Angell, Norman. 1910. *The Great Illusion: A Study of the Relation of Military Power in Nations to Their Economic and Social Advantage*. London: W. Heinemann.

Angell, Norman. 1928. *The Money Game: How to Play It: A New Instrument of Economic Education*. London: J.M. Dent & Sons.

Angell, Norman. 1935. "Peace and the Public Mind", Nobel Acceptance Speech, Oslo.

Baudrillard, Jean. 1994. *Simulacra and Simulation*. Ann Arbor: The University of Michigan Press.

Beira, Eduardo. 2014. " 'Visual Presentation of Social Matters' as a Foundational Text of Michael Polanyi's Thought", *Tradition and Discovery* 41(2): 6–12.

Berces, T. 2003. "Polányi Mihály a reakciókinetikus", *Polanyiana* 1: 55–62.

Beveridge, William. 1942. *Social Insurance and Allied Services*. London: His Majesty's Stationery Office.

Bíró, Gábor István. 2017a. *Projecting the Light of Democracy: Michael Polanyi's Efforts to Save Liberalism via an Economics Film, 1933–48*. PhD dissertation. Budapest: Budapest University of Technology and Economics.

Bíró, Gábor István. 2017b. "Projecting the Light of Democracy: Michael Polanyi's Efforts to Save Liberalism via an Economics Film", Working Paper for the Trade, Employment, and Public Policy: Polanyi Then and Now workshop (MIT – The Polanyi Society), Boston.

Bíró, Gábor István. 2018. "Changing Knowledge in the Early Economic Thought of Michael Polanyi", *Journal of Evolutionary Economics* 28(2): 207–23.

Borkenau, Franz. 1937. *The Spanish Cockpit: An Eyewitness Account of the Spanish Civil War*. London: Faber & Faber.

Borkenau, Franz. 1940. *The Totalitarian Enemy*. London: Faber & Faber.

Brock, Peter. 1983. *The Mahatma and Mother India: Essays on Gandhi's Nonviolence and Nationalism.* Ahmedabad: Navajivan Publishing House.

Burke, Edmund. 1793. *On the Death of Marie Antoinette.* N.P.

Campbell, Olwen Ward. 1924. *Shelley and the Unromantics.* New York: Scribner's.

Campbell, Olwen Ward. 1940. *The Lighted Window.* Cambridge: W. Heffer & Sons.

Carr, E.H. 1942. *Conditions of Peace.* London: Macmillan & Co.

Cassel, Gustav. 1927. "Neuere monopolistische Tendenzen in Industrie und Handel. Eine Untersuchung über die Natur und die Ursachen der Armut der Nationen", Memorandum für die Weltwirtschaftsconferenz in Gent.

Churchill, Winston. 1931. "Our Duty in India", Speech given on 18 March 1931 at the Indian Empire Society, Albert Hall, London.

Clark, Colin. 1939. *A Critique of Russian Statistics.* London: Macmillan & Co.

Cole, G.D.H. 1939. "The Decline of Capitalism", Lecture to Fabian Society.

Cole, G.D.H. 1941. *Europe, Russia and the Future.* London: Victor Gollancz.

Cole, G.D.H. 1956. *World Socialism Restated.* London: New Statesman.

Collins, Harry and Pinch, Trevor. 1998. *The Golem at Large: What You Should Know about Technology.* Cambridge: Cambridge University Press.

Cook, E. Dorothy and Cotter Rahbek-Smith, Eva. 1936. *Educational Film Catalog: A Classified List of 1175 Non-Theatrical Films with a Separate Title and Subject Index.* New York: The H.W. Wilson Company.

Craig Roberts, P. and Van Cott, N. (1998/99) "Polanyi's Economics", *Tradition and Discovery* 25(3): 26–30.

Crosby, Norman. 1948. *Full Enjoyment: The New Democracy.* London: Nicholson & Watson.

Crowther, J.G. 1944. "The Royal Society", *The New Statesman and Nation,* 2 December 1944.

Dale, Edgar; Dunn, Fannie W.; Hoban, Charles F., Jr.; and Schneider, Etta. 1937. *Motion Pictures in Education: A Summary of the Literature.* American Council on Education. New York: The H.W. Wilson Company.

Dale, Edgar and Ramseyer, Lloyd Louis. 1937. *Teaching with Motion Pictures: A Handbook of Administrative Practice.* Washington, D.C.: The American Council on Education.

Davis, Norah M. 1946. *Human Problems in Industry: The New Democracy.* London: Nicholson & Watson.

Dickens, Charles. 2005. *Hard Times.* Webster's German Thesaurus Edition for ESL, EFL, ELP, TOEFLL®, TOEIC®, and AP® Test Preparation. San Diego: ICON Classics.

Dodson, Edwards J. 2011. "How Henry George's Principles Were Corrupted into the Game Called *Monopoly*". Official website of the Henry George Institute. www.henrygeorge.org/dodson_on_monopoly.htm. Accessed 5 May 2018.

Dostoevsky, Fyodor. 1880. *Brothers Karamazov.* Moscow: The Russian Messenger.

"Economics on the Screen". *Documentary News Letter,* June 1940.

"Economics Taught by Film: New Notation for New Ideas". *Times Educational Supplement,* 15 June 1940. London.

Festré, Agnès. 2017. "Michael Polanyi's Economics: A Strange Rapprochement Between Hayek and Keynes", Working Paper for the Trade, Employment, and Public Policy: Polanyi Then and Now workshop (MIT – The Polanyi Society), Boston.

Festré, Agnès and Garrouste, Pierre. 2015. *Michael Polanyi's Economics: A Strange Rapprochement.* GREDEG Working Paper Series (WP No. 2015-36).

Feyerabend, Paul Karl. 1975. *Against Method: Outline of an Anarchist Theory of Knowledge.* London: New Left Books.

Fischer, Louis (Ed.). 1962. *The Essential Gandhi: An Anthology of His Writings on His Life, Work, and Ideas.* New York: Vintage Spiritual Classics.

Flamm, Irving H. 1935. "The Problem of Technological Unemployment in the United States", *International Labour Review*, March.

Florence, Lella Secor. 1943. *Only an Ocean Between – America and Britain, Vol. 1.* London: Harrap & Co.

Florence, Lella Secor. 1944. *Our Private Lives – America and Britain, Vol. 2.* London: Harrap & Co.

Fragment (undated) to Michael Polanyi about his portrayal in *Journey from North, Volume 2: An Autobiography of Storm Jameson*, Michael Polanyi Papers, Box 24, Folder 1, Special Collections, University of Chicago Library.

Frank, Tibor. 2009. *Double Exile: Migrations of Jewish-Hungarian Professionals through Germany to the United States, 1919–1945.* Oxford: Peter Lang.

Garton Ash, Timothy. 2003. "Orwell's List", *The New York Review of Books*, 25 September.

Giraud, Yann and Charles, Loïc. 2013. *Economics for the Masses: The Visual Display of Economic Knowledge in the United States (1921–1945).* hal-00870490.

Gollancz, Victor. 1942a. *Let My People Go.* London: Victor Gollancz.

Gollancz, Victor. 1942b. *Shall Our Children Live or Die? A Reply to Lord Vansittart on the German Problem.* London: Victor Gollancz.

Gollancz, Victor. 1945. *What Buchenwald Really Means.* London: Victor Gollancz.

Gollancz, Victor. 1961. *The Case of Adolf Eichmann.* London: Victor Gollancz.

Gollancz, Victor; Orwell, George; and Strachey, John. 1941. *The Betrayal of the Left: An Examination and Refutation of Communist Policy from October 1939 to January 1941: with Suggestions for an Alternative and an Epilogue on Political Morality.* London: Victor Gollancz.

Guilfoyle Williams, J. 1948. *The Psychology of Childhood to Maturity.* London: W. Heinemann.

Gulick, Walter. 2010. "The Social Thought of Karl and Michael Polanyi: Prologue to a Reconciliation". In Tihamér Margitay, ed., *Knowing and Being: Perspectives on the Philosophy of Michael Polanyi*, pp. 192–215. Newcastle upon Tyne: Cambridge Scholars Publishing.

Gulick, Walter. 2017. "Michael and Karl Polanyi: Politico-Economic Point, Counterpoint – Is Rapprochement Possible?" Working Paper for the Trade, Employment, and Public Policy: Polanyi Then and Now workshop (MIT – The Polanyi Society), Boston.

Hammond, John Lawrence and Hammond, Barbara. 1917. *The Town Labourer 1760– 1832: The New Civilisation.* London: Longmans, Green, and Co.

Hands, D. Wade and Mirowski, P. 1998. "Harold Hotelling and the Neoclassical Dream". In R. Backhouse, D. Hausman, U. Maki and A. Salanti, eds, *Economics and Methodology: Crossing Boundaries*, pp. 322–97. London: Macmillan.

Hands, D. Wade and Mirowski, P. 1999. "A Paradox of Budgets". In Mary Morgan and Malcolm Rutherford, eds, *The Transformation of American Economics*, pp. 260–92. Durham: Duke University Press.

Hayek, F.A. 1944. *The Road to Serfdom.* London: George Routledge & Sons.

Héder, Mihály and Paksi, Dániel. 2012. "Autonomous Robots and Tacit Knowledge", *Appraisal* 9(2): 8–14.

Heimann, Eduard. 1944. "Franz Oppenheimer's Economic Ideas", *Social Research* 11(1): 27–39.

Hennig, Christine. 2002. Online commentary about Jay Ruby on *Valley Town* in the Prelinger Archives, 10 March.

Hilgartner, Stephen. 2015. "Capturing the Imaginary: Vanguards, Visions, and the Synthetic Biology Revolution". In Stephen Hilgartner, Clark Miller and Rob Hagendijk, eds, *Science and Democracy: Knowledge as Wealth and Power in the Biosciences and Beyond*, Chapter 3. Abingdon, Oxon: Routledge.

Hogben, Lancelot. 1936. *Mathematics for the Million*. London: George Allen & Unwin.

Hogben, Lancelot. 1938a. *Science for the Citizen*. London: George Allen & Unwin.

Hogben, Lancelot. 1938b. *Political Arithmetic: A Symposium of Population Studies*. London: George Allen & Unwin.

Holme, K.E. 1945. *Two Commonwealths – The Soviets and Ourselves, Vol. 2*. London: Harrap & Co.

Illich, Ivan. 1971. *Deschooling Society*. New York: Harper & Row.

Illich, Ivan. 1973. *Tools for Conviviality*. New York: Harper & Row.

Illich, Ivan. 1994. "The Wisdom of Leopold Kohr", Fourteenth Annual E.F. Schumacher Lectures (October 1994). Yale University, New Haven, CT.

Illo, John. 1965. "The Misreading Milton", *Columbia University Forum* 8: 38–42.

Jacobs, Struan. 2017. "Projects of Social Betterment: Michael Polanyi's Economic Film Contrasted to Otto Neurath's Isotype System", Working Paper for the Trade, Employment, and Public Policy: Polanyi Then and Now Workshop (MIT – The Polanyi Society), Boston.

Jacobs, Struan and Mullins, Phil. 2016. "Friedrich Hayek and Michael Polanyi in Correspondence", *History of European Ideas* 42(1): 107–30.

Jameson, Storm. 1936. *In the Second Year*. New York: The Macmillan Company.

Jameson, Storm. 1942. *Then We Shall Hear Singing: A Fantasy in C Major*. New York: The Macmillan Company.

Jameson, Storm. 1970. *Journey from the North, Volume 2: Autobiography of Storm Jameson*. London: Collins & Harvill Press.

Jasanoff, Sheila, ed. 2004. *States of Knowledge: The Co-Production of Science and Social Order*. London: Routledge.

Jasanoff, Sheila and Kim, Sang-Hyun. 2015. *Dreamscapes of Modernity: Sociotechnical Imaginaries and the Fabrication of Power*. Chicago/London: University of Chicago Press.

Jones, Bill. 1977. *The Russia Complex: The British Labour Party and the Soviet Union*. Manchester: Manchester University Press.

Ketcham, Christopher. 2012. "Monopoly is Theft: The Antimonopolist History of the World's Most Popular Board Game", *Harper's Magazine*, 19 October.

Keynes, John Maynard. 1919. *The Economic Consequences of the Peace*. London: Macmillan and Co.

Knight, F.H. 1932. "The Newer Economics and the Control of Economic Activity", *Journal of Political Economy* 40(4): 433–76.

Kohr, Leopold. 1957. *The Breakdown of Nations*. London: Routledge & Kegan Paul.

Krahn, Frederic A. 1953. *Educational Film Guide*, 11th ed. New York: The H.W. Wilson Company.

Kuhn, Thomas. 1962. *The Structure of Scientific Revolutions*. Chicago: University of Chicago Press.

Laski, Harold. 1943. *Reflections on the Revolution of Our Time*. London: George Allen & Unwin.

Laski, Harold. 1945. Speech for the local Labour candidate, Nottinghamshire, 16 June.

Latour, Bruno. 1990. "Drawing Things Together". In Michael Lynch and Steve Woolgar, eds, *Representation in Scientific Practice*, pp. 19–68. Cambridge, MA: MIT Press.

Lovell, Maurice. 1945. *Landsmen and Seafarers – The Soviets and Ourselves, Vol. 1.* London: Harrap & Co.

Luetkens, Charlotte. 1946. *Women and a New Society: The New Democracy.* London: Nicholson & Watson.

Lyotard, Jean-François. 1984. *The Postmodern Condition: A Report on Knowledge.* Manchester: Manchester University Press.

Magie, Elizabeth J. 1904. *Landlord's Game.* US Patent 748,626.

Magie, Elizabeth J. 1940. "A Word to the Wise", *Land and Freedom,* September–October.

Mannheim, Karl. 1929. *Ideology and Utopia.* London: Routledge and Kegan Paul.

Mirowski, Philip. 1989. *More Heat Than Light.* Cambridge: Cambridge University Press.

Mirowski, Philip. 1990. "Problems in the Paternity of Econometrics: Henry Ludwell Moore", *History of Political Economy* 22: 587–609.

Mirowski, Philip. 2002. *Machine Dreams: Economics Becomes a Cyborg Science.* Cambridge: Cambridge University Press.

"Money is Star of this Film". *Evening News*, 10 March 1938.

Moodey, Richard W. 2014 "'Visual Presentation of Social Matters' and Later Changes in Polanyi's Social Theory", *Tradition and Discovery* 41(2): 25–34.

Morris, William. 1890. *News from Nowhere.* N.P.

Mooney, J.D. 1934. Apparatus designed to illustrate the laws of economics by physical analogies, patent number: US ref.1,989,878.

Mooney, J.D. 1941. Apparatus for illustrating economic principles, patent number: US ref.2,297,011.

Mooney, J.D. 1947. Apparatus for illustrating economic laws, patent number: US ref.2,488,423.

Mooney, J.D. 1948. Apparatus for illustrating relation between economic profit and loss, patent number: US ref.2,526,260.

Mooney, J.D. 1949. Apparatus for illustrating economics by physical analogies, patent number: US ref.2,526,261.

Mullins, Phil. 2010. "Michael Polanyi's Use of Gestalt Psychology". In Tihamér Margitay, eds, *Knowing and Being: Perspectives on the Philosophy of Michael Polanyi,* pp. 10–29. Newcastle upon Tyne: Cambridge Scholars Publishing.

Mullins, Phil. 2014. "Comments on Polanyi's 'Visual Representation of Social Matters'", *Tradition and Discovery* 41(2): 35–44.

Mullins, Phil. 2017. Letter of 23 June 2017 from Phil Mullins to Tihamér Margitay about Harry Prosch's *Cooling the Modern Mind: Polanyi's Mission* (Skidmore College bulletin).

Nagel, Thomas. 1986. *View from Nowhere.* Oxford: Oxford University Press.

Nedeljkovich, Brashich and Kuharich. 1911. *Pyramid of Capitalist System.* Industrial Worker. Cleveland: The International Publishing Co.

Neurath, O. 1936. *International Picture Language: The First Rules of ISOTYPE.* London: Kegan Paul, Trench, Trubner & Co.

Nye, Mary Jo. 2011. *Michael Polanyi and His Generation: The Origins of the Social Construction of Science.* Chicago: University of Chicago Press.

Orosz, M. 2014. "Isotype Mozgóképen? Polányi Mihály, az Animált Infografika Megteremtője" [public lecture], Kassák Museum, 13 February.

Orwell, George. 1937. Letter of 31 July 1937 from George Orwell to Rayner Heppenstall [XI, 381, pp. 53–4].

Orwell, George. 1940. "Review of 'The Totalitarian Enemy' by Franz Borkenau", *Time and Tide*, 4 May 1940.

Orwell, George. 1945. *Animal Farm*. New York: New American Library.

Orwell, George. 1948. *Nineteen Eighty-Four*. New York: New American Library.

Orwell, George. 1949. Orwell's untitled list for the British Ministry of Information about possible Soviet symphatizers, British National Archives, FO 1110/189.

Parker, Ralph. 1947. *How Do You Do, Tovarish? – The Soviets and Ourselves, Vol. 3*. London: Harrap & Co.

Parks, Henry Bamford. 1939. *Marxism: An Autopsy*. Boston/ New York: Houghton Mifflin Company.

Paterson, Isabel. 1943. *The God of the Machine*. New York: Putnam.

Petty, William. 1691. *Political Arithmetick*. N.P.

Pinch, Trevor and Trocco, Frank. 2002. *Analog Days: The Invention and Impact of the Moog Synthesizer*. Cambridge, MA: Harvard University Press.

Plato. 350 BCE. *Protagoras*. N.P.

Polanyi, Karl. 1944. *The Great Transformation: The Political and Economic Origins of Our Time*. Farrar & Rinehart (2001 edition, Boston: Beacon Press).

Polanyi, Michael. 1931. "Über einfache Gasreaktionen", *Zeitschrift für Physikalische Chemie B* 12: 279–311.

Polanyi, Michael. 1935a. "U.S.S.R. Economics – Fundamental Data, System, and Spirit", *The Manchester School of Economic and Social Studies*, 6 (November), pp. 67–89.

Polanyi, Michael. 1935b. A letter of 24 November 1935 from Oscar Jaszi to Michael Polanyi, Michael Polanyi Papers, Box 3, Folder 5, Special Collections, University of Chicago Library.

Polanyi, Michael. 1935c. A letter of 13 December 1935 from Michael Polanyi to John Grierson, Michael Polanyi Papers, Box 3, Folder 5, Special Collections, University of Chicago Library.

Polanyi, Michael. 1936a. Notes on a Film, Michael Polanyi Papers, Box 25, Folder 10, Special Collections, University of Chicago Library.

Polanyi, Michael. 1936b. A letter of 6 February 1936 from Michael Polanyi to John Jewkes, Michael Polanyi Papers, Box 3, Folder 6, Special Collections, University of Chicago Library.

Polanyi, Michael. 1936c. A letter of 7 December 1936 from Michael Polanyi to John Jewkes, Michael Polanyi Papers, Box 3, Folder 7, Special Collections, University of Chicago Library.

Polanyi, Michael. 1937a. A letter of 21 January 1937 from Charles V. Sale to Michael Polanyi, Michael Polanyi Papers, Box 3, Folder 8, Special Collections, University of Chicago Library.

Polanyi, Michael. 1937b. On Popular Education in Economics, Michael Polanyi Papers, Box 25, Folder 9, Special Collections, University of Chicago Library.

Polanyi, Michael. 1937c. Historical Society Lecture, Michael Polanyi Papers, Box 25, Folder 10, Special Collections, University of Chicago Library.

Polanyi, Michael. 1937d. Visual Presentation of Social Matters, Michael Polanyi Papers, Box 25, Folder 9, Special Collections, University of Chicago Library.

Polanyi, Michael. 1938a. A letter of 4 August 1938 from R.S. Lambert (British Film Institute) to Michael Polanyi, Michael Polanyi Papers, Box 3, Folder 12, Special Collections, University of Chicago Library.

Polanyi, Michael. 1938b. A letter of 3 September 1938 from Magda Polanyi to Michael Polanyi, Michael Polanyi Papers, Box 3, Folder 12, Special Collections, University of Chicago Library.

Polanyi, Michael. 1938c. A letter of 6 September 1938 from Magda Polanyi to Michael Polanyi, Michael Polanyi Papers, Box 3, Folder 12, Special Collections, University of Chicago Library.

Polanyi, Michael. 1938d. A letter of 12 December 1938 from Oliver Bell to John Jewkes, Michael Polanyi Papers, Box 3, Folder 13, Special Collections, University of Chicago Library.

Polanyi, Michael. 1939a. A letter of 27 November 1939 from Michael Polanyi to Lancelot Hogben, Michael Polanyi Papers, Box 4, Folder 2, Special Collections, University of Chicago Library.

Polanyi, Michael. 1939b. A letter of 27 November 1939 from Michael Polanyi to John Lawrence Hammond, Michael Polanyi Papers, Box 4, Folder 2, Special Collections, University of Chicago Library.

Polanyi, Michael. 1939c. A letter of 30 November 1939 from Lancelot Hogben to Michael Polanyi, Michael Polanyi Papers, Box 4, Folder 2, Special Collections, University of Chicago Library.

Polanyi, Michael. 1939d. A letter of 30 November 1939 from Lancelot Hogben to Michael Polanyi, Michael Polanyi Papers, Box 4, Folder 2, Special Collections, University of Chicago Library.

Polanyi, Michael. 1939e. A letter of 6 December 1939 from Michael Polanyi to Lancelot Hogben, Michael Polanyi Papers, Box 4, Folder 2, Special Collections, University of Chicago Library.

Polanyi, Michael. 1939f. A letter of 8 December 1939 from Lancelot Hogben to Michael Polanyi, Michael Polanyi Papers, Box 4, Folder 2, Special Collections, University of Chicago Library.

Polanyi, Michael. 1940a. Unemployment and Money: The Principles Involved. G.B. Instructional Ltd.

Polanyi, Michael. 1940b. A letter of 6 February 1940 from Michael Polanyi to John Maynard Keynes, Michael Polanyi Papers, Box 4, Folder 3, Special Collections, University of Chicago Library.

Polanyi, Michael. 1940c. A letter of 8 February 1940 from John Maynard Keynes to Michael Polanyi, Michael Polanyi Papers, Box 4, Folder 3, Special Collections, University of Chicago Library.

Polanyi, Michael. 1940d. A letter of 9 February 1940 from Michael Polanyi to Archibald Vivian Hill, Michael Polanyi Papers, Box 4, Folder 3, Special Collections, University of Chicago Library.

Polanyi, Michael. 1940e. A letter of 16 February 1940 from Michael Polanyi to Archibald Vivian Hill, Michael Polanyi Papers, Box 4, Folder 3, Special Collections, University of Chicago Library.

Polanyi, Michael. 1940f. A letter of 18 February 1940 from Archibald Vivian Hill to Michael Polanyi, Michael Polanyi Papers, Box 4, Folder 3, Special Collections, University of Chicago Library.

Polanyi, Michael. 1940g. A letter of 19 February 1940 from John Maynard Keynes to Michael Polanyi, Michael Polanyi Papers, Box 4, Folder 3, Special Collections, University of Chicago Library.

Polanyi, Michael. 1940h. A letter of 9 May 1940 from Oscar Jaszi to Michael Polanyi, Michael Polanyi Papers, Box 4, Folder 4, Special Collections, University of Chicago Library.

Polanyi, Michael. 1940i. Collectivist Planning, Michael Polanyi Papers, Box 26, Folder 3, Special Collections, University of Chicago Library.

Polanyi, Michael. 1940j. "Economics on the Screen". *Documentary News Letter*, August 1940.

Polanyi, Michael. 1940k. A letter of 20 September 1940 from Oscar Jaszi to Michael Polanyi, Michael Polanyi Papers, Box 4, Folder 5, Special Collections, University of Chicago Library.

Polanyi, Michael. 1940l. A letter of 12 December 1940 from Ruth Pedersen (Rockefeller Foundation) to Jacob Marschak, Michael Polanyi Papers, Box 4, Folder 5, Special Collections, University of Chicago Library.

Polanyi, Michael. 1940m. A letter of 16 December 1940 from Laura Polanyi-Striker to Michael Polanyi, Michael Polanyi Papers, Box 4, Folder 5, Special Collections, University of Chicago Library.

Polanyi, Michael. 1941a. A letter of 23 of March 1941 from Oscar Jaszi to Michael Polanyi, Michael Polanyi Papers, Box 4, Folder 6, Special Collections, University of Chicago Library.

Polanyi, Michael. 1941b. A letter of 29 July 1941 from Michael Polanyi to Oscar Jaszi, Michael Polanyi Papers, Box 4, Folder 7, Special Collections, University of Chicago Library.

Polanyi, Michael. 1941c. A letter of 3 October 1941 from Franz Borkenau to Michael Polanyi, Michael Polanyi Papers, Box 4, Folder 7, Special Collections, University of Chicago Library.

Polanyi, Michael. 1941d. A letter of 28 October 1941 from Michael Polanyi to Patrick Blackett, Michael Polanyi Papers, Box 4, Folder 7, Special Collections, University of Chicago Library.

Polanyi, Michael. 1941e. A letter of 3 November 1941 from Patrick Blackett to Michael Polanyi, Michael Polanyi Papers, Box 4, Folder 7, Special Collections, University of Chicago Library.

Polanyi, Michael. 1941f. The New Economics, Michael Polanyi Papers, Box 26, Folder 9, Special Collections, University of Chicago Library.

Polanyi, Michael. 1941g. A letter of 30 November 1941 from Barbara Hammond to Michael Polanyi, Michael Polanyi Papers, Box 4, Folder 7, Special Collections, University of Chicago Library.

Polanyi, Michael. 1942a. A letter of 12 January 1942 from Michael Polanyi to Tracy B. Kittredge (Rockefeller Foundation), Michael Polanyi Papers, Box 4, Folder 8, Special Collections, University of Chicago Library.

Polanyi, Michael. 1942b. A letter of 30 January 1942 and the draft article of "The Sword and the Spirit" from Hugh O'Neill to Michael Polanyi, Michael Polanyi Papers, Box 4, Folder 8, Special Collections, University of Chicago Library.

Polanyi, Michael. 1942c. A letter of 2 February 1942 from Tracy B. Kittredge to Michael Polanyi, Michael Polanyi Papers, Box 4, Folder 8, Special Collections, University of Chicago Library.

Polanyi, Michael. 1942d. A letter of 12 February 1942 from Michael Polanyi to Max Born, Michael Polanyi Papers, Box 4, Folder 8, Special Collections, University of Chicago Library.

Polanyi, Michael. 1942e. A letter of 14 February 1942 from Max Born to Michael Polanyi, Michael Polanyi Papers, Box 4, Folder 8, Special Collections, University of Chicago Library.

Polanyi, Michael. 1942f. A letter of 19 February 1942 from Toni Stolper to Michael Polanyi, Michael Polanyi Papers, Box 4, Folder 8, Special Collections, University of Chicago Library.

Polanyi, Michael. 1942g. A letter of 5 March 1942 from Arthur Koestler to Michael Polanyi, Michael Polanyi Papers, Box 4, Folder 8, Special Collections, University of Chicago Library.

Polanyi, Michael. 1942h. Outline of Book III, Michael Polanyi Papers, Box 27, Folder 8, Special Collections, University of Chicago Library.

Polanyi, Michael. 1942i. A letter of 30 June 1942 from Max Born to Michael Polanyi, Michael Polanyi Papers, Box 4, Folder 8, Special Collections, University of Chicago Library.

Polanyi, Michael. 1942j. A letter of 18 September 1942 from Toni Stolper to Michael Polanyi, Michael Polanyi Papers, Box 4, Folder 8, Special Collections, University of Chicago Library.

Polanyi, Michael. 1942k. "The Revaluation of Science", *Manchester Guardian*, 7 November 1942.

Polanyi, Michael. 1942l. A letter of 10 December 1942 from Adolf Polanyi to Michael Polanyi, Michael Polanyi Papers, Box 4, Folder 9, Special Collections, University of Chicago Library.

Polanyi, Michael. 1942m. A letter of 10 December 1942 from Geoffrey Jefferson to Michael Polanyi, Michael Polanyi Papers, Box 4, Folder 9, Special Collections, University of Chicago Library.

Polanyi, Michael. 1942n. A letter of 16 December 1942 from Max Born to Michael Polanyi, Michael Polanyi Papers, Box 4, Folder 9, Special Collections, University of Chicago Library.

Polanyi, Michael. 1942o. A letter of 20 December 1942 from Oscar Jaszi to Michael Polanyi, Michael Polanyi Papers, Box 4, Folder 9, Special Collections, University of Chicago Library.

Polanyi, Michael. 1943a. A letter of 11 January 1943 from Charles Singer to Michael Polanyi, Michael Polanyi Papers, Box 4, Folder 9, Special Collections, University of Chicago Library.

Polanyi, Michael. 1943b. A letter of 14 January 1943 from Michael Polanyi to Charles Singer, Michael Polanyi Papers, Box 4, Folder 9, Special Collections, University of Chicago Library.

Polanyi, Michael. 1943c. A letter of 22 of January 1943 from Charles Singer to Michael Polanyi, Michael Polanyi Papers, Box 4, Folder 9, Special Collections, University of Chicago Library.

Polanyi, Michael. 1943d. Comments on the "Draft Memorandum on a Planned Economy", Michael Polanyi Papers, Box 28, Folder 2, Special Collections, University of Chicago Library.

Polanyi, Michael. 1943e. A letter of 1 February 1943 from Adolf Polanyi to Michael Polanyi, Michael Polanyi Papers, Box 4, Folder 9, Special Collections, University of Chicago Library.

Polanyi, Michael. 1943f. A letter of 13 February 1943 from G.D.H. Cole to Harold Shearman, Michael Polanyi Papers, Box 4, Folder 9, Special Collections, University of Chicago Library.

Polanyi, Michael. 1943g. A letter of 13 February 1943 from Peter Thomason to Michael Polanyi, Michael Polanyi Papers, Box 4, Folder 9, Special Collections, University of Chicago Library.

Polanyi, Michael. 1943h. "Economics of Full Employment", *Manchester Guardian*, 13 February 1943.

Polanyi, Michael. 1943i. A letter of 29 March 1943 from Michael Polanyi to R.A. Eastwood, Michael Polanyi Papers, Box 4, Folder 9, Special Collections, University of Chicago Library.

Polanyi, Michael. 1943j. A letter of 5 May 1943 from Michael Polanyi to Charles Singer, Michael Polanyi Papers, Box 4, Folder 10, Special Collections, University of Chicago Library.

Polanyi, Michael. 1943k. A letter of 24 May 1943 from Charles Singer to Michael Polanyi, Michael Polanyi Papers, Box 4, Folder 10, Special Collections, University of Chicago Library.

Polanyi, Michael. 1943l. A letter of 12 June 1943 from Arthur Koestler to Michael Polanyi, Michael Polanyi Papers, Box 4, Folder 10, Special Collections, University of Chicago Library.

Polanyi, Michael. 1943m. A letter of 27 June 1943 from Lionel Charles Knights to Michael Polanyi, Michael Polanyi Papers, Box 4, Folder 10, Special Collections, University of Chicago Library.

Polanyi, Michael. 1943n. A letter of 12 September 1943 from Clifford Copland Paterson to Michael Polanyi, Michael Polanyi Papers, Box 4, Folder 10, Special Collections, University of Chicago Library.

Polanyi, Michael. 1943o. A letter of 3 October 1943 from Michael Polanyi to Toni Stolper, Michael Polanyi Papers, Box 4, Folder 10, Special Collections, University of Chicago Library.

Polanyi, Michael. 1943p. "A Review of Reflections on the Revolution of Our Time" by Harold J. Laski, *Manchester Guardian*, 8 October 1943.

Polanyi, Michael. 1943q. A letter of 12 October 1943 from Michael Polanyi to Ludwig Lachmann, Michael Polanyi Papers, Box 4, Folder 10, Special Collections, University of Chicago Library.

Polanyi, Michael. 1943r. A letter of 14 October 1943 from Michael Polanyi to Clifford Copland Paterson, Michael Polanyi Papers, Box 4, Folder 10, Special Collections, University of Chicago Library.

Polanyi, Michael. 1943s. A letter of 30 October 1943 from Toni Stolper to Michael Polanyi, Michael Polanyi Papers, Box 4, Folder 10, Special Collections, University of Chicago Library.

Polanyi, Michael. 1943t. A letter of 7 November 1943 from J.R. Hicks to Michael Polanyi, Michael Polanyi Papers, Box 4, Folder 10, Special Collections, University of Chicago Library.

Polanyi, Michael. 1943u. A letter of 13 November 1943 from Michael Polanyi to J.R. Hicks, Michael Polanyi Papers, Box 4, Folder 10, Special Collections, University of Chicago Library.

Polanyi, Michael. 1943v. A letter of 15 December 1943 from Michael Polanyi to Toni Stolper, Michael Polanyi Papers, Box 4, Folder 10, Special Collections, University of Chicago Library.

Polanyi, Michael. 1943w. The Reaction from Free Trade, Michael Polanyi Papers, Box 28, Folder 8, Special Collections, University of Chicago Library.

Polanyi, Michael. 1943x. "The Autonomy of Science", *Memoirs and Proceedings of the Manchester Literary and Philosophical Society* 85: 19–38.

Polanyi, Michael. 1944a. A letter of 18 April 1944 from Michael Polanyi to John Jewkes, Michael Polanyi Papers, Box 4, Folder 11, Special Collections, University of Chicago Library.

Polanyi, Michael. 1944b. A letter of 19 April 1944 from Michael Polanyi to Karl Mannheim, Michael Polanyi Papers, Box 4, Folder 11, Special Collections, University of Chicago Library.

Polanyi, Michael. 1944c. A letter of 26 April from Karl Mannheim to Michael Polanyi, Michael Polanyi Papers, Box 4, Folder 11, Special Collections, University of Chicago Library.

Polanyi, Michael. 1944d. A letter of 28 April 1944 from Michael Polanyi to Oscar Jaszi, Michael Polanyi Papers, Box 4, Folder 11, Special Collections, University of Chicago Library.

Polanyi, Michael. 1944e. A letter of May 1944 from Alfred Ernest Teale to Michael Polanyi, Michael Polanyi Papers, Box 4, Folder 11, Special Collections, University of Chicago Library.

Polanyi, Michael. 1944f. A letter of 2 May 1944 from Michael Polanyi to Karl Mannheim, Michael Polanyi Papers, Box 4, Folder 11, Special Collections, University of Chicago Library.

Polanyi, Michael. 1944g. A letter of 9 May 1944 from Toni Stolper to Michael Polanyi, Michael Polanyi Papers, Box 4, Folder 11, Special Collections, University of Chicago Library.

Polanyi, Michael. 1944h. A letter of 27 May 1944 from Oscar Jaszi to Michael Polanyi, Michael Polanyi Papers, Box 4, Folder 11, Special Collections, University of Chicago Library.

Polanyi, Michael. 1944i. "Science and the Decline of Freedom", *Listener 32* (1 June): 599.

Polanyi, Michael. 1944j. A letter of 27 June 1944 from Leonard Hyman to Michael Polanyi, Michael Polanyi Papers, Box 4, Folder 11, Special Collections, University of Chicago Library.

Polanyi, Michael. 1944k. A letter of 5 July from Oscar Jaszi to Michael Polanyi, Michael Polanyi Papers, Box 4, Folder 11, Special Collections, University of Chicago Library.

Polanyi, Michael. 1944l. A letter of 9 July 1944 from Michael Polanyi to Toni Stolper, Michael Polanyi Papers, Box 4, Folder 11, Special Collections, University of Chicago Library.

Polanyi, Michael. 1944m. A letter of 10 August 1944 from Karl Mannheim to Michael Polanyi, Michael Polanyi Papers, Box 4, Folder 11, Special Collections, University of Chicago Library.

Polanyi, Michael. 1944n. A letter of 13 October 1944 from Enid Bradford to Michael Polanyi, Michael Polanyi Papers, Box 4, Folder 11, Special Collections, University of Chicago Library.

Polanyi, Michael. 1944o. A letter of 23 of November 1944 from Enid Bradford to Michael Polanyi, Michael Polanyi Papers, Box 4, Folder 12, Special Collections, University of Chicago Library.

Polanyi, Michael. 1944p. A letter of 5 December 1944 from Archibald Vivian Hill to Michael Polanyi, Michael Polanyi Papers, Box 4, Folder 12, Special Collections, University of Chicago Library.

Polanyi, Michael. 1945a. A letter of 3 January 1945 from John Bowle to Mrs. Curtis, Michael Polanyi Papers, Box 4, Folder 12, Special Collections, University of Chicago Library.

Polanyi, Michael. 1945b. A letter of 9 January 1945 from William Rowntree to Michael Polanyi, Michael Polanyi Papers, Box 4, Folder 12, Special Collections, University of Chicago Library.

Polanyi, Michael. 1945c. A letter of 20 January 1945 from Michael Polanyi to John Bowle, Michael Polanyi Papers, Box 4, Folder 12, Special Collections, University of Chicago Library.

Polanyi, Michael. 1945d. A letter of 31 January 1945 from Toni Stolper to Michael Polanyi, Michael Polanyi Papers, Box 4, Folder 12, Special Collections, University of Chicago Library.

Polanyi, Michael. 1945e. A Draft Memorandum of "Our Times", A Proposed Quarterly Journal to be Published by the Manchester Literary and Philosophical Society. March 1945, Michael Polanyi Papers, Box 4, Folder 12, Special Collections, University of Chicago Library.

Polanyi, Michael. 1945f. A letter of 5 March 1945 from T.S. Elliot to Michael Polanyi, Michael Polanyi Papers, Box 4, Folder 12, Special Collections, University of Chicago Library.

Polanyi, Michael. 1945g. A letter of 6 March 1945 from Michael Polanyi to Karl Mannheim, Michael Polanyi Papers, Box 4, Folder 12, Special Collections, University of Chicago Library.

Polanyi, Michael. 1945h. A letter of 19 March 1945 from Shearman to Michael Polanyi, Michael Polanyi Papers, Box 4, Folder 12, Special Collections, University of Chicago Library.

Polanyi, Michael. 1945i. A letter of 18 April 1945 from Shearman to Michael Polanyi, Michael Polanyi Papers, Box 4, Folder 12, Special Collections, University of Chicago Library.

Polanyi, Michael. 1945j. A letter of 22 April 1945 from Andrew Bongiorno, Michael Polanyi Papers, Box 4, Folder 12, Special Collections, University of Chicago Library.

Polanyi, Michael. 1945k. A letter of 23 April 1945 from Michael Polanyi to Shearman, Michael Polanyi Papers, Box 4, Folder 12, Special Collections, University of Chicago Library.

Polanyi, Michael. 1945l. A letter of 30 April 1945 from Michael Polanyi to Franz Gabriel Alexander, Michael Polanyi Papers, Box 4, Folder 12, Special Collections, University of Chicago Library.

Polanyi, Michael. 1945m. A letter of 18 May 1945 from Toni Stolper to Michael Polanyi, Michael Polanyi Papers, Box 4, Folder 12, Special Collections, University of Chicago Library.

Polanyi, Michael. 1945n. A letter of 22 July 1945 from Oscar Jaszi to Michael Polanyi, Michael Polanyi Papers, Box 4, Folder 13, Special Collections, University of Chicago Library.

Polanyi, Michael. 1945o. A letter of 10 September from Michael Polanyi to Toni Stolper, Michael Polanyi Papers, Box 4, Folder 13, Special Collections, University of Chicago Library.

Polanyi, Michael. 1945p. A letter of 8 October 1945 from Laura Polanyi-Striker to Michael Polanyi, Michael Polanyi Papers, Box 4, Folder 13, Special Collections, University of Chicago Library.

Polanyi, Michael. 1945q. A letter of 12 December 1945 from Toni Stolper to Michael Polanyi, Michael Polanyi Papers, Box 4, Folder 13, Special Collections, University of Chicago Library.

Polanyi, Michael. 1945r. A letter of 20 December 1945 from Michael Polanyi to John Maynard Keynes, Michael Polanyi Papers, Box 4, Folder 13, Special Collections, University of Chicago Library.

Polanyi, Michael. 1945s. A letter of 20 December 1945 from Michael Polanyi to Toni Stolper, Michael Polanyi Papers, Box 4, Folder 13, Special Collections, University of Chicago Library.

Polanyi, Michael. 1946a. A letter of 28 February 1946 from Oscar Jaszi to Michael Polanyi, Michael Polanyi Papers, Box 5, Folder 1, Special Collections, University of Chicago Library.

Polanyi, Michael. 1946b. A letter of 23 February 1946 from John Maynard Keynes to Michael Polanyi, Michael Polanyi Papers, Box 5, Folder 1, Special Collections, University of Chicago Library.

Polanyi, Michael. 1946c. "Soviets and Capitalism, What is the Difference?", *Time and Tide*, 6 April 1946, p. 317.

Polanyi, Michael. 1946d. A letter of 22 April 1946 from Victor L. Block to Michael Polanyi, Michael Polanyi Papers, Box 5, Folder 1, Special Collections, University of Chicago Library.

Polanyi, Michael. 1946e. A letter of 25 April 1946 from J. Guilfoyle Williams to Michael Polanyi, Michael Polanyi Papers, Box 5, Folder 1, Special Collections, University of Chicago Library.

Polanyi, Michael. 1946f. A letter of 28 April 1946 from Gilbert Murray to Michael Polanyi, Michael Polanyi Papers, Box 5, Folder 1, Special Collections, University of Chicago Library.

Polanyi, Michael. 1946g. A letter of 29 April 1946 from unknown to Michael Polanyi, Michael Polanyi Papers, Box 5, Folder 1, Special Collections, University of Chicago Library.

Polanyi, Michael. 1946h. A letter of 30 April 1946 from E.J. McManus to Michael Polanyi, Michael Polanyi Papers, Box 5, Folder 1, Special Collections, University of Chicago Library.

Polanyi, Michael. 1946i. A letter of 1 May 1946 from Michael Polanyi to J. Guilfoyle Williams, Michael Polanyi Papers, Box 5, Folder 1, Special Collections, University of Chicago Library.

Polanyi, Michael. 1946j. A letter of 1 May 1946 from Olwen Ward Campbell to Michael Polanyi, Michael Polanyi Papers, Box 5, Folder 1, Special Collections, University of Chicago Library.

Polanyi, Michael. 1946k. A letter of 2 May 1946 from Michael Polanyi to E.J. McManus, Michael Polanyi Papers, Box 5, Folder 1, Special Collections, University of Chicago Library.

Polanyi, Michael. 1946l. A letter of 6 May 1946 from Michael Polanyi to Olwen Ward Campbell, Michael Polanyi Papers, Box 5, Folder 1, Special Collections, University of Chicago Library.

Polanyi, Michael. 1946m. "Why Profits?", *Humanitas* 1(2): 4–13.

Polanyi, Michael. 1946n. A letter of 6 December 1946 from Toni Stolper to Michael Polanyi, Michael Polanyi Papers, Box 5, Folder 2, Special Collections, University of Chicago Library.

Polanyi, Michael. 1946o. A letter from Michael Polanyi to N. Hubbard, Michael Polanyi Papers, Box 5, Folder 1, Special Collections, University of Chicago Library.

Polanyi, Michael. 1947a. The Relevance of Universities, Michael Polanyi Papers, Box 31, Folder 8, Special Collections, University of Chicago Library.

Polanyi, Michael. 1947b. What to Believe, Michael Polanyi Papers, Box 31, Folder 10, Special Collections, University of Chicago Library.

Polanyi, Michael. 1947c. British Crisis, Michael Polanyi Papers, Box 31, Folder 3, Special Collections, University of Chicago Library.

Polanyi, Michael. 1948a. *Full Employment and Free Trade*. Cambridge: Cambridge University Press.

Polanyi, Michael. 1948b. Dynamic Order, Michael Polanyi Papers, Box 31, Folder 11, Special Collections, University of Chicago Library.

Polanyi, Michael. 1949. "Mechanism of Chemical Reactions", *Endeavour* 8: 3.

Polanyi, Michael. 1962. My Time with X-rays and Crystals, Michael Polanyi Papers, Box 34, Folder 17, Special Collections, University of Chicago Library.

Polanyi, Michael. undateda. The New Outlook, Michael Polanyi Papers, Box 28, Folder 2, Special Collections, University of Chicago Library.

Polanyi, Michael. undatedb. The Limits of State Power, Michael Polanyi Papers, Box 28, Folder 2, Special Collections, University of Chicago Library.

Polanyi, Michael. undatedc. Trade Cycle, Michael Polanyi Papers, Box 25, Folder 10, Special Collections, University of Chicago Library.

Pollard, Spencer and Van Dyke, Willard. 1940. *Valley Town: A Study of Machines and Men*. Educational Film Institute of New York University and Documentary Film Producers, Inc. Sloan (Alfred P.) Foundation.

Powell, Jim. 1996. "Rose Wilder Lane, Isabel Paterson, and Ayn Rand: Three Women Who Inspired the Modern Libertarian Movement", *The Freeman Ideas on Liberty* 46(5): 322.

Powers, Kristen. 2016. "Donald Trump's 'Kinder, Gentler' Version: Kristen Powers", *USA Today*, published: 11:34 p.m. UTC, 12 April 2016. Accessed: 10:46 a.m. CET 8 July 2018.

Preda, Alex. 2009. *Framing Finance: The Boundaries of Markets and Modern Capitalism*. Chicago/London: University of Chicago Press.

Ramírez, Gracia. 2009. *Rockefeller Support for Non-Commercial Film, 1935–1939*. Rockefeller Archive Center Research Reports Online, Rockefeller Archive Center.

Ramírez, Gracia. 2013. *"In the Best Interests of the Country": The American Film Institute and Philanthropic Support for American Experimental and Independent Cinema in the 1960s*. PhD dissertation. Edinburgh: Edinburgh Napier University.

Rand, Ayn. 1943. *The Fountainhead*. Indianapolis: Bobbs-Merrill.

Rand, Ayn. 1997. *Journals of Ayn Rand*. Edited by David Harriman. New York: Dutton.

Raven, Charles E. 1943. *Science, Religion, and the Future*. Cambridge: Cambridge University Press.

Reisz, Matthew. 2013. "Softly-Softly Thought Police Brought to Book at Last: News", *Times Higher Education*, 26 September 2013.

Renoir, Jacques. 1937. *La Grande Illusion*. Réalisations d'Art Cinématographique.

Robbins, Lionel. 1932. *An Essay on the Nature and Significance of Economic Science*. London: Macmillan & Co.

Rotha, Paul. 1941. *A Few Ounces a Day*. Paul Rotha Productions. Ministry of Information.

Rotha, Paul. 1943. *World of Plenty*. Paul Rotha Productions. Ministries of Food and Agriculture.

Rotha, Paul. 1945. *Land of Promise*. Paul Rotha Productions. Bloomington: Indiana University.

Samuelson, Paul A. 1948. *Economics: An Introductory Analysis*, 1st ed. New York: McGrawHill.

Schumacher, E.F. 1943. "Multilateral Clearing", *Economica* 10(38): 150–65.

Schumacher, E.F. 1973. *Small is Beautiful: A Study of Economics as if People Mattered.* London: Blond & Briggs.

Scott, W.T. and Moleski, M.X. 2005. *Michael Polanyi, Scientist and Philosopher.* Oxford: Oxford University Press.

Shapin, Steven. 2010. *Never Pure: Historical Studies of Science as if it was Produced by People with Bodies, Situated in Time, Space, Culture, and Society, and Struggling for Credibility and Authority.* Baltimore, MD: Johns Hopkins University Press.

Shearman, Harold Charles. 1947. *Education: The New Horizon*, The New Democracy Series. London: Nicholson & Watson.

Smellie, Kingsley Bryce. 1944. *Our Two Democracies at Work – America and Britain, Vol. 3.* London: Harrap & Co.

Star, S.L. and Griesemer, J.R. 1989. "Institutional Ecology, 'Translations', and Boundary Objects: Amateurs and Professionals in Berkeley's Museum of Vertebrate Zoology, 1907–1939", *Social Studies of Science* 19: 387–420.

Slichter, Sumner Huber. 1931. *Modern Economic Society.* New York: Henry Holt and Company.

Stevenson, David. 2004. *Cataclysm: The First World War as Political Tragedy.* New York: Basic Books.

Taylor, D.J. and Smith, A. 2013. "The Orwell Wars", *New Statesman*, 29 May 2013.

Taylor, Stephen. 1944. *Battle for Health: A Primer for Social Medicine*, The New Democracy Series. London: Nicholson & Watson.

Vansittart, Robert. 1941. *Black Record: Germans Past and Present.* London: Hamish Hamilton.

Vansittart, Robert. 1943. *Lessons of My Life.* London: Hutchinson.

WEA (Workers' Educational Association). 1942. *The Film in Economics Classes: A W.E.A. Experiment.* London: WEA.

Webb, Sidney and Webb, Beatrice Potter. 1935. *Soviet Communism: A New Civilization?* New York: Charles Scribner's Sons.

Weintraub, E.R. and Mirowski, P. 1994. "The Pure and the Applied: Bourbakism Comes to Mathematical Economics", *Science in Context* 7: 245–72.

Wells, H.G. 1911. *The New Machiavelli.* London: Elkin Mathews and John Lane, The Bodley Head.

Wells, H.G. 1918. *In the Fourth Year: Anticipations of a World Peace.* New York: The Macmillan Company.

Wilder Lane, Rose. 1943. *The Discovery of Freedom: Man's Struggle Against Authority.* New York: John Day Company.

Williams, Gertrude. 1945. *Women and Work*, The New Democracy Series. London: Nicholson & Watson.

Williams, J.H. 1941. "Economics by Diagrammatic Film: A New Method of Exposition". *Adult Education*, June.

Wolfe, Burton H. 1976. "The Monopolization of Monopoly", *San Francisco Bay Guardian.*

Young, Michael Dunlop and Prager, Theodor. 1945. *There's Work for All*, The New Democracy Series. London: Nicholson & Watson.

Zemplén, Gábor Áron. 2017. "Diagrammatic Carriers and the Acceptance of Newton's Optical Theory", *Synthese*, March: 1–17.

Index

For Product Safety Concerns and Information please contact our EU
representative GPSR@taylorandfrancis.com Taylor & Francis Verlag GmbH,
Kaufingerstraße 24, 80331 München, Germany

Printed and bound by CPI Group (UK) Ltd, Croydon, CR0 4YY

01/05/2025

01858399-0003